By HIS MAJESTY's Company of Comedians,
AT THE
THEATRE ROYAL in *Drury-Lane*.
This present **T u e s d a y**, being the 16th of DECEMBER,
Will be Presented the TRAGEDY of

# OTHELLO,
## MOOR of VENICE.

The Part of *Othello* by Mr. QUIN,
*Desdemona* by Mrs. PRITCHARD,
*Brabantio* by Mr. MILWARD,
*Cassio* by Mr. WRIGHT,
*Iago* by Mr. MILLS,
*Roderigo* by Mr. WOODWARD,
*Emilia* by Mrs. BUTLER.

With Entertainments of DANCING, Particularly,
End of Act II. a New Comic Dance, call'd
## Le BOUFON.
By Signior and Signiora FAUSAN,
End of the Play, a new Comic Dance call'd
## The ENCHANTED GARDEN.
Harlequin Man and Woman by
Signior and Signiora FAUSAN.
*Shepherd and Shepherdess by*
Mons. MUILMENT and Mad. CHATEAUNEUF,
Scaramouch } Men { *Mr. Dess,* | Women, { *Mrs. Walter,*
Pierrot } { *Mr. Newton,* | { *Mrs Thompson.*
*Petit Maitre* by Mr. MACKLIN.

To which will be added, a Farce call'd
## The INTRIGUING CHAMBERMAID.
The Part of the *Chambermaid* by Mrs. C L I V E,
Col. *Bluff* by Mr. MACKLIN,
*Goodall* by Mr. WINSTONE,
And the Part of *Valentine* by Mr. LOWE.

---

tre Royal, Drury Lane.
*irst Time of the Appearance together of*
## AN & Mr. MACREADY.
MONDAY Next, November 26, 1832,
Their Majesties' Servants will perform Shakspeare's Tragedy of

# THELLO.
## THE MOOR OF VENICE.
Duke of Venice, Mr. THOMPSON,
Mr. YOUNGE, Gratiano, Mr. FENTON,
r. MATHEWS, Montano, Mr. BRINDAL,
llo, - - - Mr. KEAN,
Mr. MACREADY.
COOPER, Roderigo, Mr. BALLS,
Mr. CATHIE, Julio, Mr. EATON,
, Mr. HATTON, Paulo, Mr. S. JONES,
t, Mr. BARTLETT, Luca, Mr. BISHOP,
r. Honner, Servants, Messrs. Cowin & Rayner.
demona, - Miss PHILLIPS,
Emilia, Mrs. FAUCIT.
*To conclude with the Grand Dramatic Romance of*

# ue Beard:
## R, FEMALE CURIOSITY.
que, (Blue Beard) Mr. YOUNGE,
AYLIFFE, Selim, Mr. TEMPLETON,
Mr. HARLEY,
an, Mr. HONNER, Slave, Mr. BISHOP,
d, 2ndSpahi,Mr.Cooke, 3rd Spahi,Mr.C.Jones, 4th Spahi,Mr.Eaton
CAWSE, Beda, Mrs. HUMBY,
Fatima, Mrs. CROUCH.
**SCENERY AND INCIDENTS.**
LAGE AND ROMANTIC MO
HALL IN ABOMILIQUE'S
NSIVE VIEW OF THE COUNT
APARTMENT IN BLUE BEA
Chamber & Punishn
Y AND PART OF A BOME
INSIDE OF THE SEPUL
UCTION of the S

## ADMIRERS OF
informed, that the Traged
r. MACREADY will, for the F
ed on Monday, November
READY; and on Thursday
ago, Mr. KEAN; and to pr
n of Seats, in consequence o
cured them,) as early an ap

an Extra Pit Door will be Opene
ommodation of the Public, have be
are to set down at the Portico in
d.—Carriages to set down at the
da Drury-lane—Carriages are to
heads towards Covent Garden—
own
or Free Admission of any
on this Evening.
L FOR SCANDAL AND
act crowded audiences, will be rep

---

# NIBLO'S GARDEN
James M. Nixo............. Manager
Stage Manage............. n Cooke
Scenic Artists............. R. Smith

## SEVENTH WEEK
And 20th Night of the Engagement
OF THE EMINENT
### AMERICAN TRAGEDIAN
MR.
# EDWIN FORREST
Who will appear for the second time, these four years, as
# OTHELLO
## Wednesday Evening, Oct. 31, 1860
Will be presented, for the second time, with New Scenery, Appointments,
&c., Shakespeare's Tragedy of

# OTHELLO
## THE MOOR OF VENICE.

OTHELLO - - - - - - MR. EDWIN FORREST

| | |
|---|---|
| Iago | Mr. F. B. Conway |
| Cassio | Mr. Chas. Fisher |
| Roderigo | Mr. A. W. Fenno |
| The Duke of Venice ... Mr. Morris | Brabantio ... Mr. Canoll |
| Gratiano ... Mr. Martin | Ludovico ... Mr. Donaldson |
| Montano ... Mr. Harkins | Antonio ... Mr. Harrison |
| Marco ... Mr. Henry | Paulo ... Mr. Taylor |
| Messenger ... Mr. Beeks | Luca ... Mr. Ellis |
| Giovani ... Mr. Gouldson | Julio ... Mr. Cooke |
| Leonardo ... Mr. Andrews | Lords, Senators, Soldiers, &c. |
| Desdamona | Mrs. F. B. Conway |
| Emilia | Mme. Ponisi |

A Street in Venice................................Hillyard
The Rialto in A. D., 1400.................Hillyard
The Port in Cypress...........................Hillyard
A Room in the Citadel.......................J. R. Smith
And the Bed Chamber........................J. R. Smith

Previous to the Tragedy, the Orchestra, under the supervision of **MR. JOHN COOKE,**
will perform the overture to **OTELLO.**

### PRICES OF ADMISSION:
Private Boxes............From $6 to $10 | Orchestra Seats...................$1
According to location. | Parquette and Dress Circle.......50 Cents
Family Circle.......................................25 Cents
(entrance on Crosby Street)
in advance.

---

Theatre Royal Covent-Garden, WEDNESDAY, the 22d of MAY, 1805
Shakespeare's Tragedy of

# OTHELLO
## THE MOOR OF VENICE.

Duke of Venice, Mr. WADDY——Brabantio, Mr. HULL
Gratiano, Mr. DAVENPORT
Lodovico, Mr. CRESSWELL——Montano, Mr. CLAREMONT
Othello, Mr. KEMBLE——Cassio, Mr. C. KEMBLE
Iago, Mr. COOKE——Roderigo, Mr. FARLEY
Antonio, Mr. KLANERT——Julio, Mr. CURTIES *Jefferies*.
Mario, Mr. SARJANT.
Paulo, Mr. FIELD——Giovanni, Mr. L. BOLOGNA——Luca, Mr. LEE
Lorenzo, Mr. KING——Cosmo, Mr. REEVE
Officers of the City, Mr. DICK and Mr. POWERS
Messenger, Mr. ATKINS
Sailor, Mr. ABBOT——Leonardo, Mr. MENAGE *Rochford*
Servants to Brabantio and Cassio, Messrs. LEWISS, TRUMAN, WILDE, HARLEY.
Desdemona, Mrs. H. SIDDONS
Emilia, Mrs. LITCHFIELD

---

Performance
EST
eason
RT
AUSE
s of Niblo's.
early period, of

# THE MASKS OF OTHELLO

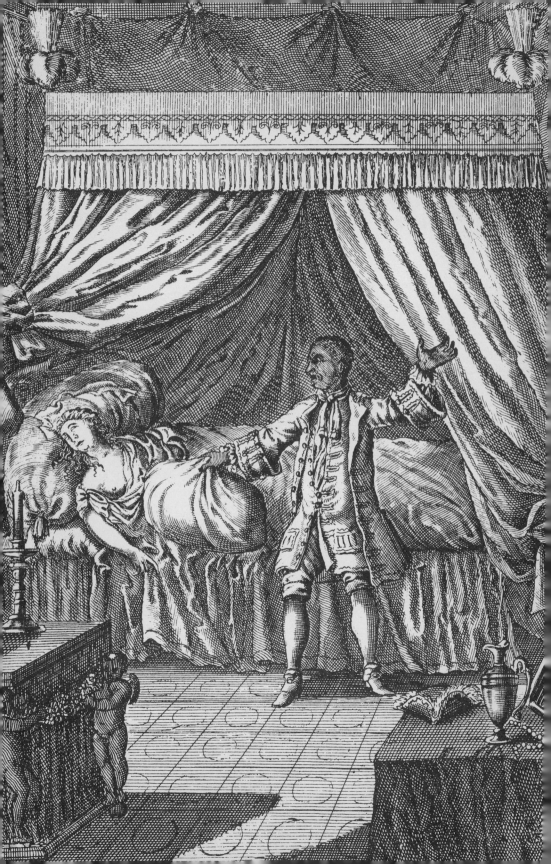

# THE MASKS OF OTHELLO

The Search for the Identity of Othello,
Iago, and Desdemona by
Three Centuries of Actors and Critics

BY MARVIN ROSENBERG

UNIVERSITY OF CALIFORNIA PRESS

Berkeley, Los Angeles, London 1971

PR
2829
R6
1961

UNIVERSITY OF CALIFORNIA PRESS
Berkeley and Los Angeles, California

UNIVERSITY OF CALIFORNIA PRESS, LTD.
London, England

ISBN: 0-520-02069-3
Library of Congress Catalog Number: 61-7521

Printed in the United States of America

*For Walter and Dorothy*
*and all the actors and critics*

# Preface

For some three centuries and a half actors and critics have been trying, in their different ways, to interpret the complex and profound characters of *Othello*. The actor has searched for characterizations that could be expressed through his physical imagery* on a stage, while the critic has tended to explain the poet's conceptions in terms of their verbal implications. Often the character images proposed by actor and critic have been curiously—even belligerently—different. I hope here to reconcile their differences, and bring together the best interpretations of both.

From the evidence of the play's stage history I try to describe—as well as words can do it—the work of art in its living form. I search particularly for the look and sound of Othello, Iago, and Desdemona; and for the inner shapes, the character essences, that the look and sound express. It will be a checkered search, for—to take Othello's case—

---

* A word about my use of "image" and "imagery." When I speak of one of Shakespeare's "character images," I refer to an artistic entity that was created to be perceived through a fusion of word, sound, and action in the theater. When I speak of "physical imagery," I refer to the actor's poetic use of voice and gesture to evoke—as verbal imagery does in another way—intellectual, imaginative, and emotional response.

few players have had the genius completely to fill
out the Moor's mighty image: the rare actors who
have succeeded were rare men, their lives often
enriched and embittered by pain and sorrow, even
by personal crises not unlike Othello's own. It was
not easy to be Othello. Or Desdemona. Or Iago.

Since a staged play is a public event, performed
before a willing audience, the actors' characterizations were partly products of their times, and to
understand their differences we must know something of how a changing society influenced them,
as it responded to them. The influences were many,
and powerful: mainly because *Othello* is the most
erotic, the most sensual of the great tragedies, and
the time came when Anglo–Saxon culture, grown
strenuously refined, tried to drive from the text its
"offensive" words and sexual atmosphere, and even
threatened the form of the play.

When I have surveyed the stage images of
Othello, Iago, and Desdemona, I will turn to the
images proposed by the critics. The critics, too,
have been creatures of their times, in acquiescence
or revolt, they too have differed sharply, and their
task has been equally difficult: *Othello*'s characters
make tremendous demands on the emotion and intellect of any who would interpret them, whether
in imagination or action. But the rewards are great
too, as we shall see.

To all the actors and critics—and reviewers—of
*Othello* this book owes much. But there are some
particular debts: to that fine scholar who first introduced me to the tragedy, and who has followed
the course of this work, Walter Morris Hart; to the
distinguished modern actors who shared with me

their artistic insights: Earle Hyman, Sir Laurence Olivier, Anthony Quayle, Paul Robeson, Abraham Sofaer, Wilfrid Walter, and Sir Donald Wolfit; to other actors I have seen in the play, and to those who played in my production of it; to colleagues who read in the manuscript and offered counsel: Arthur Colby Sprague, Moody Prior, Louis Mackay, Charles Shattuck, William Van Lennep, Philip Highfill, John Gassner, and Alois Nagler; and to many scholars alluded to separately in the notes.

I have been generously helped by many libraries, particularly the University of California Library, the New York Public Library, the British Museum, the Birmingham Public Library, the Folger Library, the Harvard College Library Theatre Collection, and the Henry E. Huntington Library—and by the company of Shakespeareans who gather in these places. For financial assistance I am grateful to the University of California Faculty Research Committee, the American Philosophical Society, and the Henry E. Huntington Memorial Library. The help of my wife has been priceless.

I am grateful, too, for permission to print material from my essays in *Shakespeare Quarterly*, *Theatre Arts Monthly*, *Studies in Philology*, *Theatre Notebook*, *Philological Quarterly*, *PMLA*, and *English Studies*.

Berkeley, California                    Marvin Rosenberg

# Contents

# PART I

## The Beginning

The *Othello* character images that actors and critics pursue were created in a curious cultural and theatrical climate. The tragedy was presented, as far as we know for the first time,[1] in 1604, for a London theater invaded by skepticism and sensuality. The time was ripe for the play, with its pervasive sexual atmosphere and byplay, its erotic and despairing language, its bold, anguished images of man and woman contending in love and jealousy. Not by accident was it a leading tragedy—perhaps *the* leading tragedy[2]—of the early 1600's.

This was a time for drama of "obscene, unendurable realities . . . revolting images of sexual appetites and activities,"[3] for dramas with "a fillip of the excessive, the devious, the perverse."[4] This mood had not come suddenly on Elizabethan literature. There had always been, on the one hand, angry or leering satires and bawdy verse and, on the other,

1

the melancholy "consolations" that told over life's mishaps and miseries.[5] If the darker mood was less conspicuous during the blooming of the sweet, Platonic sonnet cycles, it flourished in the warm, fleshy Ovidian poems and the searching satires of the late sixteenth century. About 1600 an impulse to question established values[6] erupted in the paper war on society so dogged and biting, so erotic sometimes in its flaying of eroticism, that Archbishop Whitgift burned and banned its essays and drove the energy behind it into other channels— among them the drama. A brutal examination of man's deepest commitments—personal, marital, sexual—now became an important theatrical fashion. Now Shakespeare's "sexual nausea"—or "adultery nausea" [7]—plays would be written.

There were, as always, other fashions. Happy plays were still produced, particularly in the public playhouses. It was mainly for the sophisticated, anti-Puritan society oriented to the court, as it slipped from Elizabeth's tired hands into James's inept and greedy ones,[8] that England's playwrights began to write their bitter drama, full of tainted humanity and dressed in striking metaphysical and sensual imagery: so in the private "coterie" theaters the repertory would be much more jaded, more perverse.[9] Yet, since a company like Shakespeare's had often to provide entertainment that could please the court as well as the playgoing public—which was itself growing more sophisticated—the Globe's list too would include, besides its sunnier plays, sharp satire, cynical treatment of sexuality, and dark tragedy.

*Othello* belongs to this time—and we shall see how readily Shakespeare used contemporary ma-

terials in the play—but it is distingushed from the
run of Jacobean angry drama, as it would be distinguished throughout its theater history, by its
enormous compassion. The evil in humanity, the
doubts, the despair, and the violence are strongly
projected in the chief character images; yet, as they
are treated, it is almost as if Shakespeare had deliberately adapted this brutal murder tale to dare
himself to find sympathy in the farthest extreme
of human error.[10] By contrast, Cinthio's original is
a forbidding sermon. His unnamed Moor officer
marries a beautiful Venetian woman, Disdemona,
against the wishes of her parents. The Moor's Ensign loves the lady but, unable to win her affection,
persuades the Moor that she and a Captain are having an affair. The Moor and the Ensign lure Disdemona from her bed, beat her to death with "a
stockingful of sand," and shrewdly make the violence look like an accident. They are not at first
suspected; later the conscience-stricken Moor expels
the Ensign from his company, and the Ensign informs on the Moor. The Moor, under torture, will
not confess and is sent to banishment, where Disdemona's relatives kill him; the Ensign goes on to
more villainy, is tried, tortured, and dies a miserable
death. The story's moral is explicit: the Moor and
Disdemona should never have married. Shakespeare,
in transmuting this vendetta-morality into a tragedy
of compassion, spared none of its horror and guilt.
The play probes far more deeply into the fearful
and malign motives of men; its three chief characters do grave—the gravest—wrong; and yet,
plunged as they are into an atmosphere of sensuality,
betrayal, and terror, to murder, lie, and scheme, they
have yet persistently commanded the involvement

and pity of their audiences. Herein would lie a
crucial question for critics and actors seeking the
true images of these characters: how can—and
often, for the critics, why should—three such
wrongdoers as Othello, Desdemona, and Iago win,
so surely, so much care and compassion?

# I

## The Actor's Share

From the beginning, men wept at *Othello*. A rare "review" from 1610 tells how, when Shakespeare's company went down to Oxford to play the tragedy, the actors "drew tears not only by their speech, but also by their action. Indeed Desdemona, though always excellent, moved us especially in her death when, as she lay on her bed, her face itself implored the pity of the audience." [1]

So Shakespeare's own actors achieved an effect that would be many, many times repeated: they moved an audience beyond attention and involvement to compassion, and "drew tears." How did the playwright do it? What was his artistic design? Centuries of critics and actors have tried to answer; and in their answers the outlines of the essential character problems may be seen.

First, the problem of Othello. Basically, it is this: how can he be both noble and a murderer? What kind of sympathy, what empathy, can he evoke? His act of killing is somewhat less calculating, less brutal, than that of Cinthio's Moor; but there is still

5

calculation and brutality in it, and the playwright's vision in him of man's murderous passion is far more terrifying than anything in the original. Is the Moor who commits his crime, on Iago's urging, as noble as he—and everyone else—says he is? Or, to consult some critics, is he perhaps an insecure, oversexed soldier, experienced in adultery—with Emilia, among others—who is more than ready, even eager, to believe wrong of his wife? Is he a self-deceived impostor, fooling himself as well as all the others? What about his romantic tales: the antres vast, the cannibals, and the men whose heads grow beneath their shoulders? Or the magical handkerchief—protected by a witch's curse—woven by a Sybil from hallowed silk dyed in an ancient liquor made of maiden's hearts? Is this all lying and boasting? When he stops the brawling night clash with Brabantio, when he puts down the riot in Cyprus, does he command, or bluster? Then Iago deceives him—too easily? Is he a fool? Is he a neurotic eager to be deceived? Once deceived, and his surface disintegrates, what is to be made of the violence that erupts from the cellar of his being? The turbid sexual fantasies that sweep him into his "trance"? The stormy assaults on Desdemona, and then the killing? Is this the inner shape of a barbarian? Of Anyman? What is the meaning of his dark skin?

As many problems are found in Desdemona by actors—and especially by critics. How different she is from Cinthio's pious Disdemona, who fears "that I shall prove a warning to young girls not to marry against the wishes of their parents, and that the Italian ladies may learn from me not to wed a man whom nature and habitude of life estrange from us." Desdemona declares her faith in marriage to the death, and even in a faint reprise beyond it. Yet she too is partly responsible for the catastrophe. She has taken the initiative in marriage, has virtually proposed to Othello; she has deceived her father, has eloped against his wishes with a man of another race and color. She is certainly not "proper"; and she too is touched with the erotic ambience of the play: when she listens to Iago's rowdy jokes on the Cyprus quay, when she lets Emilia discuss the virtues of adultery, in her love play with Othello, and in her undressing and bedroom scenes. She "meddles" in her husband's business, presses him to reinstate his dismissed officer—presses him at the worst moment, when he most needs understanding. Finally, she lies to him, and destroys their hope of love. Is this quite a heroine? Or, as some critics have suggested, is she perhaps to be scorned for her filial ingratitude, for her lies, for her forwardness, for her spinelessness? Is there something "unnatural" in her love? Does she deserve what happened to her? Conversely, is she perhaps the very essence of goodness? A symbol of divinity? A Christ figure? Can any of this explain why audiences would weep for her, as they did at Oxford?

Most complex of all for actors and critics is the Iago problem. This villain is much more dangerous than Cinthio's. He not only betrays the Moor and the Captain (Cassio); he injures everyone in his vicinity. How can so evil a man be plausible? How can he win the confidence of so apparently noble a man as Othello? And more important, what is his motivation? Why should any man hurt others so much? Is he simply a dramatic mechanism? A symbol of the devil? The devil himself? Or is he in fact a good man who has been provoked to revenge by wrongs done him? Was he unfairly denied promotion by Othello? Cuckolded by him? By Cassio? Why is his language so charged with erotic allusions: the lascivious wordplay directed at Brabantio, at Roderigo, even at Desdemona; the insidious, then blatant images of carnality, nakedness, and intercourse with which he overwhelms Othello; and, most of all, the brooding sexual fantasy that pervades his soliloquies? Does he really lust after Desdemona? Is he driven by a repressed homosexual attachment to Othello? Finally, how can a character who does so much wrong involve audiences so deeply in his fate?

The scanty theater record in Shakespeare's time gives us only part of the answers to these character problems. But we could not hope to know all, even if the Jacobean acting experience were whole before us. Shakespeare, wise in his craft, must

have known when he provided the great characters for his
actors that even he could not begin to realize their ultimate form
until his young man-Desdemona, and Burbage as Othello, and
someone—Lowin?—as Iago came on the stage and lived out the
language. And these actors could provide only one glimpse; for
again the playwright must have known that the human instrument on which he played was a variable one: that even in his
own lifetime, someone of different height, weight, size, voice,
temper than Burbage might play Othello, and though the core
of the character would be the same, it might be manifested in
different tones, with new insights into meaning, and still be a
true Othello.

Here is a central point—that actors *can* bring personal interpretations to these characterizations. Critics often look for a
single pattern for the big roles—a one "real" Othello, or Iago,
or Desdemona. In support of this approach, a school of "formalists" argues that acting in Shakespeare's theater must have been
so conventional that only one fixed visualization of a character
was possible—a visualization projected in a formal, non-natural-
istic, even operatic or balletic style;[2] the players did not try to
*be* the characters, they only let the lines tell what the character
was: "Given two actors of equal talent, each would be able to
perform the same speech in exactly the same way, apart from
differences in voice and personal appearance." [3] To accept this
is to believe the actors were not actors at all, as we know them,
but puppets—and indeed a formalist once called them exactly
that.[4]

If the first Othello, Iago, and Desdemona were such puppets,
then every subsequent actor who brought his own intuitions to
the roles—and every great one did—was unfaithful to the playwright's form. Certainly later Othellos differed sharply in
style and personality and originality of interpretation. Though
they were all masters of technique, they labored through inspiration as well as method to penetrate the humanity of the Moor,
to *be* him while acting him, and they were proud to the point
of competitiveness (as critics too are) over the authenticity of

their interpretations. Why, then, were the master artists for whom Shakespeare wrote willing to subdue their great talents to stock patterns? And to play Othello, say, in one formal way? Since it is my thesis that an actor of genius can bring illumination to the characters in *Othello*, we must consider whether Shakespeare intended his play for so sterile an acting instrument as the formalists say.

Their strongest argument builds on a deduction: to play Desdemona—and the other women's roles—Shakespeare had to use a "boy" actor, from whom he could not hope to get naturalistic acting; hence all acting must have been impersonal, patterned.[5] This is far from fair to the "boy" Desdemona who drew tears at Oxford, or to the nameless others who played this and the other great feminine characters of the day. They were not, as they sound, *little* boys; many were well past boyhood, and in legal documents of the time were sometimes called young men. Some were mature men; two who played women's parts in 1635 were at least twenty-four, perhaps as old as twenty-eight.[6] From the Restoration come further hints: Colley Cibber tells how Charles II complained of the lateness of a first curtain, only to be fairly told that "the queen had not shaved yet." [7] There was probably much jest, but not all jest, in the prologue spoken before the first appearance of a woman as Desdemona:

> For (to speak truth) men act, that are between,
> Forty and fifty, Wenches of fifteen;
> With bone so large, and nerve so incomplyant,
> When you call *Desdemona*, enter Giant.[8]

Many of these adult male actors of women's parts were artists in their own right. They introduced to the stage some of its most powerful women's characters. Of the Restoration's famous Kynaston—described by Pepys as "clearly the prettiest woman in the whole house" [9]—John Downes wrote: "It has been disputable among the judicious, whether any woman that succeeded him so sensibly touch'd the audience as he." [10]

In special theaters in our major cities today, skilled men actors play women's parts—though the parts are usually so shabby, so cheap, the context so special, that the players seem to be mocking themselves. Their audiences often receive with a nervous embarrassment what was taken for granted by the Jacobeans— except those of Prynne's Puritan persuasion. Men who wanted to act like women then must have seen the stage as a kind of natural home. I do not mean to suggest that most—or even many —of Shakespeare's boy actors were homosexual, though there may well have been some truth in Prynne's furious assaults on the "sodomiticall" theater. On the stage they were simply part of the play. Note again the report on *Othello* at Oxford: "as [Desdemona] lay in her bed, her face itself implored the pity of the audience." The illusion is complete: the observer does not comment on the actor playing the part—it is Desdemona who is to be pitied. And note this: it was the great Burbage's own company, but what is remembered is the emotion conveyed by the player of the woman. Do we need to doubt that the actor of Desdemona could communicate the true passion Shakespeare demanded of him without formalizing or symbolizing his actions to disguise age or sex?

Some mocking speeches have been pointed out by formalists to prove that actors were stilted and conventional rather than creatively natural. Thus in *Othello* Iago mocks a stage cliché: "What's he then that says I play the villain?" And thus Buckingham, in *Richard III:*

> Tut, I can counterfeit the deep tragedian,
> Speak, and look back, and pry on every side,
> Tremble, and start at wagging of a straw,
> Intending deep suspicion. Ghastly looks
> Are at my service, like enforced smiles . . . (III, v. 5)[11]

What better proof that good acting was anything *but* such hackneyed stuff! How secure Shakespeare must have been in the creativity of his Iago and Buckingham to make them allude to the stereotypes of second-rate actors! Of course there were second-raters; there are always hacks where there is art. We have our own hacks; George Jean Nathan described one, a well-known actress, in her routine for "panic"—and note its family resemblance to Buckingham's histrionics:

> Panic: rapid looks to left and right, nervous paddling of thighs, wild brushing of hair up from ears, more rapid looks from right to left, execution of a few steps of the rhumba, and rapid inhalations and exhalations as if uncomfortably anticipating the imminent approach of a glue factory.[12]

Here, as in Shakespeare, the criticism of hack acting clearly implies that "natural" acting is known and valued. True, in *Othello* the playwright did occasionally dictate bits of business: Othello "gnaws his nether lip" in rage. But this does not mean that the business was rigidly patterned. A formalist tells us firmly: "Joy was expressed by cutting capers," because in Chapman's *Charlemagne* an actor cuts capers to show he is unaffected by bad news.[13] Othello, then, would caper at his meeting with Desdemona at Cyprus? The mind reels at the thought. The *Charlemagne* business was a bit Chapman thought would suit this character in this action, and sometimes such universal sign language does convey the emotion demanded. Eugene O'Neill has Mildred Douglas in *The Hairy Ape* "biting her lip angrily"; Wilde has lips chewed to shreds in *The Ideal Husband;* so Shakespeare has Othello gnaw his lip—but we need not assume therefore that any of them expected their players to act like puppets.[14]

In Shakespeare's time the playwright wanted his actors to play a part "as if the Personator were the man Personated." [15] What else did Stanislavski want? In *Othello* the lines and the characterization clearly call for this kind of "natural" assumption of the humanity of a role. It may well have differed in degree from what we think of as "natural," but not in kind. Shakespeare's time, like ours, attacked rhetorical, inflated, artificial performance, and praised as "natural" what seemed recognizably close to human behavior, what conveyed, in the close—almost arena-like—quarters of the period's theaters:[16]

Things never done, with that true life,
That thoughts and wits should stand at strife
Whether the things now shown be true,
Or whether we ourselves now do
The things we but present (*Ram Alley*, Prologue).[17]

Of course "natural" acting did not mean then, as it was sometimes to mean to nineteenth-century Othellos, a studied repro-
duction in all characters of commonplace details of everyday
life. The actor creates not a person but an art object that distills
the playwright's vision of humanity in the form of a recognizable
dramatic personality. Clearly Shakespeare's players understood
that in their art different character designs were communicated
differently: Brabantio's servants did not behave as the Duke did;
the clown, joking, was not like Iago joking. Othello behaved as
Roderigo never could. At a more important level, the complex
characters varied within themselves as they met different situations. Thus the tremendous challenge Shakespeare presented to
the actor who played Desdemona: at first a young girl, braving
her father's anger for love; then an amorous bride; then a wife,
humorously tending her husband's affairs; then a wronged,
frightened woman; and at last, a desperate mortal, fighting for
her life. Shakespeare depended on the "boy" who played so
many parts in one to convey through the lines and action a continuous personality design in which all the changing moods
could cohere.

This essential contribution of the actor is a hard fact for the
formalist to accept. Back of the formalist attitude, clearly, is a
wishful preconception: that Shakespeare must be fixed, immu-
table, not subject to the variable of theater interpretation. T. S.
Eliot said this in its raw form: "I rebel against most performances
of Shakespeare's plays because I want a direct relationship between the work of art and myself, and I want the performance
to be such as will not interrupt or alter this relationship any more
than it is an alteration or interruption for me to superpose a
second inspection of a picture or a building upon the first." [18]

But this is to deny the art form that made the plays what they are. In the theater for which Shakespeare wrote, the great words were only one part of a larger imagery that had to be expressed through a physical personality. The formalists say the players simply let the lines tell what the character was—but what *do* the lines tell us the character is? What is Othello, for instance? What two scholars agree? Yet these scholars are only seeking what Shakespeare expected the actor to find: a frame of reference in which the character's experiences may be organized.[19] The critics who were to solve Othello's character problem by writing him down a braggart, puffed up with self-delusion, managed with an easy stroke of the imagination to frame a context for the hero's every act. The actor must not only seek such a "center" for the Moor; he must create an art object in which every gesture, every vocal and facial sign, confirms the wholeness and meaning of the design. This is the only way Othello can be fully known. Clearly, from the critical arguments over his nobility, or lack of it, his true quality cannot be found simply in the lines; it lies in how the lines and necessary accompanying gestures are experienced; and Shakespeare meant them to be experienced through the medium of acting. At the Globe it was up to Burbage to synthesize the role's verbal-visual-aural imagery into the image that was the aim of Shakespeare's art. The great actor's special genius for this task was in his sensitivity to the poetry's meaning and emotion as it had to be expressed in voice and action. This sensitivity matures and is refined, so that an actor, like a scholar, continually discovers new riches in Shakespeare: thus Laurence Olivier recently told how, after years of playing, a minor phrase of Hamlet's suddenly became meaningful to him. Burbage was a lucky Othello because when he worked out his Moor, he could ask the playwright about nuances in the character's essential image; but Shakespeare was lucky too in that he knew he had, in Burbage, an artist inspired to complete the act of drama, often by expressing in a total characterization meanings that even the playwright may not have recognized as being there.

With all the magic in *Othello*, there was never this magic: that the lines, merely by being spoken well, would create a personality for whom the spectators might weep, as the Oxonians wept for Desdemona. But there *was* this magic: that the lines evoked superlatively a creative form-drive in the actor, as a piece of eloquent marble does in a sculptor; and it was by the actor's organization of the poetic material in *Othello*, his expression of its felt essence through physical imagery, that he moved people in the theater to tears and laughter and reflection as Shakespeare intended them to be moved, and as they can be moved in no other way. We look now to the theater history to find how it was done.

Shakespeare's boy actor at Oxford in 1610 established one of the dominant elements in the Desdemona image—a presence so appealing to an audience that at her tragic appearance men would weep—"her face itself implored the pity of the audience." And this is all we know, for now, of her stage image.

We have one indirect glimpse of Burbage as Othello. Burbage was one of those actors who entered deeply into the identity of his characters, and *stayed there*, in a manner again suggesting Stanislavski: "A delightful *Proteus*, so wholly transforming himself in to his Part, and putting himself off with his Cloathes, as he never (not so much as in the Tyring-house) assuim'd himself again until the play was done." [20] The center or key he found for his Othello characterization is suggested by a phrase in its praise: a "Greued Moor." Another eulogy to the actor expanded this:

> But let me not forget one chiefest part
> Wherein, beyond the rest, he mov'd the heart,
> The grieved Moor, made jealous by a slave,
> Who sent his wife to fill a timeless grave.[21]

"Grieved Moor" here suggests an inner shape, of affliction, of pain, of a governing agony that "mov'd the heart" for Othello.[22] The glimpse is of a "noble murderer."

Of the Iago image, two hints are suggestive. First, he *was* a "slave," a villain—such a villain that actors of the role were nearly tarred with his pitch:

> How often is a good Actor (as for instance the Jago in the *Moor of Venice*) . . . little less than Curst for Acting an Ill part. Such a natural Affection and Commiseration of *Innocence* does Tragedy raise, and such Abhorrence of *Villainy*.[23]

Yet apparently there was a softening humor along with the evil in the image.[24] Evil colored by humor: evil abhorred, and yet touched with a kind of mirth. Is there a hint here of the villain's motivation? Of his plausibility?

It is a temptation to go on to deduce, from the text and the known historical background, the scene-by-scene effect and meaning of the *Othello* characters in Shakespeare's time. But such deduction is the province of the critic; and until later, when we enter the stormy arena where the critical battles are fought, we are committed to the evidence of theater experience and audience reaction. Our next clues will be found in the Restoration. Again they will be few; but they will begin to give us a sense of the historic look and sound of the play.

# 2

*᭫ Rude am I in my speech . . .*

# Othello in the Restoration

Almost nothing is known of how the Restoration actors expressed the inner shapes of the characters in *Othello*; but there is evidence of a curious, paradoxical treatment of the surface images. Hero and heroine were apparently made a touch more dignified, less humanly frail, to satisfy a growing critical "Decorum." At the same time there was an intensified exploitation of the play's erotic physical imagery, to satisfy the voracious Restoration appetite for staged sensuality.

An out-of-the-way clue suggests the bold display of the visually erotic elements. The often prurient playwright Aphra Behn, piously indignant that she should be charged with pruriency, wrote hotly:

> . . . they cry, *That Mr. Leigh opens his Night Gown when he comes to the Bride-chamber;* if he do, which is a Jest of his own making, and which I never saw, I hope he has his Cloaths on underneath? And if so, where is the Indecency? . . . Another crys, *Why we know not what they mean, when the Man takes a Woman off the Stage, and another is thereby cuckolded:* is

16

that any more than you see in the most celebrated of your
plays . . . So in that lucky Play of the *London Cuckolds,* not
to recite Particulars . . . In *Valentinian,* see . . . Valentinian
all loose and ruffld a Moment after the Rape . . . and a thousand others, *The Moor of Venice* in many places . . . all these
I name as some of the best Plays I know . . .[1]

"*The Moor of Venice* in many places . . ." *Othello* was able
to share in the general erotic treatment of drama largely because
of a great, simple discovery the Restoration impresarios had
made: there is no substitute for a woman. In the Jacobean period
a young man with a gift for female impersonation might lilt in
skirts across the stage as Desdemona, and the audience would accept him as such even when he kissed Othello on the Cyprus quay,
even when he undressed in a bedroom scene, or welcomed
Othello to bed, or took a wound in his breast. But if the audience
had a whipped-up hunger for the erotic implications of exposed
female flesh, then, as Cibber observed, "real beautiful women,"
including several who "had charms sufficient at their leisure
hours to mollify the cares of empire," [2] were much more satisfying.

The revelation of actresses broke on England slowly. Preju-
dice against them had been deeply fixed:[3] not until Charles II
and his fugitive court returned from France did "those women"
begin to act professionally in London. Even then they were not
universally welcomed. Convention was convention; and even a
man so fond of females as Pepys at first objected. But there was
no resisting the obvious advantages to that licentious theater,
or the obvious advantage to the women themselves: for the respectable ones, a creative outlet; for certain pretty, practical
ones, like Moll Davis and Nell Gwyn, a showcase—a first rung
up the ladder from whoredom to mistress-ship. The rakes were
delighted; and Pepys, the would-be rake, quickly followed suit.
*Othello* very soon had a woman Desdemona; and the event was
important enough for a proud prologue. No longer would English audiences have to see "men act, that are between forty and

fifty, wenches of fifteen." This time, when Desdemona was called, no Giant would enter. The prologue leered:

> . . . I saw the Lady drest.
> The Woman plays to day: mistake me not;
> No man in gown, or Page in petty-coat;
> A Woman to my knowledge, yet I cann't
> (If I should dye) make affidavit on't.[4]

We know almost nothing of how the first women Desdemonas played their part; though we can assume they allowed it the sensuality suggested by Aphra Behn's comment, and by the lines and business of the contemporary drama. In this theater, limbs and breasts were prominently displayed and fondled, in the serious drama as well as in the comic.[5] Hence Mrs. Behn could link *The London Cuckolds* with *Othello* and *Valentinian* because of the way performances of the comedy and the tragedies treated their sensual undress and bedroom scenes. *The London Cuckolds* is a bawdy play, whose premise is that women naturally seek intimacy with any men not their husbands. In one bedroom scene a lover and his mistress are twice interrupted, first by the husband, then by a second lover; the first lover hides in the sheets while the wife pulls together her rumpled gown, sits up, and piously reads her prayer book. In *Valentinian* Rochester transmuted Fletcher's erotic Jacobean tragedy into one musky with the language and action of sexuality. Valentinian tries to take Lucina by force; she strenuously resists (Adulteries, Steele wrote in the *Tatler* [134] are "wrought up to such a height upon the stage, that they are almost put into execution before the actors can get behind the scenes"); a plot is laid to bind her for seduction; the curtains are drawn, music is played to cover (and emphasize) the implied action, and at once seducer and fair victim are disclosed: "See . . . Valentinian all loose and ruffld a Moment after the Rape," Mrs. Behn says; while Lucina, according to the stage directions, is "newly unbound"—she undoubtedly also bewitchingly "loose and ruffld."

Perhaps even more typical of the play's atmosphere is Rochester's startling homosexual love scene in Act V:

> *Valentinian and the Eunuch discover'd on a Couch*
> (Val); Oh let me press these balmy lips all day,
>     And bathe my love-scorched soul in thy
>         moist kisses . . .
>     And thou shalt be the altar of my love,
>     Upon thy beauties hourly will I offer,
>     And pour out pleasures and blest sacrifice . . .

The treatment of love in *Othello* must have had a different tone, but it probably shared the openness of the amorous passion and the unashamed use of erotic language and particularly the sensual action Shakespeare intended: Desdemona undressing, Bianca wooing Cassio, Desdemona in bed for her death—all opportunities for "loose and ruffld" costuming.* The full measure of Othello's sexual jealousy must have been presented, plainly motivating the passion that drove him to murder. This is important: it will be the last time for more than two hundred years that professional theaters try to present this part of the play's visual imagery with a frankness close to the playwright's own.

We know very little of how the actors in this permissive theater worked out the play's character problems, because no production of *Othello* is reported in detail. We do know the play was most popular: even Rymer, who despised it passionately, had to acknowledge: "From all the tragedies on our English stage, Othello is said to bear the bell away." And Pepys told charmingly an instance of its power to move: ". . . a pretty lady, that sat by me, called out, to see Desdemona smothered." So there must have been the passion and pity again, probably evoked by characterizations closely related to those Shakespeare himself had worked out at the Globe;[6] but we have almost no

---

* Rowe's first illustration for *Othello* (see frontispiece), which may reflect actual stage practice, shows Othello ready to smother Desdemona in her bed, her breast exposed by her loose gown.

details as to how this was done, except for a brief report on Betterton's Moor.

Betterton must have been influenced by the style demanded in the new formal, heroic drama, in which rant and rave, and the chanting of verse, threatened to become fashionable. But players still learned to act "as if the Personator were the man Personated," [7] and Betterton was the foremost of them. He was caught in the actor's eternal dilemma between technique and individual artistic expression: he may have thought in patterns of voice and movement, but the reports of his Othello, and of other characterizations, suggest that he achieved a deep penetration into character and a personal quality of expression that seemed to the judicious "natural" as opposed to the conventional "roar of passion" of the hacks. [8]

Betterton brought a hero's front to Othello: ". . . his Aspect was serious, venerable, and majestic . . . His Voice was low and grumbling, though he could time it by an artful Climax, which enforc'd universal attention, even from the *Fops* and *Orange-girls* . . ." He was restrained, but in his very restraint there was power: "He kept this Passion under, and shew'd it most." [9] How effectively he projected from beneath the hero's façade an image of a "grieved" Othello's inner torment is suggested by Steele, in the *Tatler:* "The wonderful agony which he appeared in, when he examined the circumstances of the handkerchief . . . the mixture of love that intruded upon his mind upon the innocent answers Desdemona makes, betrayed in his gestures such passions, as would admonish a man to be afraid of his own heart . . ." Again we catch a glimpse of a "noble murderer"—and little else.

Indirectly we get some idea of the Restoration images of *Othello* from the only contemporary theater text—from the Smock Alley Theatre in Dublin, a transplanted London playhouse. [10] The relatively few cuts seem to point up a particular effect: the "refinement" of Othello (and secondarily of Desdemona). Thus the theater moved to appease the new clamor in criticism for Decorum—as voiced, for instance, by Rymer, to

whom Othello's language and behavior were not even remotely
those of a hero. Rymer damned Shakespeare for this tasteless
creation: "There is not a Monkey but understands Nature better, nor a Pug in Barbary that has not a truer taste of things." The
Smock Alley text seemed to be trying somewhat to improve
Shakespeare's taste for the Rymers. The chief changes in Othello's lines emphasize his nobility, dignity, poise. Thus, speaking
to the ducal council, Othello is not allowed to say a few lines
beginning

> For since these arms of mine had seven years'
> pith . . . I, iii, 100–104 *

apparently because a seven-year-old warrior sounded more like
incredible boasting than romance. Similarly, Othello does not say
the indecorous:

> Let housewives make a skillet of my helm . . .
> (300–302)

Nor is he allowed the vulgar figure,

> Exchange me for a goat . . . (III, iii, 209–212)

nor a few lines later,

> Nor from mine own weak merits will I draw
> The smallest fear or doubt of her revolt;
> For she had eyes and chose me. (216–218)[11]

The Smock Alley Othello may have partly controlled the
overt evidence of his inner trouble, for Iago, deceiving him, is
not permitted to say:

> But I do see y'are moved . . . (253–256)

---

* Except in quotations from secondary sources, line numbers are from the
Furness *Variorium Othello* with language modernized.

And Othello may not say to him, at the end of their first round:[12]

> Set on thy wife to observe.

The great general cannot set a spy to his wife. The point of Othello's greater age is lost with the cut lines:

> or for I am declined
> Into the vale of years—yet that's not much—
> (309–310)

And perhaps that he should not seem to descend too low, too soon, this is also cut:

> She's gone. I am abused and my relief
> Must be to loathe her. (311–312)

Gone too is the final note of self-pity in the speech,

> Yet 'tis the plague of great ones . . . (317–321)

A little later, the romantic farewell speech is stripped of what again seemed too unmanly:

> I had been happy if the general camp,
> Pioners and all, had tasted her sweet body,
> So I had nothing known. (401–403)

Extravagance is further muted by the deletion of the speech's great baroque ending:

> Farewell the neighing steed, and the shrill trump,
> The spirit-stirring drum, the ear-piercing fife,
> The royal banner, and all quality,
> Pride, pomp, and circumstance of glorious war:
> And O you mortal engines, whose rude throats
> Th' immortal Jove's dread clamors counterfeit,
> Farewell: Othello's occupation's gone. (407–413)

In threatening Iago, Othello loses a few violent, "horrid" phrases: "Than answer my waked wrath"; "Or woe upon thy life . . . On horror's head, horrors accumulate." The Folio's "my name, that was as fresh as Dian's visage, is now begrim'd and black . . ." becomes the Second Quarto's less self-conscious "*Her* name . . ."

As Othello nears his trance in Act IV, i, his speech gives way to desperate, incoherent babbling, full of suppressed sexual images. The revelation was too naked, too indecorous for Smock Alley, and after his first "Lie with her! Lie on her!" at one time or another the text cuts through:

> We say lie on her when
> They belie her. Lie with her: Zounds, that's
> fulsome. Handkerchief: Confessions: Handkerchief!
> . . . It is not words that shake me thus, pish!
> Noses, ears, and lips: Is't possible? Confess?
> Handkerchief?                    (44 ff.)

All that is left in the text is "O devil!"—and Othello falls in his trance. A terrible moment has been cut out, a moment charged with uncanny free association, in word and thought. It was a special step in Othello's march to catastrophe, and Smock Alley breaks a gap here—though, in fairness, a tinier one than was to come.

Later in Act IV, ii, a cut steals half of another of Othello's troubled speeches, which begins:

> Had it pleased Heaven
> To try me with affliction, had they rained
> All kinds of sores and shames on my bare head . . .
>                         (57 ff.)

In Smock Alley, this ends:

> But alas, to make me
> A fixed finger for the time of scorn
> To point his slow unmoving finger at! (65)

The remainder is cut, as if there were too much of indecision, of the turning and searching of Othello's tormented mind. Gone then is the moment of yielding;

> Yet could I bear that too, well, very well.

And then his recoil, as he is overwhelmed by his sense of loss;

> But there where I have garnered up my heart,
> Where either I must live or bear no life . . .

and he turns fiercely upon Desdemona in his passion again.

Very little more is cut. In Act V, i, after Cassio and then Roderigo are stabbed in the dark ambush, Othello appears long enough to hear the tumult and to assure himself of Iago's "noble sense of his friend's wrong." But in the Irish version he ends:

> Thou teachest me, Minion, your dear lies dead . . . (41)

Cut is the savage remainder:

> And your unblest Fate hies: Strumpet I come:
> For of my heart, those charms, thine eyes, are
> blotted.
> Thy bed, lust-stained, shall with lust's blood be
> spotted.

After Othello has killed Desdemona and learned how wrong he was, in his volcanic outburst, after "Cold, cold my girl" (338), lines are cut that we know offended a century later by their "extravagance," and apparently were already in bad taste:

> Even like thy chastity. O cursed, cursed slave!
> Whip me, ye devils!
> Wash me in steep-down gulfs of liquid fire! . . . (339–343)

Finally, in his "journey's end" speech, Othello is not allowed to weep; these lines are excised:

> . . . of one whose subdued eyes,
> Albeit unused to the melting mood,
> Drops tears as fast as the Arabian trees
> Their medicinable gum. (422–425)

He goes to his death without tears—or without the words for them. The altered text tries to make him die as it made him live: somewhat less human than Shakespeare's Othello, even greater of heart, closer to Decorum's image of a hero.

Desdemona changes a little too, away from wifely humanity toward the image of a more conventional heroine to suit the dignified hero. Her cuts are few but consistent, and suggest how distressing her occasional homely domesticity was to the decorous. (Thus Rymer: "No woman bred out of a pig-stye could talk so meanly.") In Act III, iii, assuring Cassio that she will try to influence Othello, she is not permitted:

> His bed shall seem a school, his board a shrift . . . (29)

And a little later, pressing Cassio's suit to Othello, she loses the housewifely:

> Why this is not a boon:
> 'Tis as I should entreat you wear your gloves,
> Or feed on nourishing dishes, or keep you warm,
> Or sue to you to do a peculiar profit
> To your own person. Nay, when I have a suit
> Wherein I mean to touch your love indeed,
> It shall be full of poise and difficult weight
> And fearful to be granted. (89–96)

In Act III, iv, when she has gently reproved Othello to Emilia, Shakespeare has her reprove herself for doing so (163–176), makes her remember that her husband has serious matters on his mind and cannot always play the bridegroom. This is a tender moment, too tender for the Smock Alley concept—it is out. A large part of her important Willow Song scene is also gone. Some of Emilia's dialogue is refined, to make the scene more ladylike. Since the women are not allowed to call lightly on heaven, Emilia's little joke as to when she might commit adultery becomes "Nor I neither by this . . . light. I might do't as well i' the dark." Curiously, her price for adultery is also changed. In Shakespeare's text she would not do it merely "for a joint-ring, nor for measures of lawn, nor for gowns, petticoats, nor caps, nor any petty exhibition. But for all the whole world!" Smock Alley leaves out the measures of lawn, joint-ring, and caps. Is there something too common about such bribes for chastity now—or too old-fashioned? Emilia also loses much of her last speech, urging the rights of wives to be as promiscuous as husbands. Finally, the Willow Song itself is excised. The loss of this most touching of all Desdemona's scenes, when the troubled girl dreams back on her childhood and recaptures it in the heart-breaking song, further reduces the gentle femininity of the part.

Thomas Rymer voiced absolute Decorum's notion of the hopeless flaw in Iago's image—how dare Shakespeare make a soldier a villain ". . . instead of [the] open-hearted, frank, plain-dealing . . . character confidently worn by them for some thousands of years." Obviously nothing could be done to remove this occupational blemish; and Smock Alley leaves the villain's image almost untouched. Iago's loose, erotic language, the obsessiveness with sex that belongs to his motivation, is almost intact. As to how this motivation was realized, or made plausible, we know almost nothing. Some slight cutting in the Smock Alley temptation scene (III, iii) may have been an attempt to increase plausibility, through diminishing some of his more conspicuous hypocrisy. He does not say:

> Who has that breast so pure,
> but some uncleanly apprehensions . . . (162–165)

and:

> (As I confess it is my nature's plague
> To spy into abuses, and oft my jealousy
> Shapes faults that are not) . . . (171–173)

and (as noted above):

> —but I do see y'are moved:
> I am to pray you not to strain my speech
> To grosser issues nor to larger reach
> Than to suspicion. (253–256)

He loses only one long speech in this crucial scene. After Othello muses, "And yet how nature erring from itself—" and Iago, "Ay, there's the point . . ." all that follows, centering on Desdemona's cross-racial choice,

> Foul disproportion, thoughts unnatural . . . (269–279)

is pared out. This may have been to increase propriety, and to protect the hero's image.

The attack by Decorum on the images seems to have begun. In its widest sense, Decorum was a fruitful concept: what functions organically in the art form is artistically right. But some of the English neoclassicists, misusing their cue from Horace, would narrow Decorum to a system of types: a king is always lofty, a prostitute is shameless, and so on. Hence Rymer complained of Iago's character—a villainous soldier! English drama for two centuries was to suffer from this critical typing. So Desdemona is made a touch more dainty as a heroine, and less a wife—a process that is inexorably to continue: a century later, critics complained when she sewed domestically on the stage. Othello seems to be "refined" to make a more noble, more dignified hero. Yet our one actual glimpse of a theater Othello— Betterton's—asserts a greatly "grieved" Moor, in the Burbage tradition. The hero's dignity was infused with agonized passion. This still leaves the central character problems unanswered: how and why could so noble an Othello be betrayed into such grief? How overt may his passion be, how intense, how violent, visually and aurally? The answers lie ahead.

As for the hero's dignity, it is interesting that the London of Charles II had a chance personally to appreciate the image of a grave, lofty Moorish stranger when a new ambassador came from Barbary. He was, observes John Evelyn, "a handsome person, well-featured, of a wise look, subtle, and extremely civil . . ." He and his men, wearing white mantles, dazzled Hyde Park with their horsemanship. Their courtly dignity was tested when Charles' "French whore," the Duchess of Portsmouth, entertained them at a gala banquet. She tried to enliven the party by scattering the strangers among the King's bastards and

> Nelly [Gwyn], concubines, and cattle of that sort, as splendid as jewels and excess of bravery could make them; the Moors . . . drank a little milk and water, but not a drop of wine . . . did not look about or stare on the ladies or express the least surprise, but with a courtly negligence in pace, countenance, and whole behavior, answering only to such questions as were asked with a great deal of wit and gallantry and so gravely took leave . . .[13]

Nature was imitating Shakespeare.

But "taste" was getting ready to "improve" him. Morality and Decorum were sharpening their knives: there would be much in the language and passion in *Othello* to offend them. The play was on the threshold of a severe trial.

# PART II

## The Eighteenth Century

The eighteenth-century actors who sought to project the *Othello* images were confronted with a curious new moral decorum that threatened the play's form and meaning. The conscience of England seemed to be stirred by a deep inward tremor, perhaps symptomatic of the many social ferments: the rise of middle-class power against old authority, of new knowledge and belief against old superstition and dogma, of a new assertion of a man's powers against his old humility, of a newer, more personal religion. With his new freedoms, man seemed to need new guilts, new shames. There was a preoccupation with the shows of "morality." By the eighteenth century, certain words and actions newly became profane, and were prohibited. Other words and actions—usually those related to sexual functions—became "bad," and were prohibited. Other words and actions were horrid—offensive to the sensibilities—and were prohibited. This emergence of a new coded behavior did not change man; below the level of "society," in the subculture, the prohibited things were regularly done—and often by the class that most professed propriety, as a comparison of Boswell's *Johnson* and his *Journals* amusingly shows. Side by side with "refinement" went still such rowdy farces as Foote's and the lusty mid-century novels, with some of the abiding pornography in the language. Gentlemen "talked bawdy" at the dinner table. Satire was never sharper. Poetry ranged widely in mood and form. Given the variety of morals and manners, and the striking changes in the hundred-year span in social, economic, political, and artistic life, only by a calculated risk may a scholar speak of the century—any century—as an entity. But men then, as always, did bind time by passing on attitudes to a next generation, and in perspective, clusters of these attitudes can be identified. The changing content of formal drama and specifically the changes in *Othello* indicate an unmistakable tide moving strongly toward the rigid pattern of outward behavior and language that would be called "Victorianism."

Why this social phenomenon emerged in England makes an interesting study. There was a social vanguard that thought of itself as seeking the ultimate in "refinement." Mandeville shrewdly guessed that the governing classes fastened a rigid social morality on the masses to keep them from impinging on the liberties of the elite. Orthodox theologists, viewing man's arrogant new attempts to understand and master the universe, might well say he was suffering guilt pains for the sin of pride. Freud would suggest that a tribe intensifies its taboos when it destroys the father figure—something the British had done both literally and figuratively.

Whatever the cause, drama was the victim. It began the decline that—except for the flashes of Goldsmith and Sheridan—would continue for almost two centuries. Partly the stage "but echoed back the public voice," as Johnson said; but partly too the "refiners," the licensers, and the literary brahmins "made" taste, which the public learned to follow. There was never, of course, a single monolithic attitude: the taste makers quarreled among themselves as well as with the common foe, "indelicacy"; and a few alarmed contemporaries, Goldsmith among them, cried the dangers of the excessive new "refinement," the "feeble commonplace morality" degrading the theater;[1] but as the great talents of the century escaped to other literary forms, it was left mainly to hacks to try to provide, in new pure plays, or in purified versions of old ones,[2] a reassuringly conventional drama, peopled by decorous types and relatively free of "touches of real, inward probing."[3]

*Othello* inevitably suffered. Depending so much upon spoken thoughts and physical action involving the sexual act, the play troubled a culture self-conscious of "indelicacy." As the theaters worked to eliminate verbal and visual imagery that was erotic or in "bad taste," many references to physical love came to be deleted and the erotic implications of Othello's jealousy and of Iago's evil were diminished.[4] But not eliminated; and what remained was apparently still found so disturbing as to rouse the sensitive, shame-excited imaginations of these audiences as powerfully as the full text had roused the Jacobeans.

The essential form of the play was threatened by those decorous and proper spirits who wanted to improve it with the kind of "'poetic justice" that

Tate's happy ending had inflicted on *King Lear*. "Some critics," the *Theatrical Review* observed, "have been disgusted with the distresses and unhappy fate of the virtuous and innocent *Desdemona* . . . they say she had not been guilty of the least fault or failing, and therefore, her fate is too horrible to be borne." [5] The extent of the pressure toward altering her destiny may be estimated from the tragedy's experiences on the Continent. In France, Ducis's adaptation, though it properly obscured that indecorous villain Iago, had at first the temerity to let the heroine be killed. *Horror!* When the great Talma, as Othello, did the deed, he roused

> a universal tumult. Tears, groans, and menaces resounded from all parts of the theatre; and what was still more demonstrative, and more alarming, several of the prettiest women in Paris fainted in the most conspicuous boxes and were publicly carried out of the house. Ducis was alarmed for his tragedy, for his fame, and for his life.

The ending had to be changed. The heroine's father, not dead after all, rushed in and prevented her death. But after several nights Talma, to his credit, could not bear the false conclusion, and changed it back, "to the surprise of the general audience, and to the peculiar agonies of the most obviously handsome and fashionable; but there was so much truth and dramatic feeling in his performances that Death became the established mode . . ." [6]

In Germany, in Schröder's adaptation, with the deaths included, the women were similarly overcome. Fainting spell followed fainting spell: ". . . the premature and unsuccessful confinement of this or that well-known lady in Hamburg was the result of seeing and hearing this over-tragic drama." [7] Schröder gave in, like Ducis, and let Othello and Desdemona live; and since there was no Talma to help him resist, Propriety's victory was final and the ending remained "happy."

No English actors agreed to such a defacement of the play. Though they allowed the deletions of "indelicate" language to stand (and even expand), there were some attempts at restoration in the "character" cuts. Barton Booth used some lines deleted by Smock Alley; Garrick tried to put back a bit regarded in his own time as "shameful"; Kemble restored some of the passion of Othello removed earlier in the century. In fact, the actors present us with a puzzle: their successes and failures as the Moor will not easily be reconciled with the conventional notions of a restrained, a neoclassic, a "man of feeling" audience.

# 3

*My parts, my title, and my perfect soul . . .*

# The Eighteenth-Century Actors

Men wept at *Othello* in the eighteenth-century theater. Men wept, and women shrieked; and a gentleman wrote: ". . . [women] who cannot be moved at Othello's story so artfully worked up by Shakespeare, and justly played by Betterton, are capable of marrying again before their husbands are cold, of trampling on a lover when dying at their feet, and are fit to converse with tigers only . . ." [1] The world agreed there was no greater play, no higher test of an actor's powers. A few of the best players projected the Moor's surface and his depth, his dignity and his agony. But some of the greatest failed. Why?

The contemporary theater text, which diminished the humanity and exoticism of the Moor, seems to indicate that a proper, neoclassic hero was aimed at. By mid-century at the latest [2] he could no longer speak, in his round, unvarnished tale, of antres vast and desarts idle, of the cannibals, the anthropophagi, and the men whose heads grew beneath their shoulders.

For a while, until Kemble restored the lines at the end of the
century, he could not even say at the Cyprus riot:

> Now by heaven
> My blood begins my safer guides to rule,
> And passion having my best judgement collied,
> Assays to rule the way. (II, ii, 229–232)

But the deepest and cruelest cuts were made to reduce the
atmosphere of sexuality into which Othello was betrayed. This
was done partly by refining the erotic lines Iago says to him,
partly by preserving Othello from the ultimate depths of his
physical agony. Hence in Act IV, i, where Shakespeare developed the sexual imagery to a crucial pitch, the acting texts of
about 1760 indicate a standard, bone-deep incision. At first the
initial twenty-nine lines were left intact; but the later eighteenth
century removed the offending dialogue at:

> Iago: Or to be naked with her friend in bed,
>         An hour or more, not meaning any harm?
> Oth:  Naked in bed (Iago) and not mean harm? . . .
>                                              (7–9)

A few lines later came the really major surgery, at the moment
of Othello's trance. He begins his incoherent speech, with
fevered visions of Cassio topping Desdemona: "Lie with her!
Lie on her! Lie with her!" (44), but before he can sink into
frenzy the scene cuts through to 218, with Othello's "I'll chop
her into messes." Gone are the delirium and the trance, so full
of the sight and sound of Othello's psychic and physical strain
(by 1700 it seemed "unnatural for a Hero to Swoon" [3]); gone
the humiliating eavesdropping on Cassio, Iago, and Bianca; gone
even the touching and suspense-filled moment of wavering before Othello renews his resolve to murder Desdemona:

> . . . but yet the pity of it, Iago! Oh, Iago, the pity of it, Iago!

It would seem that with these cuts, the great play must surely have begun to bleed; yet even this did not preserve the hero image safely enough for the finer sensibilities of the time. Francis Gentleman, a journalist and editor of acting texts who reflected faithfully the taboos of his culture, described the act opening as "tedious, confus'd trifling, and often indecent . . . the Moor has already been sufficiently wrought on." Gentleman wanted to eliminate everything up to Othello's "I'll not expostulate with her" (222): ". . . beginning here would save delicacy a blush or two, and be, in that sense, an improvement." [4] Kemble and the nineteenth century saved the blushes.

In Act V, Othello's image was relatively untouched, although he does not appear at all for that brief, ironic moment when he is supposed to hear the street scuffle and take heart in the integrity of his friend Iago. Fortunately the killing of Desdemona involved no serious "indelicacy" to need cutting, and later there is only one refinement for "taste"; Othello's defense to Emilia, "Cassio did top her," becomes either Pope's softened "tup" or the less specific "use." But aesthetic propriety was offended by the extent of the grieved Othello's despairing remorse, and Gentleman especially complained about the lines (cut by Smock Alley) beginning: "Whip me ye devils . . . Blow me about in winds, roast me in sulfur, Wash me in steep-down gulfs of liquid fire." Said Gentleman: ". . . as they convey very horrid ideas, we could wish them omitted." [5]

This suggests something of the image of the Moor the century seemed willing consciously to perceive. The uncanny welling up of instinctual drives evoked by Shakespeare's language had now to be started even more by the physical imagery and emotional means of the actor; yet the actor was supposed to bear the air of Decorum's hero. As acting tended toward a formal, declamatory style, it was a routine matter for hack players to project the surface of such a figure. "The ordinary Method of making a Hero," Addison observed (*Spectator*, 42) "is to clap a huge Plume of Feathers upon his Head, which rises so very high, that there is often a greater Length from his Chin to the Top of his Head, than to the Sole of his

Foot." Could actors penetrate deeply below such a hero's surfaces of manner and dress to an authentic disclosure of both
Othello's nobility and his murdering fury?

Unfortunately very little is reported about the early-eight-
eenth-century Othellos.* Betterton, acting into the first decade,
clearly conveyed the Moor's grief, but how, we hardly know.
Barton Booth's Moor certainly "moved the heart": "In the
distressful passages . . . all the Men, susceptible of the tender
Passions [were] in tears." But the few details that survive to
illuminate his Othello do little more than add to the puzzle. Here
was certainly the front of a hero: ". . . he had a manly Sweetness in his Countenance . . . His Attitudes were all picturesque,
he was noble in his Designs . . . the *Blind* might have seen him
in his *Voice*, and the *Deaf* have heard him in his *Visage*." In
playing Othello, as Benjamin Victor observed, Booth had to go
beyond appearance and technique to convey "all the various
passions of the soul." One sample gives a first real glimpse, in
sight and sound as well as language, of the inner Othello struggling through the outer restraint. In Act III, iii, Iago has just
left, on "I once more take my leave." Then

> . . . *after a long pause, the Eye kept looking after him, Booth
> spoke . . . in a low tone of Voice:*
> "This Fellow's of exceeding Honesty,
>   And knows all Qualities with a learn'd Spirit
>   of human Dealings."
>         *Then a Pause: the Look starting into Anger.*
>         "If I do prove her haggard,
>   Though that her Jesses were my dear Heart strings,
>   I'd whistle her off, and let her down the Wind
>   To prey at Fortune!"
>         *A long Pause, as to ruminate.*
>         "Haply, for I am black,
>   And have not those soft Parts of Conversation

---

* The theatrical record of the century resides mainly in a mass of vague and
random praise and blame in letters, memoirs, and periodicals (the great reviewers were yet to come). I have synthesized the meaningful comments on
*Othello*.

That Chamberers have—Or, for I am declin'd
Into the Vale of Years—Yet that's not much—"
> *After a Pause, the following Start of*
> *violent Passion.*
"She's gone! I am abused! and my Relief
Must be to loath her; O Curse of Marriage!
That we can call those delicate Creatures ours,
And not their Appetites!"
> *What follows in a quicker, contemptuous Tone.*
"I'd rather be a Toad,
And live upon the Vapour of a Dungeon,
Than keep a Corner in the Thing I love
For other's Uses!"
> *A Look of Amazement, seeing Desdemona coming.*
"Look where she comes!"
> *A short Pause, the Countenance and Voice*
> *softened.*
"If she be false, O then Heav'n mocks itself!
I'll not believe it." [6]

This Othello then was "violent" in his passion, and moved fluidly through "the highest expression of Fury and Distraction" —and was applauded by audiences in an "age of restraint." But it was said in his praise that in the "most heartbreaking anguish of his jealousy" he never "whindled, whined, or blubbered . . . all his Grief, though most feelingly expressed, was never beneath the Hero." [7] This confronts us with a rephrasing of a central problem of the character: How much grief—and what ultimate visual, aural signs of it—could the "grieved Moor" express and still *be* a hero?

At one extreme James Quin seemed intent on expressing the least possible grief. Quin, who dominated the London theater before Garrick's stardom, projected a large, heavy, slow-moving Moor whose surface seemed ideal for the times—a kind of ultimate in the outer image of a neoclassic hero. Here was an imposing, spectacular figure—a big, black Moor all in white: white

wig, white British officer's uniform, white gloves—a famous
piece of business was his slow peeling off of one pale glove from
a black hand. His forte was "speaking the sublime," the stolid,
massive effect: for example, "as calm as a marble statue" while
addressing the Duke.[8] His ponderous hero's surface in tragedy
was well suited to restrained heroics; but it was not enough for
Othello. Even physically Quin seemed "too cumbersome and
unwieldy" for the active Moor;[9] more important, the role demanded an inner passion, a grief that his "hoarse monotony" [10]
could not convey.

> His eyes in gloomy sockets taught to roll,
> Proclaim'd the sullen "habit of his soul":
> Heavy and phlegmatic he trod the stage,
> Too proud for tenderness, too dull for rage.[11]

In the judgment of Foote, an Othello himself, Quin was particularly deficient in tenderness. Foote (who believed firmly
that the Moor should win even more audience sympathy than
Desdemona) thought that Quin, where he should have been
loving and grieved, was "brutal, unfeeling." [12] Others agreed:
the gentleness, the pain, the inner fire in the vessel of the hero
seemed to be missing.

At the other extreme from Quin's ponderous Othello was
David Garrick's new, tempestuous one. Recurrently in the history of acting, a school arises to make the old one seem "unnatural," "old-fashioned"—and this happened now. The pioneer
of the new "natural" style, Charles Macklin, had at first met
strenuous resistance: "I spoke so *familiar* . . . and so little in the
hoity-toity tone of the Tragedy of the day, that the [London]
Manager told me I had better go to grass [the provinces] . . ." [13]
Both styles had faults: the typical old actor strutted stiffly and
waved his arms "in a continual see-saw"; the new, livelier player
sometimes seemed "afflicted with St. Vitus dance . . . [or] so
miserably distressed that a deaf spectator would be apt to imagine

he was complaining of the cholic." [14] When Garrick successfully championed the new manner, the jealous Quin prophesied: "The people who go to chapel will soon go to church again." [15] Instead, Quin's style as Othello was soon regarded as "old," inflated, loaded with "false majesty," while the "new" actors conclusively proved themselves better at exciting "pity and terror"; and Garrick was easily the best of them, agile in movement, sensitive in feeling, violent in passion—the greatest actor of the century.

Given his other triumphs, Garrick's success as Othello seemed almost inevitable. Certainly his conception of the Moor was as far as possible from Quin's mediocre one, and it was carefully thought—and felt—out. Garrick sensed the need to project through the Moor a violent—even horrid—inner agony that could not be contained in the customary envelope of a proper hero. In defending the overt terror in his conception against a doubter, Garrick argued that Shakespeare

> had shown us white men jealous in other pieces, but that their jealousy had limits, and was not so terrible . . . [in] Othello, he had wished to paint that passion in all its violence, and that is why he chose an African in whose being circulated fire instead of blood, and whose true or imaginary character could excuse all boldnesses of expression and all exaggerations of passion.[16]

So daring was Garrick that he even presumed to restore some of the now-standard textual cuts, which had probably affected Booth's performance and certainly had Quin's. Thus he revived Othello's trance, so shocking to many contemporary sensibilities —and the scene won him applause. In this instance at least, audiences were less responsible than the ruling taste makers for the deletion of "indelicacy," judging from Macklin's anger when a welcome was given to "that shameful scene of Epilepsy in the fourth act, which instead of being applauded, ought to have been exploded with indignation and contempt for his impudence . . . in offering such an absurd passage to a thinking and supposed judicious public . . . a passage which . . . on and off the stage must be looked on as an excrescence of the worst sort." [17] Alas, the taste makers would triumph; the trance would disappear for more than a century.

So Garrick's Othello was daring, violent, suited to the pyrotechnics of the great actor's "new" style—and it was over all a failure. Why? Was the interpretation faulty? Was the audience not ready for such a show of grief?

Several contemporaries felt that Garrick was simply trying too hard to be different from Quin,[18] that, in escaping the stuffed hero, he went too far and shattered the image of the Moor in fragmentary excitements. Victor advised him—after first larding him with praise (". . . it would be ridiculous to make the least doubt of your ability to act this character in the utmost perfection") that he was too busy, too flighty, lacking in dignity. Victor jested that Quin expressed little because he felt little: ". . . you are perhaps, too apt to run into the contrary extreme. I could wish . . . your gestures were less violent . . . your proper and pathetic manner of speaking would charm more successfully, if those violent, and seeming artful emotions of body were a little abated." Garrick retorted that tremendous passion was called for; Victor agreed that the jealousy needed "winding up . . . to a stature of horror and despair . . . but the error lies in being too *early*, or too *frequent*, in that violence of emotion." [19]

Henry Aston similarly attacked Garrick's action in addressing the Duke's council: ". . . it was not suitable to the occasion . . . the dignity of the action consists in modesty, not pomp . . ." And the jealousy and indignation later seemed without dignity: the "little wincings and gesticulations of the body were much below it; they were fitter for a man under the impressions of fear, or on whom some bodily torture was inflicting . . ." Aston tried to end all happily: ". . . [but] you have so eclipsed your rival [Quin] that he may be able to say, like Othello, 'his occupation's lost.' " [20] The observation was as inaccurate as the quotation. Quin was not yet eclipsed, and he himself dealt Garrick's Othello the most unkindest cut of all by comparing Garrick to a little Negro slave in a Hogarth picture: "Othello! . . . Psha! no such thing! There was a little black boy, like Pompey attending with a teakettle, fretting and fuming about the stage; but I saw no Othello!" [21] Malicious as this was, it struck home. Garrick had tried to support his conception of a barbarian stranger by adding a turban to Othello's now customary British army officer's uniform. The towering hero's turban was probably also meant to make Garrick seem taller than he was—he was not tall. He may have looked not unlike the little blackamoor page in Hogarth's *The Harlot's Progress*, who, wearing a laced jacket and oversized turban, bears in the kettle— for Quin's remark was remembered widely. It was not Garrick's shortness that was fatal; Kean was little, and a great Othello, and would have survived Quin's witlash. But apparently Garrick's Moor looked little because his actions were little and fretful; the massive shape of the character was lost.

Another possibility exists: this Moor may only have been too strange and violent, too "grieved" for men of refinement and feeling. Consider how Aaron Hill objected to ardent affection in a stage meeting of Othello and Desdemona:

> . . . when, at your arrival in *Cyprus*, you ran so eagerly to the arms of *Desdemona*, that *love* made you unmindful of your *greatness*, which might, however, be well enough preserved here, by a certain stately, yet tender, advance, not tripping lightly, to her *embrace;* but a little quickening the *step*, more strongly extending the arms, gently inclining the *breast*, not the *head*, and sending your look, as it were, before you, with a kind of amorous delight, in approaching her.[22]

For such a cooler image of a hero, "never unmindful of his *greatness*," let us look ahead for a moment to the ranking Shakespearean star at the end of the eighteenth century—stately John Philip Kemble.[23] Kemble seemed born to play heroes: he was tall and lordly, with "the front of Jove." His manner, too, was lordly; though he was sometimes praised for sudden, illuminating moments of familiarity, of "naturalism," his style represented mainly, as Sprague observes, a kind of "splendid formalism." [24] To his critics he seemed excessively rectilinear:

> . . . Lo Kemble comes, the Euclid of the stage;
> Who moves in given angles, squares a start,
> And blows his Roman beak by rules of art;
> Writhes with a grace to agony unknown,
> And gallops half an octave in a groan. [25]

This "teapot school" style (one hand on the bosom, one extended) fitted well the austere Roman heroes he played best—Brutus, and Cato—images of neoclassic Decorum. He tried to make it do for Othello by conceiving the Moor as a "slow man." For fiery emotion he substituted majesty—and mystery: ". . . he wrapped that great and ardent being in a mantle of mysterious solemnity, awfully predictive of his fate." [26] He seemed almost to be aiming at a timely paradox: a kind of Gothic, Roman Othello, the brooding mystery of emergent romanticism struggling under the formal restraint of neoclassicism. But the formality triumphed too completely, and circumscribed the image: the agonized man never broke through the hero. [27] So Kemble joined the company of premier actors who did not triumph as Othello.

Washington Irving thought that: ". . . in many parts he was cold and laboured, in the tender scenes he wanted mellowness." [28] Macready found one soft moment: at " 'Not a jot! Not a jot!' there was a tearful tremor upon his voice that had pathos in it; not a single [other] passage . . . excited the audience to sympathy . . ." [29] Hazlitt[30] and Kemble's famous sister, Mrs. Siddons,[31] doubted that Kemble felt the necessary passion for Othello's love and jealousy. The most rounded estimate came from Kemble's loyal biographer, Boaden. He said the actor had never "identified with" the role: "Mr. Kemble was grand and awful and pathetic. But he was European: there seemed to be philosophy in his bearing; there was reason in his rage . . . One of the sublimest things in language, the professional farewell of Othello, came rather coldly from him . . . It was, at most, only a part very finely played." [32]

What, then, did the eighteenth century want of Othello? If not the ponderousness of Quin, the excitement of Garrick, the mystery of Kemble? Could a hero's nobility, and then his awful passion and murder, be synthesized by an actor in this culture? Yes. In the middle of this restrained age, the great Othello, Spranger Barry, was a Moor of overpowering emotional force, the fiery, ardent essence of "the Hero and the Lover," who could go from "heart-rending" softness to the most extreme "extravagance of passion" [33] in love, in jealousy, and in killing. The tremendous thrust and stature of his emotion, in sight and sound, seemed completely to fill out Othello's form, in spite of the textual cuts.[34] Even Garrick's partisans, bitterly hostile to Barry, admitted that here was a true Moor.[35]

Barry could unleash the kind of violent passion Garrick had conceived, but not expressed; instead of being fretted away in separate moments, it rose and climaxed in an organic movement. With the famous tenderness—the "silver cadence"—of his voice, and his majestic physique, Barry projected an indestructible human dignity, not only in repose, but also in his expression of passionate love; and later too, when a fearful agony so shook his body and mind as to convey, even without the trance, the terrible deeps of Othello's inner being.

Barry took great care to assert the calmness and dignity of the early Othello. His first speech, "Tis better as it is," evidenced "a pre-eminence of judgement . . . a dignified and manly forbearance of temper." [36] His dignity in quelling the riot was "commanding." [37] Addressing the Duke, he was everything Garrick and Quin were not. He began "Rude am I in my speech" in tones "as soft as feathered snowflakes . . . as they fall." [38] His recitals of "feats of broils and battle" were "full of gallantry and heroism; but when he recalled Desdemona's

> In faith 'twas strange—'twas passing strange!
> 'Twas pitiful, 'twas wondrous pitiful!

his voice was so melodiously harmonized to the expression that
the sigh of pity communicated itself to the whole house . . ." [39]
The speech was greeted with "three rounds of applause . . .
and when the Duke . . . observes, 'I think this tale would win
my daughter too,' the hands came again, as their hearts had done
. . . in echo of his sentiment." [40] On Cyprus, Barry greeted Desdemona "with the voice of love itself; describing that passion
in so extatic a manner, as seemingly justified his fear

> That not another comfort like to this
> Succeeds in unknown fate."

The "vehemence" of this Othello's "tender passion for Desdemona seized every imagination." [41]

But Barry's special genius lay in the power of his grief.
Tempted by Iago, he was torn "between doubt and tenderness,
confidence and resentment. . ."

> His first tendencies to jealousy are beautifully expressed and
> are finely smothered, till at length they burst out with an amaz-
> ing wildness of rage . . . when he collars Iago, it is actually
> astonishing how his powers carry him through such a long con-
> tinued climax of terror, and yet . . . a little after he bursts out
> with "If there be cords or knives, poison or fire," etc. with the
> impetuous ferocity natural to one of Othello's complexion, still
> improved with the wildest harmony of voice . . .[42]

As the mold of the hero cracked and the naked man showed
through, there was a fearful authenticity in the release of emotion, powerfully suggestive of the visual and aural image Shakespeare had in mind—a bloody passion did indeed shake his very
frame:

> You could observe the muscles stiffening, the veins distending,
> and the red blood boiling through his dark skin—a mighty flood

of passion accumulating for several minutes—and at length,
bearing down its barriers and sweeping onward in thunder, love,
reason, mercy all before it. The females, at this point, used invariably to shriek, whilst those with stouter nerves grew up-
roarious in admiration; for my own part, I remember that the
thrill it gave me took my sleep the entire night.

And yet—

The very antithesis of this was the manner in which he gave the
words, "Oh, Desdemona—away—away—away—away—!" . . .
he looked a few seconds in Desdemona's face, as if to read her
feelings and disprove his suspicions; then, turning away, as the
adverse conviction gathered in his heart, he spoke falteringly,
and gushed into tears.

A few lines later, when "looking tenderly on her" he "exclaims

But there, where I have garnered up my heart,
Where either I must live or bear no life . . .

the extremes of love were so powerfully painted in his face . . .
and in his tones, that the audiences seemed to lose the *energies
of their hands,* and could only thank him *with their tears.*"
Even in the terrible moment when he was finally moved to murder Desdemona, the intensity and size of his agony—"his whole
visage became inflamed . . . he seemed to raise himself above
the ground"—swept the audience to empathy. "The very frame
and substance of our hearts was shaken, as if . . . we swelled
and trembled as he did." The realization of his loss:

My wife! My wife! What wife! I have no wife!

came as a "piercing lamentation." To the end this Othello was
one of "excruciating tenderness . . . [and] grief." [43]
    Here, then, was how much grief a hero-Othello could release
in this century of restraint and sensibility: the very utmost
"extravagance of passion"—as long as it was under aesthetic
control, "Decorous" in the true sense (emerging from the core

of the character)—grief as much as a man's body and spirit might bear, a total grief.

### ⌘ *I am not what I am* . . .

The Othello problem is interlaced with Iago's. To know how a noble man may be betrayed into murder, we must know the motives and manner of his betrayer. An excellent reverse example of what he must be was Colley Cibber's classic demonstration of what he must *not* be. So obvious was Cibber's wickedness, as he "shrugs up his Shoulders, shakes his Noddle, and, with a fawning Motion in his Hands, drawls out" his lines, that "Othello must be supposed a fool, a stock, if he does not see thro' him." [44]

As with Othello, Iago's problem was complicated by textual cuts. The missing lines contained part of an important motivating dimension—part of that uneasy, diseased element in Iago that turned again and again to thoughts of the sex act and made him seek to fasten similar thoughts on his companions. Along the thread of his journey through the play can be found the main cuts for "indelicacy."

Surprisingly, in mid-century he was still allowed to speak three early lines that were soon to be found intolerably shocking—his taunts to Brabantio:

> an old black ram
> Is tupping your white ewe . . . (96–97)

> You'll have your daughter cover'd
> with a Barbary horse . . . (123–124)

> your daughter and the Moor are making
> the beast with two backs . . . (128–129)

While this *Othello* was being performed in the 'sixties, Samuel Johnson wrote refinedly, "Iago bellows . . . in terms which a modern audience would not easily endure"; but that audience was apparently more tolerant than its tastemaker, for a decade later Francis Gentleman complained that the lines ". . . for the

sake of delicacy, should be omitted, though usually spoken." [45]
Acting versions printed them through the 'eighties; finally Kemble cut the ram and Barbary horse figures—though curiously enough he let the "beast" remain.

At the end of Act I, iii, where Shakespeare begins intensively to weave the erotic into his design, deep cuts were made in Iago's speeches contrasting lust with reason (351–363) and anticipating the cooling of sexual desire in Desdemona and Othello (374–390). Still, now—and even through the Victorian period—Iago was allowed to keep his pointed sexual allusion,

> I hate the Moor,
> And it is thought abroad, that 'twixt my sheets
> He has done my office . . . (410–412)

This rationalization of his motivation could not be dispensed with.[46]

In Act II, i, composing his erotic rhymes on the Cyprus quay, Iago—according to Gentleman—"expresses himself most indecently to his wife, and barefacedly impudent to Desdemona." [47] Kemble's theater still allowed such lines as "Players in your housewifery, and housewives in your beds" (132) and "You rise to play, and go to bed to work" (136); but the rest of the suggestive verses are gone (as all would be in the Victorian period), and Iago's attempts shortly after to rouse Roderigo's mind with sexual images, leading to an "incorporate conclusion" between Cassio and Desdemona, are severely cut.

In Act III Iago's similar attempts to inflame Othello are generally intact but under attack. Gentleman comments on Iago's doubts of catching Desdemona and Cassio in the act:

> It were a tedious difficulty I think,
> To bring them to that prospect: damn them then,
> If ever mortal eyes do see them bolster . . . (458–460)

"We wish the greater part of this speech was omitted. Nothing material would be lost, and delicacy would be better sustained . . ." [48] Later this would be done. Kemble began to clean up this scene by refining Iago's:

> Would you the supervisor grossly gape on?
> Behold her topp'd? (455–456)

to an interruption:

> Behold her—

Iago shares with Othello the great chop at the beginning of Act IV, where his prurience is so insistent. In Act V, with the banishment of Bianca (Gentleman of course applauded the ejection from the play of that "excrescence, Cassio's mistress"),[49] Iago loses the moment of wicked improvisation when he shifts the blame to her.

The loss of these evidences of Iago's secret nature was unfortunate; they did not, however, compel so obvious and implausible a villainy as Cibber's. Macklin was aware of this, and with his newer "naturalistic" technique he made Iago believable, particularly in "his gradual disclosure of the character; his seeming openness and concealed revenge; and above all, his soliloquies . . ." [50] He spoke the soliloquy when he plots Cassio's fall [If I can fasten but one cup upon him] "Plainly and without ornament," though it had usually been done with "a world of unnatural contortion of face, and absurd by-play"—and, because he was still villain enough, drew the "indisputable, involuntary applause" of many audience curses.[51] Garrick, who followed Macklin in many things, was his disciple in minimizing Iago's overt wickedness the few times he played the part.[52] Judicious critics always welcomed this plausibility in Iagos, and yet actors sometimes returned to the Cibber mode: thus Ryder ". . . wore his villainy on his sleeve and evinced nothing of the insidiousness ordinarily expressed [in] the part";[53] and Cooke betrayed "so much of the workings of cunning and deceit, as makes it seem . . . a miracle how Othello can be deceived at all . . ." A sample of his physical imagery in the temptation of Othello interested Washington Irving: "Cooke grasped Kemble's [Othello's] left hand with his own and then fixed his right like a claw on his shoulder . . . drawing himself up to him with his short arm, he breathed his poisonous whispers. Kemble coiled and twisted his hands, writhing to get away, his right clasping his brow, and darting his eye back on Iago." [54] There was no mistaking this villain.

On the other hand, there was danger in too much plausibility if not accompanied by Iago's motivating passion. Thus Henderson's impressively "earnest" Iago could "turn the inside of the design outward toward the spectators, and yet externally seem to be cordial and sincere and interesting among the victims"; but his Iago was so bland that it was said he had "too much disguise"—in contrast with a villain like Cooke's, who had too little.[55] The dignified Kemble, too, demonstrated the error of plausibility without motivation. He assumed "an open, frank and not disinterested air, which would better comport with the shrewd villainy of the character, were it mixed with a little more of the restlessness inseparable from it." Here was the old trouble: Kemble did not dive into the subsurface workings of passion: as a contemporary noted, "On the whole, [he] wanted . . . that perturbed spirit or natural agitation which is so consistent with the . . . plottings of a treacherous and revengeful breast." [56]

There is no record of a great Iago matching Spranger Barry's great Othello. Probably Barry suffered for it as much as anybody. As Foote observed, "I defy the greatest *Othello* that ever was born, unless he be well provided with an Antient, properly to express either the Hero or the jealous Lover . . ." [57] Fortunately, the next century's detailed reviews would describe superb Iagos, who amply showed how to justify Othello's descent to murder.

*Excellent wretch: Perdition catch*
*My soul but I do love thee . . .*

We have seen that spectators wept at Desdemona at her moment of death, or cried out to see her smothered; now we get

glimpses of her character. Gracious, dignified, sensitive, strong
in—and because of—her love even when abused, she can subordinate her resentment to her devotion for her husband. She is
a focus for pity.

Surprisingly, the actress who conveyed this image of sympathy
was the awesome, majestic Mrs. Sarah Siddons, legendary as
Lady Macbeth. (There were other fine Desdemonas—notably
Mrs. Cibber and Mrs. Barry—but only the Siddons conception
comes to us in detail.) Few regarded Sarah a likely candidate for
the tender role, and audiences were amazed at the transition from
her erstwhile tragic majesty to sweet tenderness. The part even
seemed to change her physically, "absolutely [lowering] the
figure of the lovely being which had been so towering in Eu-
phrasia, or terrific in Lady Macbeth." [58]

True, one critic felt that Mrs. Siddons in an early performance
evoked only shallow sympathy: "What ought to be tender is
only tenderness . . . the affections being but half touched
excite in our souls but imperfect movements." [59] Boaden retorted
to this furiously: "Half-touched!" He cites "some of her striking
physical imagery in the performance of "this gentle sacrifice":
first her "generous warmth in begging to go with Othello to the
wars; then

The elegant deportment, cordial manners, and smothered anxiety, on the landings at Cyprus, previous to the arrival of
Othello . . . [her] *endurance* of Iago's ribaldry. The interces-
sion for Cassio, beyond measure winning . . . The second
scene of the third act . . . where Othello, holding her hand,
exclaims—

> This hand of yours requires
> A sequester from liberty, fasting and prayer . . .
> For here's a young and sweating devil here;
> That commonly rebels.

The surprise arising to astonishment, a sort of *doubt* if she heard
aright, and that being admitted, what it could *mean;* a hope that

it would end in nothing so unusual from him as *offensive* meaning; and the slight relief, upon Othello's adding—

> 'Tis a good hand, a frank one.'

all this commentary was quite as legible as the text.

The second scene of the fourth act, where Othello speaks too plainly to be misconceived, had beauties that cannot be described; the highest . . . the deep concern that *Othello* should so grossly err, a feeling that subdued all petulance at being unjustly accused. The delicacy that quite electrified the house in the subsequent address to Iago—

> Des. Am I that name, Iago?
> Iago. What name, fair lady?
> Des. Such as, she says, my lord did say I was.

. . . the kneeling adjuration, the pathos that swelled upward, as she uttered the words—

> 'Or that mine eyes, mine ears, or any sense,
> Delighted them in any other form;
> Or that I do not *yet*, and ever *did*,
> And ever *will*, though he do shake me off
> TO BEGGARLY DIVORCEMENT, love him dearly.' [60]

Throughout, Boaden wrote, she woke "the most intense sympathy."

Because of the theatrical cutting, it was more difficult for the Desdemonas, as it was for the Iagos and the Othellos, to project the playwright's image. The heroine again loses her pleasantly domestic "Why this is not a boon . . ." speech. Now, further refined, she may not say, as she looks for the handkerchief, "I had rather have lost my purse full of crusadoes." Her firm promise to Cassio, "If I do vow a friendship I'll perform it . . . (III, iii, 26–31), is out, and so are her later troubled but sturdy reassurances,

> . . . What I can do, I will: and more I will
> Than for myself, I dare. Let that suffice you. (III, iv, 147–152)

She can no longer make her little pun on "whore." * As in Smock
Alley, she loses the womanlike scolding she gave herself for
thinking ill of Othello. Worst of all, in Act IV she loses the
whole touching Willow Song scene. The talk with Emilia of undressing, of sheets on a bed, of adultery, and Emilia's frank discussion of men had much to do with this; Gentleman notes
piously that the pages are "judiciously curtailed." [61] In a rare
note of opposition, Boaden thundered that such censorship
denied the century its right to be called "enlightened."

. . . where, curtailing fiends, is the foreboding direction to
Emilia as to certain sheets;

> "If I do die before thee, prythee, shroud
> me in one of those same sheets."

The recollection of her mother's maid, poor Barbara? The song
of "Willow"

> "An old thing 'twas, but it express'd
> her fortune,
> And she died singing it: that song tonight
> Will not go from my mind," etc.

The wandering away from Barbara to notice delicately the
"proper person" of Lodovico. The return to the "silly sooth"
of the willow, and . . . singing in dirge-like strains immediately
before her death. The interruption to the strain—"Hark, who is
it that knocks?"

> Emil. It is the wind.

No hint of one of these things to be found.[62]

---

* I cannot say whore,
  It does abhor me now I speak the word . . . (IV, ii, 190–191)

# PART III

## The Nineteenth Century

The eighteenth-century actors who undertook the character problems of *Othello* were clearly faced with a nearly complete "Victorian" refinement of the play's imagery long before Victoria's century began. In the nineteenth century there was refinement on that refinement, to complicate still further the process of characterization. In 1808 the *Monthly Mirror* was scolding almost obsessively even Kemble's strenuously cleansed version:

> . . . as it is at present altered for the stage, we contend that it can never be played without committing such a violence on the modesty and decency of the house as is altogether intolerable. Numerous instances might be pointed out, which have not even the excuse of equivocation, but are nothing more nor less than undisguised, palpable grossness and obscenity. *Othello* is indeed a most replenished brothel of the vilest "goats and monkeys" of Shakespeare's brain.[1]

55

It should be noted that by now refined images of *Othello* came to Englishmen from the page as well as from the stage. In the eighteenth century the most popular edition of Shakespeare was Francis Gentleman's collection of expurgated theater versions—which far outsold such editions as those of Pope and Johnson.[2] A great flood of separate acting texts of the plays was published in the latter half of the century, and it continued in full tide into the 1800's. As an *Othello* preface in 1838 explained: "In many of Shakespeare's plays . . . we find language used which cannot be spoken on the stage . . . In consequence of the objectionable language . . . the works of Shakespeare have been banished entirely from many families, but the same excuse cannot in the future be made, for the 'English Stage' will comprise all his plays as acted."[3] Even Thomas Bowdler, whose censored "Family Edition" of Shakespeare has made of his name a nasty adjective, cut less of Shakespeare than the theaters did; as I suggest in the Appendix, in a brief defense of Bowdler, if a name is needed for the act of censoring Shakespeare, a much better one would be "plumptrize," after a real Jack the Ripper of literature, the Reverend James Plumptre, who not only outdid the theaters in reducing the imagery of *Othello* but also tried to distort the whole meaning of the play by giving it a happy ending. Fortunately his attempt was aborted.

What distinguished the Victorian influence on the verbal imagery in *Othello* is not so much word elimination as word change—and in particular, one special word change. The reformers allowed themselves a veiled recognition of certain things but forbade certain words denoting these things. Thus Thackeray, chafing under the concealment by lan-

guage, had to borrow from *Othello* to convey, in
the Virginians, a terrible epithet for a woman. " 'I
certainly shall request you to do so when you are
. . . with that person,' said Colonel Wolfe, angrily;
but he used a word [referring to the woman] not
to be written at present, though Shakespeare puts
it in the mouth of Othello." The word was
"whore." Ironically, by the time Thackeray wrote
his novel in the late 1850's, even Shakespeare was
no longer allowed—on the stage and often in print
—to use the word. The sensitive attitude toward
this monosyllable reflects a peculiar crisis in the
process of Anglo-Saxon culture—and in the production of *Othello*. In Shakespeare's time the word
was only another symbol for a recognized fact. The
gentle Desdemona did not like to say it, but she
could make her graceful pun on it:

> It does abhor me . . . (IV, ii, 191)

The word was regularly used in plays and titles of
plays. A century before Victoria it was still available for casual use; in *Tom Jones*, Squire Western
could introduce it freely into table conversation
with his sister and daughter. Fifty years *after* Victoria, by the middle of the twentieth century, the
word had so given up its forbidden values again that
a character in a Broadway play, *A Hatful of Rain*,
describing a night "club," says to a woman:

> I've been in chippie joints in my time . . . [this
> one's] more like a cat house. [*Ashamed, he substi-
> tutes a euphemism.*] Excuse me, I mean whore
> house.

So pass the taboos of the world.

By 1850 the need to avoid hearing "whore"—and a few other words—spoken from the stage was pressing. Considerable ingenuity went into providing substitutes, as Lacy's standard acting version shows. The awful monosyllable is preserved only once, when Othello threatens Iago:

Villain, be sure thou prove my wife a whore.

Elsewhere, when he speaks of Emilia:

yet she's a simple bawd
That cannot say as much. This is a subtle
whore . . .

Lacy has "a simple friend" and "a subtle one." The line

made to write whore upon?

changes to "write shame upon?" Later, "that cunning whore of Venice" becomes "that cunning she." Emilia's "my lord hath so bewhored her" changes to "becalled her." Three lines are cut to avoid the next "whore," and in its next occurrence it is changed to "strumpet." Other words are similarly avoided. "That cuckold lives in bliss" becomes "that husband." "Players in your huswiferie and huswives in your beds" becomes "huswives in your play." The "bawdy wind" becomes the "common wind." Iago has long since lost the third of his indecent speeches to Brabantio about the "beast with two backs." It must seem, with all these changes, that no more refinement could be visited on the play —and yet some would be, as we shall find.

And we shall find something else surprising. Now at last we have a chance to recapture nearly total physical embodiments of the Othello images, for the skilled reviewer—at his best a judicious, dedicated professional—was beginning to record splendidly detailed impressions of the visual and aural imagery of great actors.* One image that emerges from the stream of characterizations of Othello is that of a restrained, intellectualized Moor, a sorely troubled person. But another, mightier image conflicts with it: paralleling the tremendous pressure to disguise language and thought about sex in *Othello* there seemed to be a paradoxical yearning for blazing, overt expressions of its passions on the stage— of the passions of physical love and sexual jealousy that society proposed not to acknowledge. A terrible Othello was demanded on the stage, and the stage provided it.

Here, in little, is a Victorian compromise between ostensible rigid repression and subsurface libido. In the "proper" novels of the century— except for stormy undertones of passion—society worships chastity and "pure" thought and language, and clasps death before dishonor. The life of the century gives the novels the lie. There was a roaring subculture, in which the forbidden things and words were freely indulged. Thus Dickens, whose heroines almost wallowed in decency, who did not use the word "bed" in a play because "the young ladies are . . . horrified at the bare thought of anybody's *going* there" [4]—Dickens shared his later life with a mistress. Thus the word "whore" was not to be spoken, and indeed a woman could sue for divorce because her profligate husband made

---

* Out of the mass of reviews, memoirs, biographies, and similar materials, I have synthesized the descriptions of those important actors and actresses meaningful to this study, making allowances for personal and political motivations in the criticism, for differences of opinion, and for the inevitable selectivity of synthesis.

their son spell w–h–o–r–e at her; but it was a great time for whores, for the gilded, kept whores of the rich and the titled.[5] They were widely known, discussed, ogled as they promenaded in the streets or rode in carriages, much admired, envied, and sought after. Here is the same problem met with before: the century is given a name—Victorian—to suggest a recognizable cluster of formal attitudes; but throughout the "staid" hundred years men evolved amazing new departures in business, government, thought, and society; were conservatives and rebels, romantics and pre-Raphaelites, believers and heretics, and included the customary number of geniuses, madmen, and fools. For semantic convenience, I shall speak generally of the "Victorian" attitude toward *Othello* to denote the familiar one that stood for "refinement"—but inevitably there were other, contradictory Victorian attitudes. For the most "proper" Victorians resisted the Othellos who were the most popular ones: the Othellos who, playing the most plumptrized versions of the play, unleashed the fiercest passions, the rawest emotions of love, jealousy, anger, who acted out on the stage yearnings that were nominally hidden or denied. As in the "refined" eighteenth century, audiences in the "repressed" nineteenth welcomed a grieved Othello who could set dignity afire with passion, whose passion was so intense that it dignified itself.

# 4

*My blood begins my safer guides to rule . . .*

## Kean

Men wept at Othello in the nineteenth century—beginning with Kean, the first of the great Moors whose physical imagery comes down to us in detail. Kean lacked the massive physique and dignity that assert the hero's nobility in repose; yet he sustained stature throughout by the fierce intensity of his passion. His was the image of Othello that Garrick had dreamed of and Barry seemed to express: an explosion of violence, terror, love, pity. He was a great emotional instrument. Audiences trembled at his fury; Byron wept at his sobs.[1] His Moor seemed to be the flower of romanticism in the theater, questing for a passion beyond known passion.

Not all applauded, because this was the century of Victoria and Kean's tumultuous playing, and his sudden contrasts in voice and action, offended some;[2] but the sheer mass and dazzle of his exotic Moor[3] beat down the reserve and skepticism of most of his detractors. Something of the true grief of Othello was sensed and expressed by the little actor, and in the very power of his dismay there was an irresistible dignity. Clearly he meant it that way: the violence he threw into the characterization, that so amazed observers, was as much the result of thought as of emotion. He studied the sound and form of Othello "long and anxiously, often during half the night . . . he would act scene after scene, considering the modulation of the verse, and the fluctuation of the character"; then, when he had "incorporated himself" with the character until he possessed it so completely that it possessed him, his acting seemed "no simulation but revelation." [4] He could play against the strongest Iago, who only made his Othello stronger; it became "dangerous to cross his path, and death to assault him." [5] Critics had trouble finding words for the terrifying imagery he projected.[6] Hazlitt was awed:

> . . . there was all the fitful fever of the blood, the jealous madness of the brain: his heart seemed to bleed with anguish, while his tongue dropped broken, imperfect accents of woe . . .[7]

Lewes remembered the "lion-like fury, the deep and haggard pathos, the forlorn sense of desolation, alternating with gusts of stormy cries for vengeance . . ." [8] *Blackwood's* called his last act "the most terrific exhibition of human passion that has been witnessed on the modern stage." One playgoer could hardly bear it. "I was frightened, alarmed; I cannot account for what I felt. I wished to be away, and saw those *eyes* all night, and hear 'D––n her! D––n her!' still—it was too horrible." [9]

Kean's Moor took shape in a series of explosions—in "flashes of lightning." Though he declared Othello's dignity and grief with a persistent intensity, he could always rise suddenly into higher tempo or descend to ominous command. At the first brush with Brabantio, in the lofty power of

> Put up your bright swords, for the dew will rust them . . .

it seemed to Keats ". . . we feel that his throat had commanded where swords were as thick as reeds. From eternal risk, he speaks as though his body were unassailable." [10]

But Kean wrought some climaxes by slackening his pace before a sudden pounce. Thus, through the senate address, which was usually such an opportunity for grand-style actors, he rambled easily, for the sake of a sudden sharp irony:

This only is the witchcraft I have used.

dropping again to an easy grace, at

Here comes the lady. Let her witness it.

This always "startled the audience into applause." [11]

In suppressing the Cyprus riot, noble and commanding, he cashiered Cassio "solemnly and sadly, as if justifying a painful act of duty." [12] There was pathos as well as passion in his early love for Desdemona, and in the almost desperate rapture of the first Cyprus meeting. And of Act III Fanny Kemble wrote, "Who that ever heard, will ever forget the beauty, the unutterable tenderness of his reply to Desdemona's entreaties for Cassio. 'Let him come when he will, I can deny thee nothing . . .'" The very urgency of his emotion made one observer complain that he was jealous too soon.[13] He took fire midway in the temptation scene when Iago described the monster of jealousy (III, iii, 193): ". . . he started at the first whisper of this intimidation, stung by alarm, and bewildered with fury, as the whole emotion spread through his shaking frame, and tinged every look, every word, with unspeakable horror." At "not a jot, not a jot," he was clearly moved: he seemed to be holding back tears—heartrendingly, Hazlitt thought. Dismissing Iago, "One of his finest instantaneous actions was his clutching his black hand slowly round his head as though his brains were turning, and then writhing round and standing in dull agony with his back to the audience." [14]

An American was impressed by the "mixture of heart-felt sorrow and frantic rage" at

> I had rather be a toad,
> And live upon the vapor of a dungeon,
> Than keep a corner in the thing I love
> For other's uses. *Desdemona* comes.

". . . the latter part of the passage was given with a peculiar, snarling, sardonic laugh, but yet extremely quiet in manner. The sudden ejaculation, '*Desdemona* comes!', was a climax that ever struck the audience like the lightning, instantaneously." [15] The *Times* thought his jealousy took shape in the imagery— visual, aural, emotional—of his next encounter with Iago.

> [Kean] entered with the abrupt and wandering step . . . [showing] the fearful bewilderings of a heavy heart. The sound of Iago's voice broke his meditation. He suddenly raised his eye, and pronounced . . . "Avaunt, begone!" with the haughty and resentful glance of a man accustomed to authority . . . After gazing till the first burst of passion recoiled upon himself, he dropped his arms, and relaxed insensibly into a gesture finely indicative of utter exhaustion. "What sense had I of her stolen hours" was pursued in a calmer tone, till the train of thought drew on the mention of "Cassio's kisses on her lips" . . . [There had] seemed to be stealing a delicious tranquility over his mind; and he paused and dwelt upon the words, as if he was parting with images that he loved. The sound of Cassio's name gliding accidentally even from himself, broke the spell. The whole fierceness of his nature was roused; he sprung from the ground and cried the passage aloud with a wild and grinning desperation . . .

Voice, face, and mind told plainly Othello's inner conflict. At

> I had been happy if the general camp had tasted her sweet body . . .

the fondness with which the beloved object is recalled, and the loathing with which it is recalled, connected with thoughts of degradation:

> Oh, now forever
> Farewell the tranquil mind.

These pathetic words, deepened in their effect like the tears of
a man, flowing from sources not lightly used to weep, came
from the actor with the air of an alienated mind. . . ." [16]

The great farewell speech was remembered as much for its
melody as for its emotion. Here seemed to be the genuine sound
of Othello. To Hazlitt, it "struck on the heart like the swelling
notes of some divine music, like the sound of years of departed
happiness . . . [laying] open the very tumult and agony of the
soul." To Junius Brutus Booth, it was like ". . . the moan of
the ocean or the soughing of wind in the cedars." [17]
Kean flung himself fiercely on Iago at

> Villain, be sure thou prove my love a whore!

but again, his passion was explosive, orgasmic, exhausting, and
he fell back on himself, to rise again to:

> Blood, blood, blood!

Keats remembered this as "direful and slaughterous to the deepest degree, the very words appeared stained and gory . . . His
voice is loosed on them like the wild dog on the savage relics
of an eastern conflict . . ." [18]
Kean seemed quieter in the later scenes. Hunt, to whom the
actor's muted anguish was even more moving than his rage,
felt theater's greatest moment came when Kean, at

> Had it pleased heaven
> To try me with afflction . . .

stood "alone, absorbed, as if he were left desolate, and then his
voice rose with calm misery, as though he had tears in his
eyes." [19]
Kean slew Desdemona with a "noble intensity of passion,"
then descended through delicate gradations of emotion "from
the tumult which raged in his soul when he committed the mur-

der to the gloomy stillness of despair . . ." [20] But his quiet was
not like another man's quiet. To the ear he was quiet; but the
visual intensity of the image was unrelieved: "his eye wandering in vacancy, as stupefied by amazement, remorse, and despair
—and the clasped hands, palms upward, gathered across his
head, as if to crush a fevered brain, which threatened to burst
out into a volcano—exclaiming . . . with trembling, gasping
utterance, and in agonized tones: 'Fool! Fool! Fool!' " [21] Then
the "indomitable manliness of his spirit" returned: by a "fine
deliberate artifice" he diverted suspicion from his intended suicide by simulating pride in punishing the "turbaned Turk who
beat a Venetian," "as his eyes wandered from face to face in
order to see whether any suspicion as to his object lurked in
their minds." Then he killed himself with a single quick stab,
pressing the dagger horizontally as though into his heart and
after a "frozen shudder" fell at once like dead clay.[22]

An illuminating clash of critical and theatrical interpretations
developed for a while between Kean and Hazlitt. The critic
could not at first accept the extreme grief of the actor's interpretation. In 1816 he wanted it softened. Kean's passion—not
his short stature or his new tawny makeup—seemed untrue to
the Moor's inner shape:

> Othello was tall, but that is nothing: he was black, but that is
> nothing. But he was not fierce, and that is everything. It is only
> in the last agony of human suffering that he gives way to his
> rage and his despair . . . Mr. Kean is in general all passion, all
> energy, all relentless will. He wants imagination, that faculty
> which contemplates events, and broods over feelings with a cer-
> tain calmness and grandeur . . . He is too often in the highest
> key of passion, too uniformly on the verge of extravagance, too
> constantly on the rack.

But a year later, Hazlitt was capitulating. Kean's Moor was
now the "finest piece of acting in the world," particularly in
portraying the ". . . agony of [Othello's] soul. . . . On his
fixed eyelids 'Horror sat plumed.' . . . where a gleam of hope

or of tenderness returns to subdue the tumult of his passions, his voice broke in faltering accents from his over-charged breast. His lips might be said less to utter words, than to bleed drops of blood gushing from his heart. . . ." [23]

Oddly, the time came when Kean, perhaps moved by Hazlitt's earlier moderationism, played the role with variations, diminishing its grandeur with a kind of small frailty. But when he began to sound less than Othello, Hazlitt was the first to note it. "In his famous Farewell speech, he exchanged his usual organ stop . . . as if his inmost vows and wishes were ascending to the canopy of heaven, and their sounding echo were heard upon earth like distant thunder [for a] querulous, whining, sobbing tone . . . he pronounced the 'not a jot, not a jot' as an hysteric exclamation, not with the sudden stillness of fixed despair." Hazlitt felt now that Othello's very weakness had to have a strength and dignity to it, that any dilution of Kean's grieved Moor jaded it. "There is but one perfect way of playing Othello, and that was the way . . . he used to play it." [24]

Unique as was his portrayal of Othello, Kean was content to follow the text of the then standard Kemble editing with the modern refinements, except that he brought back enough of Othello's wavering to sound to its depths the Moor's central agony. "The voice on some nights would be more irresistibly touching in 'But, oh! the pity of it, Iago!' . . ." [25] His great break with the past showed in his genius for compensating for the other cuts. Kemble had tried to fill in the gaps of motivation with a surface of dignity; Kean did it—had to do it[26]—Barry's way. His metier was dash, passion, lightning, thunder; he could not be merely tender—his Romeo was a failure. He dropped the Roman from Kemble's Othello and bore the audience on pure Gothic surges past any abyss of doubt of the Moor's nobility. His was another kind of dignity: the dignity of native humanity helpless in emotion.

The effort needed to create such an image was tremendous, physically as well as emotionally, marked by "convulsed motion of the hands . . . involuntary swellings of the veins of the forehead." [27] After one performance a friend found him in the dressing room "stretched out on a sofa, retching violently and throwing up blood. His face half washed: one side deadly pale and the other a deep copper colour." [28] It was not easy to be Othello.

The stormy emotions that charged his acting of the Moor troubled Kean's private life, where the play seemed to haunt him: he became tragically involved in a sensational sexual infidelity. By some of the elite, Byron among them, he had been made much of—but only as a kind of toy from the theater, an exotic stranger in a supersubtle society that cared only for his professional skill. Hungry for admiration and love, he fled for comfort to the taverns where men of his own proletarian background worshipped him; until a nymphomaniac of "class" caught his attention by fainting at his Othello, drew him away from his wife, and pursued him so overtly that her most complaisant of husbands finally sued Kean for criminal conversation with the woman. Kean lost. The *Times* called Kean an adulterer, an "obscene little personage." [29] His wife separated from him and never rejoined him, although in his failing days he begged her to return. Often drunk, infatuated with an Irish whore, his health running out with his money, he had to act for his very life. After his trial for adultery, audiences at first found Othello's laments on a wife's unfaithfulness mocking in Kean's mouth, and hooted; he beat them down with the sheer smash of his personality, and played on—to his death. The last winter of his life he acted to the Iago of Macready, who hated—envied?— him, called him "low." Kean was very sick, but Lewes wondered at

how puny Kean appeared beside Macready, until, in the third act, when roused by Iago's taunts and insinuations, he moved toward him with a gouty hobble, seized him by the throat, and in a well-known explosion, "Villain! Be sure you prove . . ." etc., seemed to swell into a stature which made Macready ap-

pear small . . . such was the irresistible pathos—manly, not tearful—which vibrated in his tones and expressed itself in look and
gestures that old men leaned their heads upon their arms and
fairly sobbed.[30]

*Othello* was his journey's end. Needing money, he agreed to
play opposite his son Charles' Iago. His final exit on the stage
had the drama of the Moor's own tragedy. The evening of the
play, Charles went to his father's dressing room and found him

> shivering and exceedingly weak. "I am very ill," said he; "I am
> afraid that I shall not be able to act." But he went on. After the
> first scene . . . [he] was very feeble . . . brandy-and-water
> was administered to him . . . [At] the commencement of the
> third act . . . he said to his son, "Mind, Charles, that you keep
> before me. Don't get behind me, in this act. I don't know that
> I shall be able to kneel; but if I do, be sure that you lift me
> up." . . . He went off with Desdemona; and no one observed
> any change. But on entering, where he says, 'What! false to *me*,'
> etc., he was scarcely able to walk across the stage. He held up,
> however, until the celebrated 'farewell,' which he uttered with
> all his former pathos, but on concluding it,—after making one
> or two feeble steps towards his son (who took care to be near
> him) and attempting the speech "Villain, be sure," etc.,—his
> head sank on his son's shoulder, and the tragedian's acting was
> at an end. He was able to groan out a few words, in Charles' ear
> —"I am dying—speak to them for me;" after which (the audi-
> ence refusing in kindness to hear any apology), he was borne
> from the stage.[31]

# 5

## Macready, Fechter, Irving

At the other extreme from Kean's sorely grieved Moor was a characterization that seemed more suited to the "repressed" Victorians: a quieter Othello, a "troubled person," more controlled—and contrived—in dignity and passion. In his mildest manifestations, this Moor would be petulant, irritable, whining: not noble, not murderous. By an interesting coincidence, at about this time a German scholar would stimulate a critical fashion by proposing a "true" Othello very much like this. Hence when, a little later, we confront actors and critics, these "restrained" interpretations—by Macready, Fechter, and Irving —will be significant. Although these three leading Victorian "method" actors were smashing successes in other major Shakespearean roles—all were brilliant Iagos—they all fell short as Othello.

Macready, the best of them in the role, is the most difficult to assess. A terrible-tempered snob, he had such a genius for making enemies,[1] and on the other hand he was so shrewd and powerful a personal force, that he attracted both puff and pure

70

malice. His "intellectual" Othello was not a hopeless failure: it was praised by friends, and warmly applauded on an early tour of France (though less so on a later one);[2] but he was never a great Moor to English audiences, to his professional colleagues, or—more important—to himself. A younger actor who "revered" Macready concluded: "His comparative failure [as Othello] may have risen from the fact that he never liked the part—so, at least, he told me." [3]

Certainly Macready demonstrated, as an American observed, that Othello's grief cannot be put together from bits of insight, oratory, and acting tricks, however strenuously thought out. The result was "scholarly"—and uninspired: ". . . he could not veil his self-consciousness . . . After all, it was Macready in turban and pointed shoes, wailing over Desdemona stained, but really intent upon the next syllables of his elocution." [4]

Macready's Othello was handicapped partly by his own egotistic personality, partly by his indecision between two worlds of acting: for once more, in the usual way, an old, "grand" style was being challenged, this time by the "new," "natural" style of a theater growing domestic after the fashion of the French *drame*. The art of acting was more and more learned; players schooled themselves in experiencing the personality and emotions of character with techniques surprisingly "modern"—so Dickens smiles at a Stanislavski-like Othello in the great Crummles' company who blacked himself all over the day of the play to get into the spirit of the part.[5] Macready tried to "enter" his characters; but mainly this "most intellectual of tragedians" combined a methodical domesticated style, made up of "familiar little touches," [6] with calculated flashes of the lofty and violent to achieve his many popular characterizations. His Macbeth and Iago in particular were great successes; but the Moor had a passion he could not express, and his studied "Macready pause," his artificial technique of sudden, artificial *fortissimos* only distorted the shape of the character. "His force in the violent passages is more bullying than raging, and has a

loud, noisy ranting air . . . In the quiet and composed parts he
has a kind of hurly-burly, quick and abrupt manner . . . still
more contrary to all notions of greatness." [7]
Hazlitt missed the Moor's massive, tidal sweep:

> The movements of passion in Othello resemble the heaving of
> the sea in a storm . . . but Mr. Macready goes off like a shot,
> and startles our sense of hearing. One of these sudden explo-
> sions was when he is in such haste to answer the demands of
> the Senate on his services: "I do agnise a natural hardness," etc.,
> as if he was impatient to exculpate himself from some charge,
> or wanted to take them at their word lest they should retract.
> There is nothing of this in Othello. . . . Another fault . . .
> was that [Macready] whined and whimpered once or twice,
> and tried to affect the audience by affecting a pitiful sensibility,
> not consistent with the dignity and masculine imagination of the
> character: as where he repeated "No, not much moved," and
> again, "Othello's occupation's gone," in a childish treble.[8]

Other judicious critics agreed. Macready was too weak, too "effeminate." [9] Lewes: "His passion was irritability, and his agony
had no grandeur." Archer: "He was deficient in . . . majesty
of character and passion." His very physical image of Othello
was degrading, another actor thought, "like an elderly negress
of evil repute, going to a fancy ball!" [10]
Macready himself sensed his lack of stature, and particularly of
inner passion, and labored to coax them into being—without
success. In his long diary, full of self-appraisal—and self-pity—
he wrote of a performance (March, 1833): "There was not
exactly a lack of spirit in the early scenes, but a want of fresh-
ness and freedom in its flow must have been manifest." Two
years later: "Practised part of Othello, to which I do not find I
yet give that real pathos and terrible fury which belongs to
the character . . . Studied Othello, which I find difficult—the
management of my time and force. How little do they know of
this art who think it is easy!" That fall: "The criticism I passed
on Malibran's Fidelio will exactly suit my own Othello—it was

'elaborate but not abandoned.' " The next year he felt once that he had almost lost the part altogether; and a decade later the Moor's image still eluded him, and an inadequate performance set him brooding: "Acted Othello, really striving, labouring to act it well; partially, I think, I succeeded; but the labour is very great . . . My money is not got without some equivalent of toil . . ." Then the little spur of his self-pity again: "Called for [by the spectators' applause, after *Othello*], but the audience seemed to me cold and difficult to excite . . ." And the final rationalization: "It may be raised prices depress their spirits." [11]

It was not the raised prices. The shape of Othello could not be formed by the calculation of this egotist who made of the play a personal ornament. He even masked Desdemona in her important first speech to the Duke, hid her from the audience with his robe.[12] Old Foote would have guessed Macready's failure from this account by a bitter fellow-actor:

> . . . when he played Othello, Iago was to be nowhere! Othello was to be the *sole* consideration: the sole character to be evolved, the all-engrossing object to the eye and the heart of the audience. Iago was a mere *stoker*, whose business it was to supply Othello's passion with fuel, and keep up his high-pressure. The next night, perhaps, he took Iago; and lo! presto! everything was changed. Othello was to become a mere puppet for Iago to play with . . . If the Othello-side was in the ascendant, Iago stood all night with his back to the audience; his face unseen; his expression lost, sometimes even his words unheard.[13]

It was not just the prices.

The next troubled person was a great deal worse. Charles Fechter, the Frenchified Englishman, displayed a "clever" Othello, full of shrewd bits of business and "naturalistic" surface movements. His "French style" had already begun to penetrate Victorian England, behind the flag of the Gallic "modernists" whose drama now dealt freely with "ordinary" people. Macready had been leading British acting toward this technique by the time Fechter arrived with his Othello, but London was still amazed by it.

Not by the words: Fechter's text is even "purer" than that of his predecessors. Thus the last "whore" left by Lacy is eliminated; Iago's provocative "man-talk" to Cassio about Desdemona and her wedding bed (II, ii) is out; and so are the erotic elements from Iago's description of Cassio's dream when he lay with the lieutenant:

> (then would he) kiss me hard,
> As if he plucked up kisses by the roots
> That grew upon my lips, laid his leg oer my thigh,
> And sighed, and kissed, and then . . .
>
> (III, iii, 482–485)

Fechter's daring showed in other ways.[14] He introduced tricky business, and restored bits of cut scenes for shock or surprise. He revived the Willow Song—but only as a background "mood" effect for the beginning of Desdemona's death scene. He brought back Bianca—though barely long enough for Othello to see her with Cassio and the handkerchief. He worked in a manifestation of Othello's "trance"—with a glimpse of the unconscious Moor who might as well have been asleep. He tried to emphasize Othello's racial insecurity by looking in a mirror at "Haply for I am black," and "It is the cause"—but his acting of the business demeaned the character.

His brand of showmanship served Fechter well in *Hamlet*, a tremendous London success. Apparently the actor's intelligence helped him fill out sufficiently the form of the moody prince. But Othello drooped about him, and the play sagged with the character, showing up the tawdriness of the staging. George Eliot thought: "Fechter's Othello . . . was lamentably bad . . . the play is so degraded by his representation that it is positively demoralizing . . ."[15] Lewes, who greatly admired Fechter's *Hamlet*, thought the *Othello* one of the worst he had seen.[16]

Intelligent as Fechter was—and terrible as was his temper—

he could not command Othello's depth or passion. He could not even assume the role's heroic surface. He was tall enough, and handsome; but he made Othello merely "an affectionate but feeble young gentleman" [17]—"young, half-caste, familiar." [18] His diminishing of the character began with the visual imagery of his first meeting with Iago. Anxious to return to Desdemona, Othello says he must "spend a word here in this house"—whereupon Fechter took out a golden key, unlocked the door, and later, coming out, relocked it. To Lewes, "the effect is to make us forget the 'noble Moor,' and to think of a sepoy." [19] *Once a Week* protested against "the tameness and conversational tone assumed in the Address to the Senate . . . Mr. Fechter mars this splendid oratory . . . by a flat and monotonous delivery, a provoking nonchalance, a careful carelessness." [20]

Meeting Desdemona on Cyprus, Fechter offered none of the sound and gesture the Moor's love demanded:

> The entrance of Othello, with the flame of victory in his eye, eager to clasp his young wife to his breast . . . was an opportunity for being *natural* which Fechter wholly missed. Never was there a tamer meeting . . . I only recall a vision of him holding his wife at most "proper" distance, kissing her hand, his tone free from all tremulous emotion, though he has to say:
>
> > O my soul's joy! . . .
> >                 If it were now to die
> > 'Twere now to be most happy . . . [etc.]
>
> And from Desdemona he turns to the gentlemen of Cyprus, as affable and calm as if he had just come home from a morning stroll.[21]

He was merely "petulant" at the night riot, quelling the bell with "impatient irritability." [22]

Some praise was given Fechter's more subdued moments: his shame at setting a spy on Desdemona, his tenderness with her before the final anger in the handkerchief scene; but the impact

was always diffused into "over-sentimentalized melodrama." [23]
Intellectually, Fechter knew the need for passion well enough;
he called for it in his elaborate and interesting acting edition.
Brooding of "Cassio's kisses on her lips," the stage direction has
him in "a ferverish agony of rage." When Iago mentions the
handkerchief as a clue to adultery, he "crosses with the fierce-
ness of a tiger, and with action as if destroying Desdemona's
work." At "Oh, blood . . . !" "he rushes about as if seeking his
prey." The directions indicate other angry movements and "infuriated" glances in the crisis; but even these do not mold the
shape of Othello's massive anguish, and the actor fell short of
"grief" as he fell short of nobility: the torrent of passion broke
into "numerous petty waves." He was "loud—and weak; irritable, not passionate." [24]

The great stir created by Fechter's "naturalistic" style and
his tricks of business[25] momentarily deceived some of the judicious as to the merits of his Othello. The thoughtful *Athenaeum*, dazzled at first, credited him with initiating a helpful
"revolution in the English style of acting . . ." [26] But the journal
was soon praising faintly; and ended in opposition:

> Shakespearian characters (such as "Othello") . . . are eminently
> ideal and involve, as Coleridge has said, "the universal in the
> individual." [The actor] may soar on the wings of imagination
> and passion to heights where mere intellectuality cannot follow
> . . . Now, this in England we are accustomed to regard as act-
> ing of the highest sort, not the mere copying of conventionali-
> ties.[27]

The fault was not in "naturalistic" acting as such but, as Lewes
saw, in Fechter's failure to understand and convey the essence
of the Othello image: "When he appears leaning on the shoulder
of Iago . . . when he kisses the hand of Desdemona, when he
employs that favourite gesticulation which reminds us . . . of
a *gamin* threatening to throw a stone, he is certainly *natural*—
but according to whose nature?" Another critic had the answer:
". . . certainly not that of a Moor; it is scarcely that of a *man*.

It is rather the maudlin and hysterical emotion of a hero of French melodrama who is continually whimpering and whining about his mother." [28]

The failure of the next troubled person's Othello was even more remarkable—and reminiscent, in its way, of Garrick's. Sir Henry Irving, in his time as much Britain's leading actor as Garrick had been, also brought to *Othello* great talent for production, a fine interpretative intelligence, and a genius for acting —and was defeated by the role. Like Garrick, he failed partly because he tried too hard to differ from the current great Moor, the Italian Salvini, whose fearfully grieved soul set a standard for the late 1800's: "Hence . . . [his] Othello was so conceived that the sensual qualities, as well as the storm and stress of passion, were rendered comparatively inconspicuous." [29]

The result was that Irving's Othello, like Macready's and Fechter's, was neither noble enough nor murderer enough, neither sounded nor looked like the Moor. The *Athenaeum* scolded "The too plaintive and lachrymose side of Mr. Irving's Othello . . . the intellectual stays and starch." [30] He too seemed merely a sepoy—"an infuriated sepoy." His attempt at a lover's softness, to offset Salvini's force, ended in mushiness: "He becomes curiously effeminate in the presence of his bride; there is . . . moral weakness in his obsequious uxoriousness." Trying to be greatly troubled, he wasted his power: "The mine of passion is sprung too soon and too suddenly." [31] Ellen Terry had even harder words: "He screamed and ranted and raved—lost his voice, was slow where he should have been swift, incoherent where he should have been strong." [32] There seemed to be no center to his characterization. [33]

Irving was doubly handicapped. He was slight of build, weak of voice, and his features were ". . . cast in too delicate a mould to give full expression to the higher passions." [34] Then he indulged in curious mannerisms—perhaps ingrained from his apprenticeship in burlesque—that audiences sometimes found ludicrous. But with amazing energy and determination he had trained himself effectively to the Macready–Fechter line of acting, the use of realistic, domestic detail. His interpretations were masses of picturesque minutiae, dartings of representation that were generally warmly applauded. But the passion of Othello, as Coleridge and Hazlitt observed, spreads massively, in a great tide; Irving flitted from scene to scene, building no momentum, "and it is [only] . . . after the death of Desdemona, [when] he assumes a stare of desperation, that he allows any one emotion to hold possession of his face long enough to be quite intelligible." [35]

Individual bits were praised: this Othello was commendably slow at jealousy; his utterance of " 'O blood, blood, blood' was electrical . . ."; in the trance scene—which Irving restored— "the signs of swooning were faithfully conveyed . . . and the blank desolation of the concluding scene was impressive." But the *Athenaeum* mentioned a few good bits, it said, because the faults were too many, notably in the passionate crises.[36] What passion there was seemed restless and shrill, totally unsuited to the Othello image, the *Academy* reported. In the street clash with Brabantio, Irving "restrains the combatants by throwing up his arms in an excited manner certainly not in accord with the serene self command of the address to his defenders . . ." In the address to the Senate, he spoke "with I know not how many stampings of the foot, or how much uplifting of the arms, or patting of the breast." [37] The acerb *Saturday Review* likened him to an "Ojibbeway," relentlessly detailed his distortions of the role's shape: "[when] he is roused to jealousy by Iago, his appearance and manner are those of a sham Indian about to perform his war dance in a booth at a country fair . . . when he speaks before the Senators, and the Duke says, 'I think this tale would win my daughter too,' we can only say that we do not think so . . ." Like Garrick, Irving seemed to fret and fume away the Moor's dignity:

When Mr. Irving says, "I'll tear her all to pieces," he probably feels called upon to emulate the traditional intensity of Kean, and accordingly, his fingers not only perform . . . the comminuting process, but also appear as if they were distributing

the fragments among the audience . . . All that clutching of
the throat, rumpling of the hair, and twirling of the fingers
. . . In the [Farewell] speech . . . he does not look as if he
belonged to the calling which he is giving up . . . it is aston-
ishing how hard the whole performance is. "The pity of it"
is just that which we nowhere feel.[38]

Archer thought it ridiculous even to compare "the great Italian
(Salvini) with the physical and intellectual feebleness" of Irving's "ghastly" failure. And he repeated a mean jingle about the
"fiasco":

> For I dare not repeat
> The things that were said—
> Of a mop stem on feet,
> In one weekly I read—
> With its arms like a pair of pump handles
> And the mop dipped in ink for the head . . .[39]

These were harsh words for the greatest actor-manager of his
day; but for all his intelligence, effort, and hired puffing, as
Othello he never earned much better ones. He made his most
serious try after his fame was well established, when he was an
accepted standard for Hamlet, Macbeth, and Lear. And he did
it in the most spectacular context the theater could then offer.
He and Edwin Booth, the two ranking English-speaking actors,
exchanged the tragedy's leading roles, with Ellen Terry as Desdemona. The show was a great commercial success—but Irving
came out of it knowing he could not fill out the image of Othello.
After his last performance with Booth, Ellen Terry watched as
"he rolled up his clothes that he had worn as the Moor, one by
one, carefully laying one garment on top of the other, and then,
half humorously and very deliberately said: 'Never again.' " [40]
    It was not easy to be Othello.

# 6

## Booth

Now a fierce difference developed over the Othello characterizations. Many Victorians would welcome the thunder and lightning of sorely grieved Moors; others, outraged by so much overt emotion and sensuality, but unsatisfied with the cooler "troubled person," demanded the full measure of Othello's grief in a "refined" guise. Between the two factions there would be bitter arguments. The former would be generally satisfied by the tempestuous Salvini, the latter by Edwin Booth.

Booth was able to lift Othello above "trouble" to a sense of true grief by transmuting the wild, stark "extravagances of passion" of the Barry–Kean Moor into emotions more felt, less shown—through a more "gentlemanly" expression of anguish. Booth himself was deeply a gentleman in the Victorian sense: grave, dignified, earnestly respectable. He had known grief personally: as a child he played guardian to his hard, hard-drinking actor-father; two cherished wives died young, the second in madness; and his brother committed one of history's most awful crimes—the murder of Lincoln. Grief drove Booth into a retirement; but his gift was too precious to hide. And his grieved Moor was one of his greatest roles.

Booth's brooding nature, his slight figure, and his musical voice, with its "exquisite feeling for the sweetness of words," [1] suited the image of the poetic murderer he usually made of Othello. Usually—for he was an intelligent, versatile experimenter, and would try even to match the great rival characterization, the stormy Moor of Salvini. Once in Boston, where usually "he did not roar so loud as most" Othellos,[2] he projected almost as fiery an image, sweeping on in "demonaic transports to murder";[3] and on his German tour, he tried manhandling his Iago, almost in the Salvini fashion, with "the ferocity of the jaguar." [4] But it was the gentler agonies of his "sweeter and tenderer" [5] Othello that normally touched audiences. Avoiding the boldest overt action, he practiced tirelessly *becoming* his character, penetrating imaginatively to its core,[6] expressing its "deep, subdued emotions";[7] and there were not many he failed to move with his passionate gentleness, his restrained grief.

Conversely, it was his very restraint that troubled the doubters of his characterization: he seemed almost too noble, not murderer enough.[8] *Macmillan's* found him "tumultuous, fierce, passionate, but never grand, never terrible";[9] and a German critic missed "that elementary ferocity which should break loose after *Othello's* African nature is once aroused . . . [in] the murder scene . . . Booth seemed too much like a sacrificial priest." [10]

This hit in fact the core of Booth's conception; and for the many Victorians to whom Salvini's Othello was too frightening for pity, it seemed the essence of the Moor. William Winter praised one of the actor's greatest performances precisely because the killing of Desdemona seemed "in her husband's belief, a righteous immolation";[11] the *Saturday Review*, which had quartered and drawn Irving's "Ojibbeway" Moor, and was made uneasy by Salvini's terrible, sensual Othello, welcomed Booth's dreamer:

[He] takes the poetical view of Othello, the view which has always seemed to us the true one. Unless the romantic nobleness of the character is insisted upon, it surely becomes difficult to find any acceptable explanation either of Desdemona's love for the Moor or the complete confidence placed in him by the Seigneury . . . [Mr. Booth] has thrilling bursts of passion, but it is passion . . . of a noble nature led astray by the diabolical wiles that work upon its freedom and openness . . .

When Booth did succumb momentarily to fury, the *Review* was pleased by "the many indications that the giving way to such passion was repugnant to the soul of the valiant Othello." As against Salvini's savagery, the *Review* applauded Booth's "chivalry," "poetry," and "dignity." [12] But Booth's Othello was "not too tame neither," the *Academy* insisted, in an oblique insult to Irving. "His refined tenderness toward Desdemona . . . carefully avoids the super-sentimental uxoriousness [of] certain Othellos . . ." [13]

Even the *Athenaeum*—which doubted that any living Anglo-Saxon could bring enough grandeur to Othello—softened to Booth's portrayal, "the best of the present generation . . . the psychological processes of Othello are shown with singular clearness, and the violence and obstreperousness that have disgraced our stage disappear." [14] Between the passion of Booth's dignity and the dignity of Salvini's passion, the issue was now clearly drawn. Both were warmly applauded Othellos; and yet to fierce partisans of each, the other was hardly Othello at all.

Late in life, Booth spelled out for Furness the physical imagery he used to create his dark poet Othello. The notes suggest a Byronic Moor, quick to sadness, melancholy, foreboding—though with a curious admixture of playfulness; a noble man, pained to find himself lost in violence, and able to kill only under the justification of sacrifice. He was—and this, to Booth, was the "keynote" of Othello's nature—"a modest, simple-hearted *Gentleman*." [15]

In quieting Brabantio's gang, Booth urges: "Be very respectful to Brabantio, resent his abuse, merely with a look of momentary anger." Address the Senate without "a breath of bluster." And yet, when the Duke believes

> . . . this tale would win my daughter, too,

Othello should "Playfully acknowledge this compliment."

On Cyprus, the contending elements in Booth's Moor show more sharply. He meets Desdemona lovingly—but properly, embracing her "with delicacy. There is nothing of the animal in this 'noble savage.'" They do not kiss; ". . . *heart throbs* are better than kisses. Holding Desdemona clasped to his breast, Othello feels the quick beating of her heart against his own." (The *Review* lauded his "deep and chivalrous tenderness" here.) But this dignified amorous joy already lives under a faint shadow; for Othello's

> If it were now to die,
> 'Twere now to be most happy . . .

is "uttered in low, foreboding tones." The Oriental imagery, which Booth emphasized in his make-up, in his melancholy, and in his actor's *feeling* of the Moor's kinship with mystery, enchanted his partisans almost too much, as this paean suggests: "That . . . proud, beautiful . . . dark face, to which the Eastern robe was so becoming, seemed at once to be telling its mighty story of adventure and conquest. *Desdemona* was not worthy of it." [16] But he radiated power as well as beauty: "In the interruption of the brawl and the subsequent rebuke to Cassio, the actor gave another proof that dignity and command are not necessarily associated with a big physique . . ." [17]

His Othello's playful humanity emerged for the last time—to emphasize his later misery—when Desdemona first pleads for Cassio:

> What? Michael Cassio,
> That came a-wooing with you? And so many a time
> (When I have spoke of you dispraisingly)
> Hath taen your part . . .

Booth's Othello must "Reprove her playfully. Throughout this colloquy gaze lovingly in her face, and seem to encourage her to *coax* by your teasing silence." And when she goes on

> . . . to have so much to do
> to bring him in? Trust me, I could do much.

Booth: "Here she begins to 'pout' at her failure to obtain his consent, and he, fearing that she has misconstrued his silence during her last appeal, stops her with a kiss."

This is the end of joy. As he watches her leave, the foreboding refrain returns:

> Excellent wretch; perdition catch my soul
> But I do love thee: and when I love thee not
> Chaos is come again.

This is said "with joyousness—yet there should be an undertone of sadness—as at their first embrace in Cyprus."

Then Iago begins. But though Othello is melancholy, he is slow to jealousy, cannot conceive Iago's drift for a long time. And then he is more troubled than jealous. Deep in the scene, at Iago's "O! beware my lord of jealousy . . ." he still does not understand that the reference is to himself; and later, when he does, he shakes it off. But at last he is infected. He smothers a "moan" at Iago's

> But, I do see you are moved

and groans at the Ancient's

> Cassio's my worthy friend.

When he must say "Set on thy wife to observe," the *Review* thought "the greater agony of remorse which follows it marks the natural nobleness of a man who has been driven into a deed which is abhorrent to his contemplation the moment that he had done it, but which he still will do in pursuance of what seems to him the just discovery of a vile crime." [18] Now he is deep in melancholy. When Desdemona comes to take him to dinner with the islanders, and kneels to offer him the handkerchief for the pain in his forehead,

> Take time, gently push the handkerchief from her hand as she is in the act of binding it on your forehead. Pass her, while on her knees, with forced indifference, but turn lovingly, and holding your arms for her to enter them, say "Come, I'll go in with thee!" Then with a soulful look into her eyes, fold her tenderly to your heart and go slowly off.

Returning, unaware of Iago, Othello says *Ha ha, false to me?* "mournfully." After the farewell speech, aware of Iago's possible duplicity, he speaks "with smothered intensity, not loud, gradually increasing, till 'If thou dost slander her'—when the full force of Othello's wrath breaks forth in violent tones and he seizes Iago, who cowers." The *Review* was impressed by his remorse at this act: "He falls back in a reaction of horror and shame in which he manages to lose none of the general's dignity." [19] Booth himself pictured his Othello falling upon a garden seat "with a flood of tears." He rises to anger; but at the moment of his terrible oath of revenge, "although the savage blood is up, let a wave of humanity sweep over his heart at these words. Breathe out 'Tis gone' with a sign of agony which seems to exhale love to heaven." [20]

Waves of humanity break often on this poet-Othello, and leave him groaning, weeping, or moaning. Even the *Review* was troubled by his long-drawn-out sobbing;[21] and the *Börsenzeitung*, so impressed by his jaguar-Moor, nevertheless was bothered that "Booth too frequently employs inarticulate wailing . . . We of Central Europe are accustomed to the dumb rather than to the audible expression of pain." [22] But to his partisans, as in Boston, part of the "rich fabric" of his Othello was this vocal imagery— "the thousand variations of tones and inarticulate tones, of tremblings, starts, and checked gestures." [23] Thus, in III, iii, at

Damn her lewd minx:

he urges—rather daringly, for so refined a gentleman—"Take a liberty here and 'damn her' four times; the first savagely, the second less so, melt with the third, and choke with tears at the fourth." [24]

Booth's audible, visual grief was a poetic sublimation of Salvini's violence, which Booth normally shrank from. At

I'll tear her all to pieces

"Here you may let the savage have vent—but for a moment only; when Othello next speaks, he is tame again and speaks sadly." In the handkerchief scene he tries to be harsh with her—

Oh, hardness to dissemble!

—but his manner must change "from indifference to sadness." Booth's gentleness was warmly welcomed by his most famous Desdemona, Ellen Terry. She felt it had precisely the right quality for her—and for the play. "It is difficult to preserve the simple, heroic blindness of Desdemona to the fact that her lord mistrusts her, if her lord is raving and stamping under her nose! Booth was gentle . . . until *the* scene where Othello overwhelms her with the foul word and destroys her fool's paradise." [25]

Booth himself found it hard to confront Desdemona in the later scenes "without being too tame or too violent." He helped himself by eliminating the actual striking of Desdemona before Lodovico. As between fury and agony, his Othello steadily chose agony. "I must weep, but they are cruel tears," the Moor says, before waking Desdemona. Booth, who had restored these lines, often unpopular, notes that weeping was part of Shakespeare's image of Othello: "Remember how often he is moved to tears—therefore, I do not attempt to restrain them in the excess of passion here, in Act III, and elsewhere." [26]

Only this kind of Othello could reconcile men of ultimate

sensibility to his terrible killing. To Samuel Johnson the scene
had been dreadful, painful to work on, not to be endured. Furness, Booth's contemporary, who had to edit so many editings,
suffered even more: "I do not shrink from saying that I wish
this tragedy had never been written. The pleasure, however keen
or elevated . . . does but increase, the unutterable agony of
the closing scene." [27] Only a gentlemanly "grieved Moor" could
make this terror palatable to men of Booth's kind. And, at Desdemona's death, grieved Booth was

> . . . weighed down with woe, tender behind his grim and fatal
> purpose; his heart breaking beneath the hands lifted to strangle
> at once his inward and his outward love.[28]

Now the troubled poet took on the image of a priest: "a priest
at the altar. There is then no anger in his conduct. The man has
passed through a hell of anguish and passionate conflict . . .
and at last he is calm, in the concentration of despair . . . He
confidently supposes himself to be fulfilling a sacred duty of
*sacrifice*." [29]

At the last, when he sees what he has done, Booth's Othello
"Opens the curtains—pauses—kisses Desdemona—slowly and
with deepest feeling of remorse"—

> Then must you speak,
> Of one that lov'd not wisely, but too well.

Restrained to the end, after he stabs himself he cries simply
" 'O, Desdemona!' makes an effort to reach the bed, clutching
(not much) for the curtains as he falls back dead." [30]

Booth was as tender of words as of physical violence. He refined beyond all other theater refiners, carefully eliminating such
words as "sheets," "bed," and "body," changing "whore,"
"bawdy," "strumpet," and obscuring the details of sexual relationships.[31] Again the sensitive Victorian imagination was relied
upon to supply the implied details. Booth's excessively restrained
text was too plumptrized [32] even for some Victorians;[33] but

many approved, and some thought it was still too indelicate to be presented.[34] To minds as threatened as theirs were by impropriety, euphemisms seemed to carry the weight Shakespeare's franker speech had for minds more free, and every hint was explosive. They wanted the whole of Othello's fierce passion; but the physical sensuality of Salvini's tormented soul was to them almost obscene; while Booth's troubled, poetic murderer seemed to convey all that was left unsaid, was the very image of a "grieved Moor," ". . . the best Othello and truest to Shakespeare on the native and foreign stage . . . You pity him not less than Desdemona from your inmost soul; his agony wrings your heart; his tragedy is yours, and that of all humanity." [35]

# 7

🍃 *My wife! My wife! What wife? I have no wife!*

## Forrest

For those Victorians—among them Henry James—who sought
in the stage Othello the naked passion their culture was trying
to repress, the image of a titanically grieved soul plunging from
love into agony would best live out their buried lives. Eventually
they would be satisfied by Salvini, passionately sensual in his
love and volcanic in his grief; but they were prepared for him
by the fiercely noble murderer of an American actor who seemed
destined to play out a fearful jealousy not only on the stage but
in life too. This was Edwin Forrest, the first great American
tragedian. He curiously demonstrates the influence of an actor's
life on his interpretation of character. When Forrest made audiences tremble at Othello's grief, and weep at his betrayal, he
was working out, over and over, a private agony.

Friends—and critics—thought it was Forrest's personal experience that made Othello his particular part:

His life, too like the Moor's, had been scorched in going
through the hell of deception in marriage . . . His nerves and

89

fibers had been stretched to their utmost tension of agony, and
all his finer sensibilities had been tortured and awakened . . .[1]

Like Kean, Forrest had risen from poverty to win a place in
"society." He was forty-four—about Othello's age—when one
day in 1848, after ten years of married life with a gay, talented
English girl, Catherine Sinclair, he returned unexpectedly to his
hotel room—and grief. "[I] found Mrs. Forrest standing between the knees of Mr. Jamieson, who was sitting on the sofa,
with his hands on her person. I was amazed and confounded,
and asked what it meant. Mrs. Forrest replied, with considerable
perturbation, that Mr. Jamieson had been pointing out her
phrenological developments."

Forrest was "for a time quieted by this explanation"; but he
was made uneasy by his wife's habit of entertaining at late and
noisy parties while he was away on tour. Her father and mother
were intemperate, her sisters were frivolous and more—one bore
an illegitimate child—and he worried that he might be cuckolded.
He himself consorted regularly with prostitutes and actresses;
but he could not bear the thought that his wife might be unfaithful. Finally he opened her private drawer, and found a love
letter from Jamieson. It was sugary and sentimental, speaking of
vague ecstasies that might have been "Platonic" rather than
physical, but it infuriated Forrest. For four hours he harangued
his wife. Finally he spoke of her sister's degradation. She said,
" 'It is a lie . . .' the words fell into his irascible blood like drops
of molten iron . . . 'If a man had said that to me he should die.
I cannot live with a woman who says it.' " He stormed out.

In their last months together, they slept in the same bed, but
presumably as "brother and sister." He treated her like an "upper
servant," and brooded.

In his proud, sensitive, and tenacious mind, recoiling with all its
fibres from the fancied wrong and shame, the poison of the
. . . letter worked like a deadly drug, burning and mining all
within. By day or by night, he could not forget it . . . jealousy
. . . gnawed and tore him . . . For more than a year he kept

his dark secret in silence, not saying a word even to his dearest friends, secluding himself much of the time, brooding morbidly over his pent-up misery. Now he learned to probe in their deepest significance the words of his great Master—

> But oh, what damned minutes tells he o'er
> Who dotes yet doubts, suspects yet
>     strongly loves!

When Forrest was unable to contain his secret longer, he complained to a friend that "he had begun life as a poor boy, had struggled hard to reach a pinnacle," and a betrayal from the woman he loved seemed hardly fair. The friend defended Mrs. Forrest's spiritual and physical beauty; Forrest, echoing Othello, exclaimed, "She now looks ugly to me: her face is black and hideous."

Finally he ordered her from his house, but both solemnly vowed to keep the cause secret. Soon he charged her with failing the oath, and she denied it. He was adamant, sued for divorce for adultery, and she countersued on the same grounds. From this distance their letters suggest that she loved him and would gladly have returned, but that a mean, stored bitterness in him rejected all mutuality. The lady's "propriety of language and elegant deportment" won her many friends; Forrest made many enemies. He watched her house, waylaid one of her visitors, and, finding him the wrong man, threatened to find the other and "rip his liver out. I'll cut his damn throat at the door. You may go this time, damn you. But I have marked you, all of you, and I'll have vengeance." Forrest finally caught and beat one of his enemies in Central Park. He lost friends, turned inward; he felt more and more a lofty stranger, misunderstood and exploited by a super-subtle society.

In the divorce trial the lady was found innocent, and Forrest was declared an adulterer and ordered to pay alimony. He appealed to another court, and lost there. He appealed to another court, and again lost. Five times he appealed, over a period of eighteen years, before he finally gave up and paid. Meanwhile, he carried his rancor into the theater, where, beginning one triumphal run, he spoke to a wildly applauding audience his personal version of "It is the cause . . .":

> I submit my cause to you; my cause, did I say?—no, not "my" cause alone, but yours, the cause of every man in this community . . . the cause of every honest wife . . . the cause of everyone who cherishes a home and the pure spirit which should abide there.

His troubled biographer, Alger, acknowledges: "Justice to the truth requires the frank admission that there was also in him a rude and harsh element, a streak of uncivilized bluntness . . . ." [2]

If anything kept Forrest's Othello from the very top rank, it was this touch of something sullen and sulky, an imaginative limitation that kept him from comprehending the depths of the Moor's soul. Physically, he was ideally suited for the outer image of the role: even his enemies agreed that he had the look and sound of Othello. A bull of a man, with great, bulging muscles, he reminded a fellow actor of Michelangelo's Moses. John Foster Kirk, no partisan, said: "Of the actors whom I have seen, Salvini not excepted, Forrest alone possessed a physique such as one conceives to have been moulded expressly for . . . heroic roles." [3] His voice, in "volume, resonance, melody, and compass was phenomenal." [4] And he made full use of the great voice and body—too much so, thought his detractors, who found his sound only roaring and his action mere posture. Critics were fierce then: one called him the "greatest master of the Epigastric School of Action . . . His particular excellence seems to lie in his extraordinary power of pumping up rage from his epigastrium and expectorating it upon his audience through interstices of his set teeth." Twelve years after Forrest's death, Kirk described what then seemed the actor's dated style: "He moved at times with a certain rush, as of a boulder that has been set rolling; he beat his breast and ranted in overpowering tones—or, as an old actor expressed it to me, 'thrust his fist into the face of his audience'—by way of showing animation or passion . . ." [5]

But in Forrest's own time, his critics were far outthundered by applauding admirers respectful of the classic dignity in his style and awed by its romantic fury. The Anglo-Saxon world regarded him as easily the most powerful Othello after Kean. Some even thought him better[6]—and in the 1850's nothing could be better than better than Kean.

By both his champions and his detractors Forrest was remembered best for the mighty rages in which he vented his passions; yet, as he worked the role out he softened it, and some of his greatest moments came in quiet and tenderness. If indeed he saw himself in Othello, then he labored, through visual and audible imagery, to make the Moor of the early scenes as noble and lovable as a hero could be. Alger admired the dignity of his first appearance: the "self-possession of a free and generous nature full of honest affection and manly potency." [7] At Brabantio's onrush, he spoke

> Keep up your bright swords, for the dew will rust them

"in a tone of unruffled self-command, touched with a humorous playfulness and . . . respect." Kirk admired his voice's "calm deep sound [which] seemed to suspend the clashing weapons by some inherent irresistible sway." [8] The *New York Mirror* praised "the delicacy and modesty" of his confession of courtship before the Senate. Here by manner and voice Forrest established the loveworthiness of his romantic hero. "There was a depth in the love-tones . . . that spoke of the intensity of his passion. His utterance of 'My life upon her faith' had all the romantic fervour of the proud days of chivalry." [9] No wonder ". . . a refined and lovely young lady . . . was heard saying to her companion, 'If that is the way Moors look and talk and love, give me a Moor for a husband.' " But Alger hastens to stipulate that Forrest's passion was decent: the "high and pure character" of his "signals" to Desdemona, as she entered the council chamber, showed no "animal love bred in the senses alone, but a love born in the soul and flooding the senses with divineness." Unlike Booth's, there was no foreboding for this

Moor, no fear that so good a married love might end. "On the keen fires of his high-blooded organism . . . the exquisite sweetness of the surrendered and gentle Desdemona played a delicious intoxication . . . Life was too short, the earth too dull, the stars too dim, for the blissful height of his consciousness." [10] There was more love imagery on Cyprus. Forrest's almost unbearable happiness, the *Mirror* said, made him indeed " 'prattle out of fashion.' His arms were twined around Desdemona, his hand played with her ringlets." [11] Though still respectable, the passion of this Othello was much warmer than Booth's, the voice full of the sound of love:

> . . . the rapturous smile that clothed his face, his parted lips, his heaving breast and outstretched arms . . . worked on the spectators like an incantation. And [then] he drew her passionately to his bosom, kissed her on the forehead and lips, and gazed into her face with unfathomable fondness . . .
>
> Oh, my soul's joy! . . .
>
> uttered with a restrained, prolonged, murmuring music, a tremulous mellowness, as if the burden of emotion broke the breath into quivers.

Forrest remained nobly dignified in the riot scene, bursting into "volcanic heat" only once, when explanations came slowly. A famous bit, indicative of his restraint, was his seizing a passing soldier to order, in a low chilling tone, "Silence that dreadful bell."

By the time the great temptation began, Forrest had amply projected the image of Othello's nobility. When he was a very young Othello—known as the "American boy tragedian"— Iago's first hints left him "still all love to his fair wife." [12] But later in his bitter life, as his nature or his private experience governed him, he released his smoldering passions more quickly than most Moors. His Othello was as ready to be jealous as he himself was. In his first entrance, he looked up—at Iago's careful hint—to ask:

> Was not that Cassio parted from my wife?
> Iago: . . . No, sure I cannot think it
> *That he would steal away so guilty like,*
> Seeing your coming.

For an instant Forrest looked at Iago as if much impressed by his emphasis on the last part of the sentence; Forrest's mind from this moment was particularly drawn to all that Iago said about Cassio.[13]

After this "opening wedge," Forrest kept steadily to the scent. At Desdemona's plea for Cassio, he asked "pointedly"

> Went he hence now?

"as if searching for something hidden." When she continued,

> . . . he hath left part of his grief with me.
> I suffer with him. Good love, call him back.

Forrest was not fondly or playfully affectionate, as were other Othellos. "Somewhat displeased . . . (he) grew restless, and in haste said, as if wishing to get rid of the subject:

> Prythee no more. . . ."

Here began the great center of Forrest's interpretation, full of thunder, lightning, and whirlwind. Was he cruelly spurred now by his own undigested experience, by a recurrent image of his wife standing between the knees of George Jamieson? To many he seemed so.

When Iago asked if Cassio knew of the wooing, and then a speech later artfully seemed to try to avoid the subject:

> But for a satisfaction of my thought,
> No further harm

Forrest, "looking Iago directly in the eyes, and with intense inquiry:

*Why of thy thought?"*

From here on, though Forrest's Othello was often moved to tenderness—"the tone [of] 'if she be false, then heaven mocks itself' drew tears in the eyes of many"—he was dominated by a terrible passion. By the end of the first temptation, he seemed unmistakably the image of a jealous husband. At

> If I do prove her haggard,
> Though that her jesses were my dear heartstrings,
> I'd whistle her off, and let her down the wind
>     to prey at fortune . . .
>                       . . . I'd rather be a toad,
> And live upon the vapour of a dungeon,
> Than keep a corner of the thing I love,
> For other's uses.
> Desdemona comes!

The burst of mixed passions with which he uttered the first of these sentences was terrific. His voice then sank into tones the most touching, expressive of complaining regret. The conclusions seemed to have excited him to the most extreme pitch of loathing and disgust, and, as he sees Desdemona advancing, he, for a few moments, gazed upon her with horror.[14]

Briefly he reverted to tenderness, but soon he was in the grip of Iago again. In the great Farewell speech, he would seem heartbroken, "his voice in the tremulous minor key of the flute"; but then all the frustrations of his own emotional privations were released in an orgasm of physical imagery that marked him surely the most terrifying of English-speaking Othellos. The hands that would gladly have strangled George Jamieson or ripped out his liver could now seize openly on the naked throat of Iago, and Forrest ominously moved toward the final charge:

Slowly he appeared to indulge the suspicion of his wife's infidelity; in silent agony the conviction seemed to be creeping upon him,—his iron sinews trembling with dreadful and conflicting emotions—rapid as thought were his denunciations;

and, with all the weakness of women, he again relapsed into tenderness,—pain had a respite, and hope a prospect.[15]

Then came his fearful challenge to Iago:

> Suddenly, with one electrifying bound, he leaped the whole gamut from mortal exhaustion to gigantic rage, his eyeballs rolling and flashing and his muscles strung, seized the cowering Iago by the throat, and, with a startling transition of voice from mellow and mournfully lingering notes to crackling thunderbolts . . . shrieked,—

> > If thou dost slander her and torture me,
> > Never pray more; abandon all remorse. . . .

It was a tremendous effort, and the spectators, "with distended eyeballs and compressed lips," saw—as with Kean—Othello's complete physical and emotional dismay. "It was at the end of this speech that Kean rushed for the sofa that stood on the stage . . . and thereon threw himself to recover from his absolute exhaustion before he could go on with his next speech, during . . . thunders of applause and waving of hats and handkerchiefs . . . Forrest changed the action and rushed for [a] profiled column . . . while the audience gave him a like ovation." [16]

Here was the peak of Forrest's performance. Unlike Salvini, who kept building an image of fury through Act V, Forrest followed Kean in a diminution of passion, though intensity was maintained. "The glare of his eye when his wife could not produce the fatal napkin was almost supernatural; and a lady, who sat in the same box with me, clutched convulsively at her husband's arm for protection . . ."

Forrest's partisans felt that in Acts IV and V he was recurrently overcome by waves of tenderness and at last killed Desdemona, as Booth did, sacrificially. But others believed rather that Forrest, still seeing his own bitter self in Othello, indulged less in pathos than self-pity, felt too much a "galling relationship between him and the Moor." [17] To one observer, his personal involvement was plain from the painful intensity, the personal assimilation he expressed in . . .

> But alas! to make me
> A fixed figure for the time of scorn
> To point his slow and moving finger at—

The groan which escaped from the broad chest was natural . . . In place of interpreting Othello, he interpreted himself, enacting Forrest under a borrowed name.[18]

Whatever his motivation, Forrest emphasized—sometimes almost querulously—Othello's wavering between revenge and yearning for a lost love: ". . . he grew so pale and haggard, wore so startled and dismal a look, was so self-absorbed in misery . . . He grew less massive and more petulant." [19] At *I'll tear her all to pieces*, "His revenge began furiously, 'I will [*sic*] tear her'—when his love came over it, and he suddenly ended with pitying softness—'all to pieces.' " Forrest even brought back some of the lost *Othello* language to emphasize his whipsaw passions. In the main he kept to a "refined" text, but to show Othello's mental turmoil he dared to restore some of the trance episode.[20] Even a trace of the long-lost "wavering" scene seems to have been saved. Not the full force of the sweet nostalgia juxtaposed to the thoughts of grim revenge; nothing of "O, the pity of it" in those words; but Forrest is reported saying—in an amazing textual cut-and-splice: " 'O, the world hath not a sweeter creature': then, the imaginative associations changing the picture, he screams ferociously, 'I will chop her into messes.' " [21]

By Act V, "the pity of it" was in the ascendant. Now Forrest strove to acquit his Othello of any imputation of savagery: he killed Desdemona solemnly, delicately, "seeming to fancy himself not so much revenging his personal wrong as vindicating himself and executing justice." The curtain's rise found this transformed image—a gentle, melancholy Moor—musing beside Desdemona's bed, "the deep subdued tones of his voice . . . like the muffled bass notes of a cathedral organ." He rose, and paced the stage in restless despair. When finally he wakened Desdemona, he "showed no harshness, but acted more in the spirit of pity." Hers was the gentlest of deaths: "Forrest enclosed himself behind the curtains by pulling them together, and the struggle between him and Desdemona was not seen by the audience. It was almost noiseless; you faintly heard the words of Desdemona as if smothering . . ."; and later, at her sound, "he drew his dagger, closed the curtains, and finished the murder . . . a slight groan from Desdemona giving the final token of her death." From here to the end, his passion was generally[22] considered low-keyed but intense. After he learned at last how wrong he was, "an absolute desolation and horror of remorse, as if a thunderbolt had burst within his brain, smote him to the floor. Staggering to the fatal couch, his gaze was riveted on the marble face there, and a broken heart and a distracted conscience moaned and sobbed . . .

> Now, how dost thou look now? O, ill starred wench!
> Pale as thy smock! . . .
> O, Desdemona! Desdemona! dead." [23]

"Oh, fool, fool, fool" was "a touching cry"; and he spoke "Behold I have a weapon" with such power "that the audience shook themselves out of their silent attention and applauded . . . to the echo." [24] Then, in his suicide, "unable to reach the gentle Desdemona 'to die upon a kiss,' he dropped dead in the centre of the room, his hands outstretched and his face turned toward the bed whereon his wife was lying, the pearl he had so rashly thrown away." [25]

So the end is described by admirers. His critics felt the atmosphere of romantic nobility in the last acts was sullied by the pervasive stain of Forrest's personal experience—and personal limitations: he seemed to carry into the play his attitude toward Catherine Sinclair: "His love of his wife was the love of possession . . . Desdemona's impurity did not shock him so much as the disobedience of her nuptial vows angered him. He thought less of her sin than of the sinner who had cajoled him into trust of which she was not worthy. The hideous picture in his imagination was not Desdemona secretly bestained, but Othello publicly disgraced." [26] Forrest's friends fell away from him as he grew old and sick, and at the last he was unable even to hold an audience for a reading. He felt abandoned: once, after a performance before his gift was quite gone, when someone said, "I never saw you play *Lear* so well," Forrest retorted bitterly, "*Play Lear! . . .* By God, sir, I *am Lear!*" [27] He had no disciples, Wilson observes,[28] and his uniquely mixed classic-romantic style died lonely with him.

Once Salvini's great new Othello appeared, the audiences that had applauded Forrest so warmly greeted the Italian with even greater enthusiasm. Two frustrated biographers tried to account for this. Alger suggested Forrest was before his time in the scale and fervor of the passions he portrayed:

> They were not exaggerated or false, but seemed so to the cold or petty souls who knew nothing of the lava floods of bliss and avalanches of woe that ravage the sensibilities of the impassioned souls . . . [Salvini's] conception and performance of the part were so identical with those of Forrest . . . (hundreds) exclaimed that it seemed as if Forrest had risen from the dead . . . and although Salvini made the passion more raw and the force more shuddering and carried the climax one degree farther . . . actually sinking the human maniac in the infuriated tiger, he was greeted with wondering acclaim.[29]

Harrison was less tolerant: "Forrest did not in any part of his conversation with Desdemona treat her as if he was an Italian bandit, or a low butcher . . . We have had one actor [Salvini] in this country that the press prated about being a great Othello, and who had the audacity in the presence of a refined audience to slap Desdemona in the face with a letter he held in his hand —take Iago by the throat, throw him upon the stage, and place his foot upon his neck. This was an Italian conception of Othello. . . ." [30] But this was the conception—cataclysmic in its sensuality and fury—that polite Anglo-Saxon audiences would enthusiastically prefer. And it was not the surface that made the difference. Salvini's Moor had an inner shape that Forrest, intelligent and talented as he was, could not conceive.[31] Something in the utter honesty—as well as in the nakedness and terror—of Salvini's passion validated it. It seemed then that there must have been too much of Forrest's self in his Othello, and too little of Othello in Forrest.

# 8

∿ *I'll tear her all to pieces . . .*

## Salvini

It is time now for the entrance of the great grieved Moor of the past century, one of the theater's greatest Othellos—Tommaso Salvini. His terrible magnificence set a standard: "troubled persons" were measured by contrast with him, and the other tormented souls were inevitably scaled against his titanic characterization. He was either the best of Othellos—or the worst. He came out of Italy like a tornado, and his first performances in England—spoken entirely in Italian—almost blasted the Victorians from their theaters. He was "strongly criticized for the terrible and almost excessive demonstration of fury of his last scene," by the time Fanny Kemble saw it; and by then, though he had "much toned it down," still no English actress would submit "to the full fury of his assault . . ." [1] But his Moor was recognized as a masterpiece of passion (except by those too fearful of passion), of a frank, erotic sensuality, then of a grief that transcended violence, finally of an utter despair of nobility sunk in delusion, torment, and disaster—and yet never ignoble.

To his admirers, he presented the true form and inner image

102

of the Moor. Henry James, sensitive to Salvini's visual, aural imagery, wondered at ". . . the depth, the nobleness, the consistency, the passion, the visible, audible beauty of it . . . the perfect Othello is there." [2] So was the perfect heroic image, James added:

> His powerful, active, manly frame, his noble, serious, vividly expressive face; his splendid smile . . . He is a magnificent creature, and you are already on his side . . . you find yourself looking at him, not so much as an actor, but a hero.[3]

Then he began to act—and became, depending upon the point of view, an image of the magnificent tragic protagonist or of the primitive barbarian or wild beast. The *Athenaeum*, on the whole sympathetic, saw him as the "barbarian whose instincts, savage and passionate, are concealed behind a veneer of civilization so thick that he is himself scarcely conscious he can be other than he appears . . . In the end the barbarian triumphs . . ." [4]

But to the *Galaxy*, savagely negative,

> The Italian's Moor has little dignity, no majesty, barely a flash of heroism amid all his lurid flashes of ferocity. He is a superbly, though but physically, developed barbarian, whom the civilization of Venice has simply veneered. How dissimilar, how opposite indeed, to Edwin Booth's Othello, struggling grandly and often successfully with the jealousy he is ashamed of, but cannot hide . . . You hate [Salvini's Moor] and are impatient for his death, as you might be for the death of a mad dog let loose in the streets.[5]

So he was called an "Italian bandit . . . a low butcher." But Henry James disagreed: "It is impossible to imagine anything more living, more tragic, more suggestive of a tortured soul and of generous, beneficent strength changed to a purpose of destruction. With its tremendous force, it is magnificently quiet, and from beginning to end has not a touch of rant or crudity." [6]

Here was a curious point. Like Forrest, Salvini was remembered for his grief as Othello; yet his admirers prized "natural" moments that were quiet, touched with humor, even gay. An actor from boyhood, he had shunned the bombastic Neopolitan style for the variety of naturalism that seeks out and represents the essential "nature" of a dramatic character. He had the mind and emotion to assume great natures: he had learned humanity while guarding his lonely, aging actor father—much as Booth had done—and in denying himself in order to pay the father's posthumous debts. He had fought with Garibaldi for the Italian republic, had gone to jail for his patriotism. As a young man, he was passionately on his dignity; but he learned to be quick to forgive and be generous with praise for his fellows. Booth, acting Iago to his Othello, thought him ". . . very gentle, kind, and modest." [7] And Towse: "He exhibited the power of an Edwin Forrest in combination with the delicacy and subtlety of a Duse." [8] So light were his touches of movement and voice in the love play with Desdemona that E. T. Mason called them ". . . exquisite high-comedy effects . . . in the first three acts of this play, before Othello's suspicion is aroused, Salvini gives more of the essential spirit of high comedy than could be found in the 'Mercutio' of some noted actors." [9] So "naturalistic" were his quieter moments that Henley, partial to grand style, was troubled: "Of course it is touched with modernism, and here and there brought within range of criticism by its lapses into prose." But the poet saw, with relief, that Salvini was only faintly touched by the new "literality":

> A modern Othello would no doubt slay his Desdemona with the 'fatal calm' of one of Hugo's heroes; having done the deed, he would light a cigarette, ring for a brandy-and-soda, and tell Emilia, with a little gesture of the hand, a nod or two at the bed, and eyebrows arched with significance, to go for the police. Salvini's Othello is unconscious of Pall Mall . . . It is heroic and romantic, but it is profoundly and *terribly natural* and true.[10]

This Moor was never so quiet that the tragedy was not warm with his passion. He was lofty and imperious in suppressing the first night clash with Brabantio: "Or the dew will rust them" was "touched with gallant laughter." [11] In his address to the Senate, his action was closest to the formal and declamatory: ". . . spreading out his arms, with a sweeping gesture, to suggest the deserts; pointing upward to the hills." He told of the cannibals "expressing horror by his face, and by a gesture with both hands, as if repelling the man-eaters." And, curiously, recalling what Desdemona thought of his tale:

> 'twas strange, 'twas passing strange,
> 'Twas pitiful, 'twas wondrous pitiful

"he personates Desdemona, and speaks in a feminine voice." [12] But this was all prelude to the "passionate joy" with which, "loud and exultant," he told of his love and waited her coming.[13] Now the *Athenaeum* saw the first picture of his passion: "He covers [her] with a glance of indescribable tenderness. As she claims from the Duke permission to go with her husband to the wars his gaze becomes burning. Forgetful of all restraints, he approaches and almost folds her in his arms." [14]

To some Victorians, this visual imagery was unseemly, low. Even a partisan felt "His gloating over Desdemona ill-became the lines which displayed the depth and chastity of the hero's love"; and to the ardent negative: "The burning passion that fairly flushes from him is not what we have looked for. He consumes her with his gaze; his senses riot over her. There is complete absence of spiritual affection or sympathetic communion, of pure delight at renewed companionship. The merely physical demonstration is unpleasant, unredeemed by something higher . . ." [15] The sensitive poetess Emma Lazarus felt a different, deeper image: "The indescribable accent with which he utters the very name of the 'divine Desdemona' is in itself a revelation, and after the lurid horror of the final catastrophe the music of that first tone comes back to us with unforgettable pathos. 'I do not wonder,' said one of the gentlest of women . . . that Desdemona forgave his killing her, when she had his perfect love for a little while." [16]

Throughout the Senate scene, he was a noble man who loves and trusts. His "affectionate confidence" in Iago was emphasized by gesture and exchanged look. There was "a very patient calm in his manner with Brabantio"—until Brabantio's warning insinuation:

> Look to her, Moor, if thou hast eyes to see:
> She has deceived her father, and may thee.

This he indignantly repelled.[17] After "Come Desdemona, I have but an hour . . ." spoken with deep tenderness, he "pauses, gazes upon her; then, impulsively, and with great ardor, he embraces her and, gazing rapturously into her face, leads her away." The imagery of their action at the Cyprus meeting was equally sensuous, "steeped in Southern voluptuousness." [18] He embraced Desdemona, then, after "It stops me here," embraced her again "more closely, kisses her, and stands with his lips pressed to hers during Iago's lines, 'O you are well tuned now.' " Fanny Kemble almost wept at "the sudden choking of his utterance in his overwhelming joy when he finds his 'soul's joy' . . ." [19]

The night riot was put down with vehemence and passion, but Salvini remained in control. He was most angry when he saw that the noise had roused Desdemona; after dismissing Cassio angrily, with "vehement tenderness . . . he snatches the cloak from his own shoulders and wraps Desdemona in it . . . like the passionate, apprehensive gesture of a mother [guarding] her child." [20]

His playfulness with Desdemona in Act III was what led Mason to speak of his "high-comedy" touch. He is at his table, trying to write; and, in a pleasant domestic figure, she "reclines beside him, resting upon one knee and leaning upon his knee, insisting he set the time for Cassio's recall.

> *Des.* Shall't be tonight at supper?
> *Oth.*                  No, not tonight.
> *Des.* Tomorrow dinner, then?

> *Oth.*                           I shall not dine at home;
>    I  meet the captains at the citadel.

He goes on trying to write; she presses him until finally she takes his pen from him.

> *Des.* Why, then, tomorrow night; on Tuesday morn;
>    On Tuesday noon, or night; on Wednesday morn:
>    I prithee, name the time, but let it not
>    Exceed three days: in faith, he's penitent;
>    When shall he come?

He pauses in his work, turns partly toward her, and listens with a pleasant smile, as one might attend to the prattle of a favorite child. He embraces her at the end of the speech, interrupting her impulsively:

> *Oth.* Prithee no more: let him come when he will;
>    I will deny thee nothing."

It seemed, from the "infinite tenderness of his half-amused, unsuspicious manner . . . he only delays the granting of her request for Cassio's reinstatement in order to enjoy the luxury of hearing her sue." This recalls Booth. Before her exit, he once more embraced her, was about to kiss her, became conscious of Iago and Emilia nearby, and let her go reluctantly as if to say, "There are too many spectators here—we must wait until some other time!" As he watched her go, "Excellent wretch" was spoken with "ineffable tenderness." [21]

Now Iago began the temptation; but Othello, back at his desk, was writing in earnest. Iago found hard going; Othello presented the image of a happy, busy man, patient with his very good friend but annoyed at being interrupted; through the first four speeches he was "bothered, bored, teased, anxious to get on with his own work." His obstinacy in repelling doubt strongly impressed reviewers. "Nay, it is not until Iago has repeatedly plied his instigations that he can be said to repel doubt, since the doubt does not seem even to come. He has no suspicion to fight against, since he entertains no suspicion, at least of Desdemona." He replied to Iago's insinuations in the "quiet, kindly tone a man in his position might use toward one . . . whose officiousness is ignored because of the honesty and fidelity which prompt it." [22] Finally, realizing some trouble in his friend, he turned to Iago.

> Thou dost mean something . . .
> *Iago:* My lord, you know I love you.
> *Oth.:*          I think thou dost.

Here again the mutual trust between the two was visually emphasized. This Ancient was indeed "very dear" to his general. "Othello takes Iago's hand in both his own, clasping it warmly and releasing it as he continues:

> And, for I know thou'rt full of love and honesty,
> And weigh'st thy words before thou givest them
>      breath,
> Therefore these stops of thine fright me the more . . ."

Iago evaded again, with a hint. Othello pressed him:

> Nay, yet there's more in this.

"After a moment of keen scrutiny of Iago's face, Othello smiles, shakes his head, and waves his hand slightly, deprecating Iago's lack of frankness, and persuading him to outspoken sincerity." Even at "O misery!" where Booth had finally risen to the bait, Salvini spoke it "merely as an expression of sympathy with any poor wretch in such a plight as Iago has described." It was not until

> *Oth.* Why, why is this?
>      Thinkest thou I'd make a life of jealousy?

that he first recognized that Iago may be thinking of him; he repelled the thought. But now Iago had an opening:

> *Iago:* I am glad of this; for now I shall have reason
>     To show the love and duty that I bear you
>     With franker spirit . . .
>             I speak not yet of proof . . .
>     Look to your wife; observe her well
>         with Cassio . . .

"When Iago says 'I speak not yet of proof,' Othello shrugs his shoulders and laughs incredulously. At 'Look to your wife,' he becomes gravely attentive." At "observe her well with Cassio," he started, shook his head in angry negative, and half turned toward Iago. "He represses himself, [asks] 'Dost thou say so?' in a low, anxious tone. He says, 'And so she did,' in a still lower tone, scarcely audible . . .

> *Iago:*                    Why, go to then;
>     She that, so young, could give out such
>         a seeming,
>     To seal her father's eyes up close as oak—
>     He thought 'twas witchcraft . . .
> *Oth.:* I am bound to thee forever."

"When Iago says, 'He thought 'twas witchcraft,' Othello turns his eyes, threateningly, toward Iago, without turning his head, and moves his hand toward [his] sword . . . He immediately restrains this wrathful impulse and stands, motionless. At the end of Iago's speech, there is a pause; then, in a very low tone, tremulous with suppressed emotion, Othello says 'I am bound to thee forever.'" Iago then: "I see this hath a little dash'd your spirits"—and here a curious point of disagreement arose. Salvini, who carefully checked Mason's valuable account of the characterization, saw an image of himself "recovering" and answering, "in an indifferent tone, 'Not a jot, not a jot.'" But Mason, who often watched the performance, saw this:

Othello at first essays to speak, but cannot find his voice; then, half turning toward Iago, with a ghastly smile and a tremulous waving of his hands, he delivers 'Not a jot, not a jot!' in a tone scarcely audible, husky with hardly repressed passion.

Who knew better—actor or observer? In any event, as Henley and Frank Archer insist, the speech was a memorable one.[23]

Even in this Othello, the jealousy at last takes seed, and grows in a beautifully articulated visual, aural design. He must listen; must try to work with his pen again, but at last dash it down in despair. He rose, brooded. Desdemona came, but she could not dispel doubt, as she could not ease his "headache." Here "Othello's voice is very low, and his utterance faint and slow . . . After Desdemona's exit . . . he sighs heavily and follows her at a slow pace, with downcast looks, his head bowed upon his breast." His low-keyed despair continued until he met Iago again; then slowly it mounted through the farewell speech to his goodbye to the great cannon,

> whose rude throats
> The immortal Jove's dread clamors counterfeit . . .

(*Bocche tonanti, nunzii di vittoria*—Mouths thundering, messengers of victory) spoken "with the full force and volume of his voice. Then, as he says 'Farewell! Othello's occupation's gone!' he bursts into passionate weeping, throws himself back into the chair, falls forward upon the table, and lies there." It is "virtually a farewell to his better self," [24] the *Athenaeum* thought; for here came the famous terror of his attack on Iago. He recovered and turned on the Ancient, and began the pattern and rhythm of action in which observers saw the metaphor of a great tormented animal. "Shaking his head like an angry lion, he utters 'Villain!' in a low voice, expressing the extreme of deadly menace." Now the great center of the storm is loosed, and the hero gives way before the agonized man:

> . . . he rushes upon Iago, clutches him by the throat, and forces
> him down upon his knees . . . at times menacing him with his

clenched right hand . . . at times seeming almost to twist Iago's head from his body . . . he twists Iago violently from left to right and flings him prostrate upon the stage . . . Then, with clenched hands upraised, with distended eyes and passion-contorted face, he raises one foot, as if to stamp out Iago's life. He restrains himself, perceiving that he has gone too far [this last phrase was inserted into Mason's description by Salvini] and retires . . . He then advances again, quickly to the prostrate Iago, who raises his left hand, as if to ward off a fresh attack upon him. Othello grasps Iago's hand and raises him to his feet, with an inarticulate sound, expressive of grief, shame, regret, and then staggers blindly . . . to the lounge, upon which he throws himself exhausted.

This was too much visual passion for the negative. Winter, who described the Italian style as "using Iago as a floor-mop," said Salvini "became an incarnation of animal fury, huge, wild, dangerous, and horrible, but he was consistently common and bestial." [25]

But the general, and most of the judicious, disagreed. They saw the image of a steady, massive swell in Othello's tidal passion, the wholeness of the wave from serenity to disaster. Lewes said of the flinging down of Iago, the foot raised to trample:

. . . then a sudden revulsion of feeling checks the brutality of the act, the *gentleman* masters the *animal;* and with mingled remorse and disgust, he stretches forth a hand to raise him up. I remember nothing so musically perfect in its *tempo* and intonation, so emotionally perfect in expression—the fury visibly growing with every word, his whole being vibrating, his face aflame, the voice becoming more and more terrible, and yet so completely under musical control . . .[26]

Most amazing, the passion was renewed, mounted even higher, awing observers. Henley: "You imagine that . . . he had said his last word, and five minutes afterwards he confounds you by his tremendous interpretation of Othello's oath of vengeance, which has in it the fury and thunder of the Pontic and Hellespont at war." [27]

Between the trampling and the oath, Othello's passion was always clamorous, threatening; he held "himself in check with the greatest difficulty, likely at any instant to spring upon Iago and blot him out. He is a man upon the rack." Yet he did restrain himself; and a visual figure of his repression Mason especially noted was the curious, ghastly, "death-like" smile by which "he suggests the utmost conceivable depth of human anguish." He kept giving way: at "I'll tear her all to pieces," like Kean and Irving, he made the sundering gestures with "intense ferocity." Then "Now do I see 'tis true" came "with a sudden cry of anguish, as if pierced by a sword."

> *Iago:* Yet be content.
> *Oth.:* O, blood, blood, blood!

And then the oath.

From now on, there was no rest. Momentarily, an image of hope crept on his face, when he asked Desdemona to show him the handkerchief and she:

> Why so I can

But she must follow this with "but I will not now," and suddenly, as she sued for Cassio, she was hateful to him; her pleading arms around his neck were repellent; he thrust her from him. Back with Iago, his agony and the Ancient's incitements gave him no peace; and at last, sinking under the strain—not so far as a trance, but groaning and sobbing—he flung himself into a chair and buried his head in his hands.

There was no overhearing of Cassio.[28] Instead, he recovered from his despair enough to plan Desdemona's death and then to meet Lodovico—and strike Desdemona with the letter. Half the Victorian world was dismayed by that blow: ". . . he struck Desdemona . . . and thus indicated the taint of savage ancestry." [29] Emma Lazarus pointed out that this was the action imagery Shakespeare himself had visualized; Furness agreed, but he could hardly bear it. "This blow is the ineffaceable blot in Othello's history which leaves, upon me at least, a more painful

impression than even the smothering . . . *Fechter* strikes with
the letter . . . this is a shade better than the backhanded blow
which *Salvini* delivers full on those sweet lips, and which makes
your own lips grow white as death, at the sight." [30] But Mason
denies the hand struck her—only the letter; and Salvini footnotes, "almost involuntarily, and repents of this base action
immediately."

Now, before Lodovico, Othello again tried to mask his torment behind one of those "horrible" smiles that "produced some
of his most profoundly tragic effects"; but "the pent-up passion
which he has repressed with so much difficulty breaks loose; and
he [leaves] with loud cries of anguish, wringing his hands
wildly above his head." Once more he must face Desdemona,
in the brothel scene; again she must try to embrace him; again
he must drive her back.

O, Desdemona! Away! Away! Away!

"At '*lasciami, vanne!* [leave me, fly!]' he bursts into passionate
weeping and falls upon the chair . . . weeping and sobbing
convulsively." Like Booth, he wept often; but there was more
nakedness in his tears, more sounding grief; this Moor was as
abandoned in his sorrow as in his rage.

In building to the final great smash, in Act V, Salvini played
in lower tones, but they were all ominous; and the agony of his
very real destruction of Desdemona disturbed many. He tried
to hold his passion under restraint, "as a giant might hold a
raging tiger." But the restraint gave way as her tears, seemingly
for Cassio, maddened him; and now the physical imagery was
terrifying: "he drags her to her feet . . . grasps her neck and
head with his left hand, knotting his fingers in her loose hair,
as if to break her neck." With his Italian Desdemona, Piamonti
—"the personification of pitiful, protesting love gradually resolving into speechless terror—he pounced upon her, lifted her
into the air, dashed with her . . . across the stage and through
the curtains, which fell behind him. You heard a crash as he flung
her on the bed, and growls as of a wild beast over his prey." [31]

To proper Victorians this was intolerable. Beast, butcher, bandit, he was called, a "New York skulking assassin." The passionate reactions showed again the sensitivity to overt sensuality:

> From the hour he is fairly set on to doubt Desdemona, he surrenders his manhood to the wild beast which had peered out from his amorous gloatings in the meeting in Cyprus . . . Blind, furious jealousy tears and controls him, to the exclusion of every gentle emotion. He counterfeits a wild beast. He crouches like a tiger . . . Whenever he is with his wife, he snarls and snatches at her; can scarcely keep his hands from her throat, from dashing her to the ground . . . [In] the final and distressing chamber scene . . . he arouses only horror in his audience; he compels Desdemona to rise from her bed, where she should stay for her doom, and come to the front that he may seize her struggling and screaming—and carry her in his murderous arms back to the peaceful couch to do a butchery, not perform a sacrifice.[32]

To this, a Salvini supporter countered: "I am not a convert to the theory that Desdemona ought to be immolated in the spirit of religious sacrifice. Murder, especially when prompted by jealousy, founded or unfounded, is murder."[33]

Archer allowed "errors of taste" in the violent physical imagery of Desdemona's killing, and even more in Othello's suicide: "With a short scimitar, he literally cut or hacked at his throat and fell to the ground, gasping and gurgling." Yet, like most of the rest, Archer thought the performance "wonderfully beautiful" in spite of the gaffes: they were mere "spots on the sun."[34] To Henry James, the furious tiger in the man was a splendid part of the essential shape of Salvini's Othello. It was an "Italian Othello"—different, James was sure, from the ideal English Othello, "more charged with 'the pity of it,' more awe-stricken at what he feels himself impelled to do, hanging over Desdemona at the supreme moment more hushed to horror." But James could imagine nothing more powerful, more suitable to the tragedy, than the imagery of Salvini's famous gestures:

Some of his tones, movements, attitudes, are ineffaceable; they have passed into the stock of common reference. I mean his tiger-like pacing at the back of the room, when, having brought Desdemona out of her bed and put the width of the apartment between them, he strides to and fro, with his eyes fixed on her and filled with the light of her approaching doom. Then the still more tiger-like spring with which, after turning, flooded and frenzied by the truth, from the lifeless body of his victim, he traverses the chamber to reach Iago, with the mad impulse of destruction gathered into a single blow. He has sighted him, with the intentness of fate, for a terrible moment, while he is still on one knee beside Desdemona; and the manner in which the spectator sees him—or rather feels him—rise to his avenging leap is a sensation that takes its place among the most poignant the actor's art has ever given us. After this frantic dash, the one thing Othello can *do* to relieve himself (the one thing, that is, save the last of all), he falls into a chair . . . and lies there for some moments, prostrate, panting, helpless, annihilated, convulsed with long inarticulate groans. Nothing could be finer than all this; the despair, the passion, the bewildered tumult of it . . . My remarks may suggest that Salvini's rage is too gross, too much that of a wounded animal; but in reality it does not fall into that excess. It is the rage of an African, but of a nature that remains generous to the end; and in spite of the tiger-paces and tiger-springs, there is through it all, to my sense at least, the tremor of a moral element.[35]

Here was certainly an image of a grieved Othello; all but the terribly shocked agreed to that. Though, in his jealousy, as on horror's head horrors accumulated, there was more of terror than pity, there was much pity. A quality of humanity in Salvini's Moor matched Shakespeare's conception; the playwright's garment shaped itself to the player at most points, so well that audiences trembled at their mutual creation, their shared power.

And this in the face of appalling handicaps. Salvini spoke only in Italian, whether with his own home company or in the later polyglot performances, as with Booth, where he learned with much labor to dovetail his native language to the cues of an English-speaking cast. And he played a mutilated text: Cassio's part is reduced, and Iago's byplay with Roderigo and Cassio and even some of his soliloquizing are out. All this has the effect of centering the play on Othello and on his duel with Iago. On the other hand, Salvini all but restored the trance; and though he, too, cut deeply in the play here, he kept a few lines from the wavering scene, the Italian equivalent of:

> Here within the heart has turned to stone.
> I strike it and my hand is hurt
> O, but the world no daintier creature had!
> Get me some poison . . .

He restored part of the Willow Song scene, though the discussion of adultery was plumptrized;[36] and—most odd—at the end he let Emilia live. Should not this tumbled version, heard in Italian, or Italian-English, only have bewildered spectators? It didn't. These obstacles were usually not mentioned in the most judicious reports. The authentic aural and visual imagery of Salvini's master passion conveyed what the playwright had intended.

Here we are close to the mystery of the art. How could so noble a hero turned into so savage a murderer earn so much pity? Salvini's own conception of the role's image is suggestive.

> Although a soldier of fortune, Othello was descended from a royal race, of which honor, however, he never boasted . . . Skilled as he was in the art of war, he was simple and ingenuous in other relations, believing everybody honest who appeared so . . . Desdemona, who admires him more for his noble qualities, sees beneath his dark complexion the whiteness of his soul, and declares her love . . .

Desdemona became his whole world: ". . . the joy of the present, the sweetness and charm of the future: the rainbow of his troubled and tempestuous career." Here was Othello's hope of security—he had committed himself all in all to his wife. The imagery of physical passion noted in his performance, Salvini felt, was submerged in a much greater, total affection. "His is not a sensual love; it is the pure affection of a soul which unites itself to another and without which he could no longer exist— a sentiment so profound, so intensified, and so wide that it embraces the affection of a friend, of a brother, of a son, and of a father. It has become to him as the air he breathes, an ever-present paradise." The serpent in this paradise was Othello's battle companion, his "friend," Iago. The mutual confidence of their relationship Salvini emphasized, as we saw, in performance as well as description. Iago, "believed to be honest by everybody," had earned his trust:

> . . . hence, how could he do otherwise than listen to the insinuations with which Iago seeks to poison his mind . . . and which he makes with that assumed air of reserve, as if fearing to do her injustice? . . . And yet [Othello] refuses to hear the first insinuations of doubt as to the fidelity of his wife, so beloved and so reverenced; and it is only when Iago reminds him of the prediction of Brabantio and bids him remember the difference of color and customs between her and himself that he gives any thought to those revelations and becomes suspicious almost by force.

Salvini insists that Iago must seem utterly trustworthy and sincere; then the noblest Othello may—as he must—truly believe the murder of this all-betraying woman is a necessary execution. "The fountain of his life is dried up, and the treasure of his heart is lost . . . her death is a sacrifice which he owes to society . . . and when he becomes aware of his fatal error, with more care for his honor than for his life, he desires that his deed should be narrated in all its horrid details; then, making himself at once judge and executioner, he sacrifices himself as he has sacrificed Desdemona." [37]

There were other well-known Victorian Othellos, but they do not contribute significantly to the century's characterization. A few, however, are interesting for accenting what we have already learned from the giants. Thus Ernesto Rossi, Salvini's countryman, an actor of great physical power, coming abroad to take advantage of the "Italian" vogue with a loud, savage, sensual Othello, succeeded mainly in repelling British and American audiences. Henry James saw and heard in his Moor "a kind of bestial fury, which does much to sicken the English reader of the play. Rossi gloats in his tenderness and bellows in his pain." [38] Winter, affronted by the Italian conception, but grudgingly respectful of Salvini, found in Rossi only "gloating, uxorious animalism . . . sneaking suspicion . . . hysterical garrulity . . . The denunciation of *Iago*—who, yelling with fear, had been hurled to the floor . . . was snarled forth with blatant vehemence. The killing of *Desdemona* was effected with hideous brutality . . . Unredeemed by such personal magnetism and such colossal individuality as those of his predecessor—[his Othello] was radically wrong and supremely repulsive." [39] Fury, sensuality, violence, and terror were not enough to make up the Moor's image.

Most of the secondary English-speaking Moors were of the "troubled person" type; and as "natural" acting triumphed, their interpretations grew more domestic, more intellectual. [40] One interesting variation was John Edward McCullough's: he came on, not merely of "a free and open nature," but with a kind of happy, boyish joy, truly seeming to feel he lived in sunshine. His was an Anglo-Saxon counterpart to Salvini's robust Italian *joie de vivre;* and his romantic naïveté was followed, typically, more by troubled misery than by the fierce grief of the tormented Othellos.

The novelty of the century was Ira Aldridge, an American Negro, the more novel because he was married to a white wife. He emphasized his blackness in the role, making a visual point of enclosing Desdemona's white hand in his dark one. Though, like Salvini, he treated Desdemona roughly at the end—he would snatch her "out of bed by the hair and drag her around the stage before he smothered her" [41]—he usually seemed not the barbarian African he was rather expected to be. He had "a solemn intensity of style . . . the dark shades of his face become doubly sombre in their thoughtful aspect: a nightlike gloom is spread over them, and an expression more terrible than paler lineaments can readily assume." [42] But his interpretation was often dismissed as "intellectual." Gautier, who saw Aldridge's Othello much applauded in Russia, thought he purposely—and wisely—was not the primitive.

> We looked forward to an energetic manner, troubled, impetuous, a little barbaric and savage in the manner of Kean; but . . . doubtless to appear as civilized as a white, he has a quiet acting style, regulated, classic, majestic, recalling Macready . . . he smothers Desdemona with taste, and he roars properly . . . he seemed to us to have more talent than genius, more science than inspiration. [43]

In England, only one native Othello after Kean promised to command enough of both pity and terror to match him in the Moor's stature. This was Gustavus Vaughan Brooke, physically the image of the noble Othello—"The manly form, the leonine bearing, the well-poised head." He had a phenomenal voice that ranged from tenderness to rage, and enough, but not too much, of the grand acting style. He began triumphantly. But he drank himself to oblivion; and for too long he lived out that oblivion on the stage, where his acting grew mechanical and meaningless. Once, in the middle of the first act, he simply gave up; and an admirer wrote sadly: ". . . my last sight of the idol of my boyhood was the vision of a helpless man, head sunk upon his chest, arms hanging listless, form swaying backwards and forwards." [44]

It was not easy to be Othello, to have a sure insight into Othello's grief and the equipment to give it tangible shape: the physique, the voice, the energy, the nobility, the passion—and, beyond all these, the gift of genius that lifts craftsmanship into art. When they could not bring this last to Othello, notable Hamlets, Macbeths, Lears fell short of him. Their very failures will help as much as the successes to clarify, in my later chapters on *Othello* criticism, the far dimensions of the character and the demands it must make on any who would interpret it.

# 9

◠◠◠ *What's he then that says I play the villain?*

# The Victorian Iago

In the Victorian Iago we begin to see clearly how the essential enigmas of his character—his plausibility and motivation—were being solved in the theater. The reviews begin to show his rounded image—of pervasive evil, masked by an innocence that irresistibly corrupted the noblest Othello.

But it was not easy to be Iago. Many failed, and as many fell short. At the lowest level, the stereotyped acting mind still saw him in the Cibber tradition, as did the stereotyped critical mind —so that a "refined" writer could be amazed that a "refined" actor could undertake the role: "If once a look or a gesture denoting honor, courage, or kindly feeling, should escape Iago, the illusion would be destroyed. . . . It is undeniable evidence of Mr. [Charles Mayne] Young's transcendent professional ability that he, a gentleman of his education and polished manners, should assume a character so opposite his own and so repugnant to his nature . . ." [1]

All this probably explains why Young's Iago was called "jocular and sarcastic—nothing more." So obvious an Iago

120

necessarily made Othello "an object of contempt for his credulity." [2] Another type on the same level was a dominating, manipulating villain, at his worst in a pre-Civil War Iago in New Orleans, who "snarled, scowled, and ranted" like "some cruel Diego of a slave driver who was giving an unlucky nigger a piece of his mind." [3] At the other extreme was the hollow villain, without passion, dignity, or weight, made visual by one "dainty, mincing, elegant, dandified Iago, who appears to be actuated less by a deep fiendish hate than by a sort of feminine spitefulness." [4]

A good cut above such hacks were the "almost" Iagos who, though they did not express the Ancient's inner "perturbed spirit," made his villainy outwardly plausible. Kean in particular was noted—and imitated—for his cheerful "honesty." "We saw . . . a jocund, elastic villain, who murdered reputations with a smile, and whose vivacity and intelligence formed a cloak far more impervious to suspicion than the vulgar cut-throat aspect which [usually] . . . renders the jealousy of Othello so eminently ridiculous." [5] Kean's Iago image had the promise of greatness, and had he been willing to labor over it, as he did with Othello, he would probably have distilled its very essence. [6] But he was too eager for the major part, too anxious to escape the "dull and cloudy Othellos" he had to act against. One of them, Sowerby, was almost hooted off the stage once Kean had left it. Kean fell into one of the classic faults, playing the villain for surface laughs and excitement, and neglecting the motivating passion that should have glowed through the outer form. He seemed "*too* lightsome in his manner," his biographer wrote, "for there is a great weight of metal in our Ancient." [7] Hazlitt agreed:

> I did not mean to object to the "gay and careless air which Mr. Kean threw over his representation of that arch villain," but to its being nothing but carelessness and gaiety . . . Mr. Kean very properly got rid of the brutal ferocity which had been considered as the principle of the character, and then left it without any principle at all . . . If our Ancient had no other object or principle of action but his indifference to the feelings of others, he gives himself a great deal of trouble to no purpose.

If he has nothing else to set him in motion, he had much better
remain quiet than be broken on the rack.[8]

This would be a consistent critical view. As well as plausibility, there had to be motive: Iago has "passions of his own,
which are not to be trifled with";[9] he must be much more than
"a gay light-hearted monster." [10] But this "jolly" characterization now had the authority of Kean; and its comedy and disa-
vowal of guilt made this "careless, cordial, comfortable villain" [11]
easy for the audience to enjoy on a shallow level. So it became
one of the standard Iago patterns, until *Punch* could describe a
Sadler Wells Ancient as "semi-comic." [12] Kean's better imitators
tried to give dimension to the role, but they had trouble including the character's passion and "principle" with their gaiety;
they were too clever, too little moved. Thus Brooke, potentially
so powerful an actor, indulged in the shallows of Kean's conception. That he could have done more is suggested by a vocal
surprise he once gave his Othello, Forrest. It was in the great
crisis of Act III, iii: Forrest, who prided himself on the volume
of his voice, "put forth all the lung power at his command . . ."
Brooke countered with " 'Oh, Grace! Oh, Heaven, defend me!'
in a tone of thunder which as it reverberated through the building at once dwarfed his colleague's delivery by the contrast
. . . Forrest . . . stood perfectly stupefied. For the first time
in his eventful career he had met with a man whose voice ex-
celled his own." [13]

But Brooke squandered his strength in Iago, as in Othello; he
reduced the villain to a casual, comic image, ". . . affected an
air of easy nonchalance and familiarity of speech . . . The assumption of character proved flippant; there was no exaggera-
tion, but there was no profundity. Deep-seated malice was not
indicated . . ." [14]

Kean's imitators often failed to copy another quality in his
Iago that doubly insured plausibility—his earnestness in the more
serious scenes: his "solemn sincerity where he labored at his
proofs—indignant patience where he retorted the suspicions of
his fidelity—and . . . the deep and collected devotedness with

which he knelt and declared his friend Cassio to be 'no more for this world.' " [15] Thus he was more than believable to Othello —he was likable, trustworthy, deserving of his general's friendship. This characteristic would be a mark of all the better Iagos, and would invariably gratify reviewers, as with Forrester: ". . . it is too commonly forgotten that no gentleman, to say nothing of ladies, could have allowed himself to appear in company with such a miscreant [as Iago often is] . . . Mr. Forrester has the look, carriage, and manner of a gentleman . . ." Hence not only was it credible for his Othello to "listen to his suggestions"; [16] the two could also share a sense of intimate comradeship, so that this Iago could even show "a wheedling and cajoling tenderness in the scenes of Othello's trial." [17]

The very best Victorian Iagos learned not only to preserve an always sincere—though a sometimes blunt and jovial, sometimes kindly—plausibility, but also to use it as a mask for a passionate inner "principle" of revenge, a "perturbed spirit" that usually emerged only in soliloquy.[18] The best of the British Ancients were, curiously, the inadequate Othellos: Macready, Fechter, Irving. The volcanic passions of the hero were beyond their reach, but they could command the smoldering passions of the villain, subdued, as was their technique, to a strong intelligence.

Macready's Iago suffered visually, as did his Othello, from the egotism of the actor. When he was the Ancient,

> Othello was to become a mere puppet for Iago to play with . . . Iago's intellect, his fiendish subtlety, his specious calculating malignity were to be the sole feature of the play. Othello was to be a mere fly, a large *blue-bottle*, struggling in the meshes of the Italian spider . . .[19]

More's the pity; because where Macready's Othello could not survive a really strong Iago, his Iago could apparently stand up to anything—short of a Kean. Hazlitt said of an early performance, "[Charles Mayne] Young, [as] Othello, was like a great humming top, and Macready in Iago like a mischievous boy whipping him." [20] Still Macready went on strengthening his interpretation through long and illuminating study. Years later he wrote of one performance: "There was a want [in me] of sustained earnestness and spirit; there was no proper direction of the sight, and, in consequence, a scowl instead of clear expression . . ." [21] The next year he "acted Iago very indifferently"; he still needed work on his visual imagery, on "the habit of scowling or looking from under my brows . . . I wanted reality and directness, indeed, a revision of the execution of the character . . ." [22] Finally he "cleared" Iago's face of scowls, made him a blunt, honest soldier, and behind this sturdy mask of innocence merged intellect and passion into energetic purpose. It was a "revelation of subtle, poetic, vigorous, manly, many-sided deviltry" [23] to the very end, when "passionate with his frustrated design . . . he burst the doors open with clenched fists to make his passage free." In such a moment of passion, and in his soliloquies, he revealed the source of his wickedness: "He convinced his hearers that they need not cudgel their brains seeking for concealed causes of hatred against Othello, Cassio, or Desdemona. Iago's motive was found in his own nature . . ." [24]

Macready himself was not satisfied with his interpretation until he was sure he had penetrated to the self-motivation of Iago; and then indeed the egotist was pleased—as if he were the only actor who had ever gone beneath the villain's surface: "That last performance of Iago was . . . an elucidation and opening out of [Shakespeare's] profound conception . . . which has not been given before in the inward feeling of the part: the selfishness, sensuality, and delight in the exercise of his own intellectual power . . ." [25]

Fechter followed the outer form of Kean's conception, but with more purpose behind the gaiety; for Macready's bluffness he substituted "a bland and polished courtier, whose manner and appearance would grace the gondola of a princess or the levee of a Doge . . . It is Iago with the tiger-teeth, concealed by a smile, and the cruel claws muffled in velvet." [26] Fechter's polish gave him something of the image of Cinthio's original Ensign, "a man of the most handsome person . . . he cloaked with proud and valorous speech and with a specious presence the villainy of his soul . . . he was to all outward show another Hector or Achilles . . ." All agreed that this Ancient "could and did make friends." Dickens discovered Fechter's "honest" Iago—as so often critics discovered a plausible one—as if this were the first of the breed:

> . . . not in the least picturesque according to the conventional way of frowning, sneering, diabolically grinning and elaborately doing everything else that would induce Othello to run him through the body early in the play. Mr. Fechter's is the Iago who could . . . overpower Emilia by other arts than a Saracen's Head grimness; who could be a boon companion without ipso-facto warning all beholders off . . .[27]

To the *Times*, Fechter seemed particularly right in his relation to Othello: ". . . he is ever a benignant being . . . his manner becoming more soothing as the tempest he has raised increases in violence." [28]

Fechter sometimes marred the image with his stagy theatrics, overplaying the contrast between villainy and hypocrisy. Thus, "When he leaves *Othello* in torment of mind his fingers cast at him behind his back a swift Italian gesture of contempt, instantly followed by a servile obeisance at the threshold as Othello turns his face." But such "questionable interpretations" [29] were forgiven because of the unity of the conception[30]—the organic relation between the two faces of his villain's image: the honest surface one, and the passionately vindictive inner one below. "In the earlier scenes—so deep does his villainy lie—it seems doubtful whether he will ever rise above the pleasant hero of light comedy." But his subtle byplay and the "malice and vindictiveness of his soliloquies" caught his audiences[31] and held them through a carefully articulated development "from crime to crime until the climax of the tragedy he works." [32]

Henry Irving, Britain's most distinguished Iago, veneered the character with a gay front[33] that made even stronger the sense of inner villainy.[34] ". . . he claims our attention from the first by . . . the charm of personal confidence . . . draws us yet closer . . . by a mysterious fascination that has almost as much of admiration as of horror in it; a feeling, as Hazlitt rightly points out, akin to that which leads us always to read the accounts in the newspapers of dreadful fires and shocking murders . . ."[35] Irving being Irving, his Iago was flawed by acting tricks, "sundry little 'touches of nature,' as they are somewhat recklessly called"[36]—the hands "knocking against the stony heart, or passing through the grizzling hair . . . tormenting the thin moustache, playing with the dagger, or toying with the steel ornaments of the girdle . . ."[37] The characterization was loaded with "business" that men remembered. Many Iagos since Irving have used his action, after sending Roderigo off to sell all his land, of covering his face with his two hands, then slowly withdrawing them "revealing a face all alive with the devilish scheme which had come into his mind."[38] The *Athenaeum* could remember ". . . no finer picture . . . than that of the saturnine ruffian turning over with his foot, in indolent and mocking curiosity, the body of Roderigo to see if life were extinct."[39] Among Irving's memorable props were "those grapes which he plucked in the first act, and slowly ate, spitting out the seeds, as if each one represented a virtue to be put out of his mouth."[40] (But *Macmillan's* could not see how this imagery enriched Iago's character, and was even less happy when, in soliloquy, Irving "picks his teeth with his dagger and afterward wipes it on his sleeve.")[41]

Irving's Iago tended to overbear Othello in appearance as well as in manner—except when up against a giant like Booth. There was warrant for an Iago "to all outward show another Hector," but Irving overdid, appearing as ". . . a splendid triumphant cavalier, wearing far costlier garments than his superior officer . . . he is always the dominant figure in the scene, the one whom the eye first singles out."[42] Irving admitted this dominating impulse, and supplied an image that later Iagos—among them

Laurence Olivier—would also adopt: "To me [Iago] has also a slight dash of the bullfighter, and during the brawl between Cassio and Montano, I used to enjoy a mischievous sense of mastery by flicking at them with a red cloak, as though they were mere bulls in the arena." [43]

And like Macready and Fechter, Irving sometimes seemed to overemphasize the difference between the role's surface gaiety and its inner vindictiveness. *Macmillan's* conceded that "this deepens the tremendousness of its villainy"—but "these contrasts want no heightening, this villainy no deepening . . . Iago is no unnatural monster, no chaos of irreconcilable opposites; he is a man, and a natural man enough, if one looks carefully at his character . . ." [44]

Again, like Macready and Fechter, Irving was able to absorb the flaws in his acting into an interpretation "of such magnitude" the rest was forgiven.[45] And where his inspiration could not command the means to body forth Othello, it fully served his Iago. Thus Ellen Terry, as Desdemona, once moved him so with her plea: "Oh good Iago, what shall I do to win my lord again?" that tears filled Irving's eyes. Having succumbed to the emotion, he transformed it into character imagery:

> . . . seizing on those tears as handy properties, [he] ostentatiously dashed them away and blew his nose "softly and with much feeling," conjuring from true emotion the very essence of counterfeit hypocrisy.[46]

The master pattern that lay behind the dazzling variety of his performance was summed up by Miss Terry: "So full of charm, so sincerely the 'honest' Iago, peculiarly sympathetic with Othello, Desdemona, Roderigo, *all* of them—except his wife. It was only in his soliloquies and in the scenes with his wife that he revealed his devil's nature." [47]

Irving located the source of this interpretation in Macaulay's image of Machiavelli: "We see a man whose thoughts and words have no connection with each other, who never hesitates at an oath when he wishes to seduce, who never wants a pretext when he is inclined to betray. . . ." But most important, behind this duplicity was the passion, the inner force that was lacking in Kean and others of the too-gay school—a kind of terrible "principle" to motivate the villainy: "Hatred and revenge eat into his heart; yet every look is a cordial smile, every gesture a familiar caress . . . His face is unruffled, his speech is courteous till vigilance is laid asleep, till a vital point is exposed, till a sure aim is taken . . ." [48]

The Victorian theater's finest interpretation of the Iago problem was Edwin Booth's. Without distracting mannerisms, he conveyed a sense of driving, malignant inner passion—but screened by a splendidly plausible exterior. Here was one of the great villains of stage history—largely because Booth labored assiduously to make him appear as absolutely "unvillain-like" as possible: "To portray Iago properly you must seem to be what all the characters think, and say you are, not what the spectators know you to be; try to win even *them* by your sincerity. Don't *act* the villain, don't *look* it or speak it (by scowling and growling, I mean), but *think* it all the time. Be genial, sometimes jovial, always gentlemanly." [49] In this Iago the inner evil was strong but implicit—and implicit *always*. As with Othello, Booth worked hard to capture what the character was and to *be* it, even during moments of inaction. Thus, of Iago's position in the Act I Council scene: "Othello leaves Desdemona with Cassio . . . Iago, at back watches them curiously, but let him not be obtrusive; he must keep in the background and . . . feel the curiousness, even if only one person in the whole audience sees or understands it . . ."

It *was* seen and understood; *Macmillan's*, for instance, warmly preferred it to the restless pyrotechnics of Irving—"how much really less natural to the character than Mr. Booth's still, respectful attitude, leaning against the sun-dial . . . seeming careless of what goes on . . . yet ever watching his prey with sly, sleepless vigilance." [50] William Winter thought that Booth's villainy almost had to be *felt*, through an "indefinable but instantly perceptible . . . transparency . . ." [51] And it sometimes seemed indeed that only through an intangible glow could the evil become apparent, the signs were so rare.[52] Lucia Calhoun saw: ". . . no stage winks and grimaces. Save in his soliloquies he makes no confessions . . . If Othello had suddenly turned upon him, at any moment in their interview, he would have seen only the grave, sympathetic, respectful, troubled face that was composed for him to see." [53]

As with his Othello, there was change and development in Booth's Iago, mainly toward deepening the inner vindictiveness.[54] By the time he played against Salvini, his villain's style was more realistic, closer to "ordinary life." [55] The Salvini-Booth *Othello* ought to have been one of the theater's historic performances, but unfortunately, coming late in Booth's career, it found him lacking in the energy to support his conception. As it was, the partnership gave rise to a scandal *d'estime*. Booth was lonely as well as old now, and he rambled through one New York performance in a way reminiscent of his earlier drinking days. The *Herald* reported:

> . . . the actor seemed to find some difficulty in walking about the stage and in speaking his lines. The supporting actors gathered about him in such a substantially sympathetic way that they seemed to be leaning against him like braces.

Once he stumbled and broke the guardrail and almost fell over the footlights. The *Herald* quoted a wicked allusion to the elder Booth's habits: "[Edwin] is a great actor . . . and he is following in the footsteps of his father." [56] Salvini's manager told the newspaper the fall was caused by a rush of blood to the head. Booth claimed dyspepsia, an old complaint.[57] The brief partnership was not terminated;[58] Salvini respected Booth and thought his Iago was "absolutely admirable." [59] In Boston all went smoothly enough; though where Salvini still showed the old "overwhelming bursts of passion, the Olympian power" (except for the "famous tiger spring" for which he was now too old), critics missed the Booth-Iago's storied "personal magnetism and ophidian charm." [60]

Booth himself best described the physical imagery with which he achieved his guileless-seeming triumphs. He rigorously restrained the theatrical impulse toward sudden, stagey revelations of the leer behind the smile. Even where he used "by-play," he carefully covered it. When Brabantio's troop assaults Othello's little company in Act I, i, Iago quickly picks a target:

> You, Roderigo? Come sir, I am for you.

Booth: "This is to prevent harm to Roderigo, for whose purse Iago has a tender regard. Make the audience understand this by your manner of singling him out—a look will do it." And, at the end of the act, another firm caution against obviousness: "Be not too flippant with Roderigo, nor too eager to show the audience your villainy." In preparation for revealing his inner self in the act's final soliloquy, "Change your manner at Roderigo's exit from 'bonhomie' to seriousness."

On the Cyprus quay, Booth has Cassio kiss Emilia directly on the lips, at

> 'Tis my breeding
> That gives me this bold show of courtesy.

"Iago winces"; and in this scene, though he is gallant in manner to Desdemona, in his foolish rhymes, "All that he says till he speaks 'Aside' should be delivered humorously, to conceal his bitterness, which his features occasionally reveal." Winter was impressed by the "sweet serenity and inexorable purpose of evil" that glowed through his honest front here.

In the crucial temptation scenes, Booth repeatedly warned against the show of villainy. At the outset, when Iago and Othello enter to find Cassio leaving Desdemona, Iago's foreboding

> Ha. I like not that

is muted. "Don't growl this—let it barely be heard by the audience." When Othello reveals that in his courtship of Desdemona, Cassio "went between us very oft," Iago must "Contract the brows, but do not frown—rather look disappointed, and merely mutter in surprise, 'Indeed!' " Pressed by Othello to speak, Iago protests:

> Utter my thoughts? Why say they are vile and false?

"Don't speak this as though you held your thoughts to be really 'vile and false,' nor *look* so; be frank in appearance." And Iago's next pious homily

> Good name in man and woman, dear my lord,
> Is the immediate jewel of their souls . . .

is sincerely casual. "Don't fire this directly at Othello, but trust to the whiff and wind of it, for your effect on him, and on the audience too, although it may not gain applause from them as do the scowls and growls of the stage villain."

> Oh, beware my lord of jealousy . . .

is spoken "in a tone of solicitude."
   Finally, as Othello chokes out his shameful

> Set on thy wife to observe.

and Iago turns to go, Booth allows an overt physical image: "A quick, fiendish smile of triumph and a rapid clutch of the fingers, as though squeezing his very heart [Othello's face is buried in his hands] is quite legitimate here, but do it unobtrusively as you *vanish*." The difference between Booth and Fechter shows here. When Iago finally goes, Fechter has him, stagily, "Retire humbly—looking on from the back with a triumphant smile. At the door he raises his shoulders in contempt; and exit." Booth has none of the mock humility, or the "by-play"—quite the con-

trary: "Iago should be rápid in all his actions except at this point
—do nothing, but go slowly off with a tender respect."

In the handkerchief theft scene, he is rude to Emilia—"he is
given rather to chiding than caressing" her; but he is at once
warm again to Othello and *reluctantly* revealing. "His most per-
nicious lies . . . he administered in the most deceptive form,
that of an involuntary confidence." [61] After this, when Othello
despairingly cries for blood, "Iago affects remorse for having
put this to him." Scamp Iagos have waited for Othello's kneeling
at the oath of revenge to display behind him ironic winks and
grimaces—and even the handkerchief; Booth only watches
Othello keenly—the Moor turning suddenly would have found
"only the grave, sympathetic, respectful, troubled face." Here
is where Booth especially cautions against showing what the
spectators know Iago to be: "try to win even *them* by your sincerity." Accordingly, when he joins Othello in the oath, he is
"devotional." And when Othello asks him to provide for Cassio's
death, "Iago is shocked, of course, and slightly shudders."

> My friend is dead.
> 'Tis done at your request.

Then he speaks "beseechingly":

> But let her live.

Booth's Iago carefully avoids any slip when poor, troubled
Desdemona kneels and asks him to bring her together with
Othello again. He helps her to rise; and "Nothing could be
more absolutely specious and convincingly sympathetic than
Booth's voice, manner, and whole personality when he said,
"There's matter in it *indeed*, if *he* be *angry!*" [62] Afterward, when
he meets Roderigo, his mind is on other things, and he speaks
"with nonchalance," until the gull threatens exposure, where-
upon "he instantly plans the removal of Roderigo as well as
Cassio." He dazzles Roderigo with images: Desdemona coming

home to Venice, the death of Cassio, of which he first speaks "slowly and mysteriously"; then, to overcome the "silly gentleman's" fears, "rapidly—don't give Roderigo a chance to think." When he kills Roderigo—he would kill Cassio, too, but Lodovico and Gratiano come too soon—and then "discovers" the others, "Iago is very much overcome." But alone he is under strain, and when the rest turn to go he will watch them "well off, then take a look at Roderigo, and speak hoarsely,"

> This is the night
> That either makes me, or fordoes me quite.

The final revelation of his vindictiveness, capped sometimes by his "pointing triumphantly at [Othello's] dead body and gazing up at the gallery with a malignant smile of satisfied hate," [63] seems to have been the least of his effects. The terrible cumulative force of his wickedness came from its almost complete concealment. By conveying in soliloquy the sense of corrosive passions lurking behind the friendliest image, he powerfully engaged the repressed terrors and impulses of his audiences:

> . . . it was only when alone that his Iago revealed his frightful wickedness and his fiendish joy in it, and there was, in that revealment, an icy malignity of exultation that caused a strange effect of mingled admiration and fear . . . akin to the fascinated loathing inspired by a deadly reptile.[64]

What compounded the horror of the evil in an Iago like Booth's was the inevitable effect on Othello. This villain's Moor seemed to have a "friend" such as few men would be lucky enough to own, endless in patience and regard; Othello could confide in the friend as any man might long to confide—and more, when (as the result of *"involuntary confidences"*) faith so clearly justified more faith. This Iago's Othello, as Salvini emphasized, could not help but place an absolute trust in his old battle companion, his old comrade.[65] No wonder audiences shuddered—how could friendship seem more secure? It was through a mask of such absolute plausibility that the great Victorian Iagos revealed—in soliloquy, mainly—the passion, the "deep-seated malice," the "vindictiveness" that motivated the Ancient's villainy.

# IO

*Oh, thou weed, who art so lovely fair . . .*

## The Victorian Desdemona

Important qualities in Desdemona's character emerge in reports of distinguished Victorian performances. This in spite of considerable handicaps suffered by actresses of the role. The heroine's image was still cruelly stripped of some of its richest, most touching verse, and as always she was overshadowed figuratively and physically by "star" Othellos. The low state of the part is reflected in Macready's response when Fanny Kemble, who paired famously with him in *Macbeth*, volunteered to do Desdemona to his Othello: ". . . he expressed his astonishment at my being willing to play Desdemona: 'For,' said he, 'there is absolutely nothing to be done with it, nothing: nobody can produce any effect in it; and really, Emilia's last scene can be made a great deal more of. I could understand your playing that, but not Desdemona.' " [1]

Desdemona was not only overshadowed by Othello; she was sometimes in danger of being quite literally extinguished by him. Except when a "gentle" murderer like Forrest sought to ennoble her smothering with sacrificial restraint, Desdemona was sure

135

of at least a mauling and—as with Salvini—possibly much worse. Fanny Kemble had a wholesome fear of it: "That smothering scene . . . is most extremely horrible . . . my only feeling about acting it with Mr. Macready is dread at his personal violence. I quail at the idea of his laying hold of me in those terrible, passionate scenes." Fanny already had a broken finger, which Macready, lashing about recklessly as he liked to do for his big effects, had cruelly crushed in *Macbeth*; in *Othello* she assumed it would be rebroken, and as for that smothering in bed, 'Heaven have mercy upon me!' as poor Desdemona says." [2]

Macready was so famous for mistreating his leading ladies as well as upstaging them when he played a passion that once one of his actresses plotted a counterscheme:

> . . . in such a part, [he] gets hold of one's head and holds it in chancery under his arm, while he speaks a long speech, at the end of which he releases one, more dead than alive, from his embrace; but I shall put so many pins in my hair and stick them in such a fashion that if he takes me by the head, he will have to let me go instantly again. [3]

Fanny Kemble took more positive measures as Desdemona. She brought to the role its traditional tenderness; but she also asserted a positive inner quality that she and other outstanding Victorian Desdemonas found essential to the heroine's image. Softly feminine as this Desdemona was, she was also sturdy, brave, forthright in the face of terror. (This was not a new discovery in the character: Sarah Siddon's Desdemona had never lost her dignity, and Mrs. Cibber won applause for the "uncommon energy with which . . . she asserted her innocence"; [4] but now the actresses describe the quality themselves). Fanny observed that "the Desdemonas that I have seen on the English stage have always appeared to me to acquiesce with wonderful equanimity in their assassination. On the Italian stage they run for their lives." Fanny did not want to run: she could not find warrant for this physical imagery in the text, and besides—femininely—"the bedgown in which I had arrayed Desdemona for the night would hardly have admitted of this flight around the stage." In any event, she was determined not to submit easily. "I think I shall make a desperate fight of it, for I feel horribly at the idea of being murdered in my bed." Surely Desdemona, she thought, "should like not to be killed: and therefore, at the last, [I] got up on my knees on my bed and threw my arms tight around Othello's neck (having previously warned Mr. Macready, and begged his pardon for the liberty), that being my notion of the poor creature's last appeal for mercy." [5]

Fanny's task was probably easier because another of Macready's Desdemonas, Helen Faucit, was able to show him that a sturdy Desdemona would not steal any glory from him, but on the contrary would, by counterpoising it, strengthen his own characterization. "*Desdemona's* death under a cloud of dishonor was an acute agony, as if it had been [Miss Faucit's] own;" [6] and she was determined to resist it with all a heroine's strength:

> Desdemona is usually considered a merely amiable, simple, yielding creature . . . This is the last idea that would have entered my mind. To me she was in all things worthy to be a hero's bride and deserving the highest love, reverence, and gratitude from the noble Moor. 'Gentle' she was, no doubt (the strong are naturally gentle). . . .

Miss Faucit's Desdemona—which moved Carlyle deeply—stood up to Othello like a hero's bride indeed, and fought for her life as she fought for her love. Several actors appreciated its visual strength; one "told me that . . . it restored the balance of the play by giving her character its due weight in the action, so that, as he said, he had then seen the tragedy for the first time in its true *chiarouscure*." And Macready, her Othello, conceded that "my brightness and gaiety in the early happy scenes . . . helped him greatly, and that, when sadder, I was not lachrymose, and, above all, that I added intensity to the last act by 'being so difficult to kill.' Indeed I felt in that last scene as if it were a very struggle for my own life. I would not die . . . without the chance of disabusing my husband's mind of the vile thoughts that clouded it. I felt for *him* as well as for myself, and therefore I threw into my remonstrances all the power of passionate appeal I could command."

Miss Faucit defended her sturdy image of the heroine with as much spirit as she defended Desdemona's life:

How could I be otherwise than "difficult to kill"? *I would not* die dishonoured in Othello's esteem. This was bitterer than fifty thousand deaths. Then I thought of all his after-suffering, when he should come to know how he had mistaken me! The agony for him which filled my heart, as well as the mortal agony of death which I felt in imagination, made my cries and struggles no doubt very vehement and very real. My whole soul was flung into the entreaty but for "half an hour!" "but while I say one prayer!"—which prayer would have been for *him*. Then, when she hears for the first time that "[Cassio's] mouth is stopped," she naturally weeps the loss of the innocent man, both for his own sake and because he alone could, she thinks, prove her guiltless. All things conspire against her—her very tears, her prayers, her asseverations, give countenance to her guilt. She is hurled headlong down the precipice, but alas! not killed at once. The strong young life *will* not leave its tenement— the mortal agony is prolonged—even the dagger's thrust, which is meant in mercy that she may not "linger in her pain," is not enough. The soul *cannot* away until it asserts the purity of the sweet casket in which it has been set. It lingers on in pain until the poor lips can speak, not, as before, to deaf ears that will not listen, but to those of a sympathising woman. Then, with bitter moans and broken breath, Desdemona stammers out with her last gasp of life, "A guiltless death I die!" [7]

Ellen Terry, the darling and the last great Desdemona of the late Victorians, seemed to be the very form of tenderness in the role. Reviewers almost broke their hearts over her soft charm; she could move even Irving, as Iago, to real tears when she pleaded with him to reunite her with Othello. Yet she, too, put iron into her heroine's speech and action, and took the boldest view of all of Desdemona's character:

The general idea seems to be that Desdemona is a ninny, a pathetic figure chiefly because she is half-baked. It is certainly the idea of those who think an actress of the dolly type, a pretty young thing with a vapid, innocent expression, is well suited to the part. I shall perhaps surprise you by telling you that a great tragic actress, with a strong personality and a strong method, is far better suited to it, for Desdemona is strong, not weak.

This heady stuff Miss Terry said in her later lectures on Shakespeare, and to make it headier she quoted from the *unplumptrized* [8] play, coolly reading out "whore" and "top her" and the dialogue with Emilia on adultery. And she thought Desdemona was as unconventional as herself:

I have said she is a woman of strong character. Once she has consecrated herself to Othello, she is capable even of "downright violence" of all the conventions for his sake. But I think by nature she is unconventional. Othello's doubts that she is chaste are usually made to seem absolutely monstrous in the theatre, because Desdemona's unconventionality is ignored. She is not at all prim and demure; on the contrary, she is genially expressive, the kind of woman who being devoid of coquetry behaves as she feels.

But Miss Terry thought of Desdemona as utterly pure of heart. She cited the naïve discussion of adultery with the "curious anticipation of modern ideas in Emilia's attitude" (recalling her friend George Bernard Shaw's lament over the usual stage cutting of "Emilia's really interesting speeches, which contain some of Shakespeare's curious anticipations of modern ideas").[9] She added:

Desdemona cannot understand Emilia, as she cannot at first understand her husband's jealousy, because they are not dreamt of in her philosophy. Her purity of heart and her charity (charity "thinketh no evil") are sufficient explanation of her being slow to grasp the situation. It is not until she has been grossly insulted and brutally assaulted that she understands.

Miss Terry, an "emancipated woman" herself at a time when women were taking courage to free themselves from bondage to males, concluded triumphantly that the stronger spirits in the play were on the distaff side. "Shakespeare is one of the very few dramatists who seems to have observed that women have more moral courage than men." [10]

Thus, in the nineteenth century, though Desdemona was still robbed of meaningful lines by the refiners, a sturdy courage and a passionate dignity, as well as a deep tenderness, regularly shaped her image in the theater.

# PART IV

## The Twentieth Century

There is a fine story about a prominent British Othello of this century who took an acting company into the provinces—a good company, with a particularly talented Iago to give the show balance. At the first stop, Iago drew all the rave reviews. The Moor promptly disengaged himself of this evil man, and for his next booking took a rather less competent Iago. This substitute also proved a villain and drew the best notices, and again the injured Moor rid himself of his crafty Ancient. For the next stop, he protected himself by giving the Iago role to an untried stage hand. This time, when the reviews came out, all the critics' good words were still for the villain. The distinguished actor capitulated. He engaged the best Othello he could find, took the part of Iago for himself, and basked in glowing notices for the rest of the tour.[1]

This has not been a good century for Othellos, and the records of performances often tell us how the Moor should *not* be played. Partly this is because our actors have been less able to devote their lifetimes to the prime dramatic roles, as modern plays, films, radio, and television commandeer many of their best hours. Now, too, between the actor and his conception sometimes intrude intermediaries—the producer, and even more the director—who may enforce interpretations of their own. But Othello has seemed to suffer from something beyond this—some failure of passion, a failure to embody the Moor's total grief. Our actors are usually complimented when their performances are called "restrained"; but a restrained Othello is tempting game for an aggressive Iago—and Iago is aggressive by design.

Before I look further for the images of *Othello* in the modern theater, let me stipulate my method. Of the many recent performances reviewed, I have tried to select those that seemed either representative enough to illuminate modern treatment of the Moor (and later, of Iago), or unusual enough to add something to the characterization. Some contemporary Othellos, for instance, though satisfying, fit so completely into earlier patterns that recording them would be only repetition. As for those I do discuss, inevitably some readers will disagree with the reviews about them—as I have disagreed with some, and as the reviews sometimes disagree with each other. There have always been arguments about Othellos; but in the historic examples I have used, the distance of time bestows a synthesis, while now we must deal with live actors who are still in the process of making theater history. They have infrequently recorded their own conceptions of the character; few of them have become subjects of biographical writing; they are not quarrelled over, as actors once were—even to the point of riot—in other days. A perspective on their interpretations must be put together from scattered reviews (which are rarely as circumstantial as earlier ones). Given the large difference in critical distance, it might have been more symmetrical to ignore the present period, but, as preparation for the critical chapters to come, there is so much to learn from the praise and blame of modern actors that it clamors for inclusion. All the opinions reported are those of experienced, professional observers. Sometimes, surely, a reviewer may not have been able to perceive the total picture—in some instances through no fault of his own. (Kenneth Muir, a sensitive Shakespearean, notes that one of the best modern Othellos "never received his due from dramatic critics because his first-night performances were always spoiled by nerves and lapses of memory.")[2] Still, the reviewers are the best guide to what we are seeking: a synthesis of the Othello image as it is perceived in the theater.

In one area, both actors and reviewers are in a better position today. They do not so often need to complain that cutting of the text has shorn away motivation. The text is still cut, and Paul Robeson —who played in a pruned version—properly complained to me that any deletions diminish the total characterization of Othello; but the excisions are rarer and, when made, are not so much because of "sensibility" as to shorten the playing time. True, as late as 1922 the play was "stabbed through and through with [a] blue pencil,"[3] but more recently Orson Welles changed the language of the play to make the eroticism more explicit. Unfortunately, arbitrary or even whimsical cutting has sometimes replaced the earlier "refining"—even the important first street meeting between Othello and Brabantio has been deleted.[4] But the "indelicate" and "horrid" scenes—Bianca, the Willow Song, the trance—have regularly been restored, and over all the language that shapes the Othello images has been closer to Shakespeare's intention than for many years.

One final note. I identify the actors—here and elsewhere—only where the importance of their examples makes it necessary. I particularly try to reserve anonymity for those who serve only to demonstrate inadequacies in the approach to the central images. We are not interested in persons, but in characters.

# II

*Can he be angry?*

# The Modern Othello

The essential problem of the hero's image—the depth and quality of his nature, in repose, and then under the assaults of total passion—still challenges actors. The twentieth century has confirmed the earlier finding that Othello must be more than a hero-obstacle for a villain. Unless, while the audience admires his outer image, it is absorbed by his inner one—and by Iago's—the play slides into melodrama. And often it has done so. One of many examples was a performance wherein Laurence Olivier's Iago—recalling Henry Irving's—like "a virtuoso toreador playing a bull" dominated the Othello of Ralph Richardson:

> Richardson, one of the best actors in the English stage, plays the Moor with skill, dignity, and taste. He has a beautiful voice, and speaks his lines with understanding. But he fails to be heroic; his Othello inspires no awe; we are sorry for him, but we do not feel the profound pity that should extend from him to the whole condition of man; and the tragedy dwindles into a thriller about a villain who ruins an amiable and well-bred simpleton.[1]

145

Rarely have reviewers felt that modern Othellos burned with the clear blue-hot cone of grief needed to fire the play beyond surface excellence into inspiration. Theatergoers of the early 1900's remember fondly such performers as Forbes Robertson and Oscar Asche, who could dominate their Iagos; but reviews suggest that one fell short of the absolute power the role demands, and the other of its poetry. Asche, early in the century, had at least the "animal fury of the man," [2] though the "spiritual agony" was said to be missing. Most of his successors sinned differently: though they might touch nobility, they lacked, or could not convey, the terrible intensity, the violence, of the Moor as murderer. The description "intellectual" falls like a shroud on many modern efforts. A "Northern"—that is, restrained—Othello of the 'twenties was found touching in some moments, but where the reviewer expected visual, audible outbreaks "like the spurting of blood from a pricked artery," where the words "should leap from his mouth like a hot flame . . . [the actor] uttered them in a low tone, as you or I or any Englishman in plus-fours might utter them." [3]

One of the pitfalls of the intellectual Othello trapped an actor of the 'thirties. By his very expression of a brainy, restless subtlety, he destroyed the image of a lofty, trustful man of action at the mercy of scheming intellect, and took the life from the conflict with Iago. Interestingly, two reviewers saw a small feline shape in this performance. One: "the eager, nimble-witted watchfulness of one of the lesser and more apprehensive cats . . . [his] mind is quick with defenses against attack from all quarters." The other: "abrupt, nervous . . . his gait—feline rather than tigerish . . . we saw, not a giant on the rack, but a small man in great distress." [4]

The fault of too much brain similarly shrank the characterization of a more recent Othello: "(He) . . . begins to lose grip of the character as soon as he becomes the unsuspecting victim of Iago's villainies. For then a natural shrewdness which he cannot repress mars his presentment of the simple, open-hearted soldier who jumps with such fatal swiftness to conclusions. We cannot believe that so formidable a mind as [his Moor's] cannot help suggesting would be deceived so easily." [5]

Inevitably, the intellectual Othello lost stature as he lost passion. "Naturalness," in the sense of Fechterian casualness, humdrum, took the place of intensity. Walter Huston, who saw Othello as a "Dodsworth in cork," was understandably scolded by one reviewer for trying to make Othello "a man like other men," and by another because "his Moor is far too tame for comfort, illusion, or sense . . . suffers from all the failings which . . . Lewes long ago observed in Fechter." [6]

The alternative to the "naturalistic," intellectual Othello was the image of the grieved gentleman-poet, and he was much preferred. Thus:

> Mr. Abraham Sofaer's Othello is a structure of the greatest intricacy and intelligence. At first what he seeks is lucidity and a firm establishment of Othello as a man of tenderness and reason; then, at Iago's prompting, madness comes upon him, not in a flood of rhetoric, but like a slow poison that at last seizes his brain. In the scene of the killing, Mr. Sofaer exhibits the defect of his merits; not wishing to foam at the mouth, he is a little too cold; his love for Desdemona is perceptible in his deed, but does not shine through it. Apart from this, his performance is masterly, alike in its unsurpassed use of language and in the flowing urgency of its thought.[7]

In young performers particularly, the lack of Othello's massive stature and passion has been conspicuous. Several distinguished young actors who have tried the part for the first time have brought to it a fine sensitivity of understanding which emphasized, by its very promise, the need for the weight and power to come. In England, Richard Burton and John Neville, alternating Othello and Iago, approached the role from the two classic directions. Burton "developed the power to grasp at the barbarian . . . in anguish and uncontrolled passion." Neville was the gentleman-poet—"the civilized Moor, tender his love, sweet in recollection . . . splendid in anger and intellect, always poignant and true in grief." [8] And a brilliant young American Negro, Earle Hyman, in his first Othello "really seemed the storm-center of the play, carrying the whirlwind with him and letting Iago buzz busily at the vulnerable edges." [9] But as a critic said of the young English Othellos, these actors could hardly yet have been expected "to carry guns heavy enough for the dreadful passions of a man declined into the vale of years. Physical magnificence, weight, and power of voice are associated with Othello by custom, and for once custom is right." [10]

Generally true—with Kean the proving exception that a great little actor possessed of the true spirit of Othello can look and sound as big as need be. True, too, that "physical magnificence, weight, and power of voice" are in themselves far from enough to project a complete image of the Moor. Orson Welles brought these special personal qualities to his Othello. With his rumbling voice, his oversized gestures, and his giantized costuming, he seemed a "great, lumbering, dazed bull . . . This huge, goaded figure rolls on the stage the dreadful fog of menace and horror." [11] He further "dressed" the play by emphasizing the "sexual side of Othello's love for Desdemona" [12]—not only in action, but by what *Punch* called his "plastic surgery" [13] on the text. Thus, in "my heart's subdued even to the very quality of my lord," quality was replaced by "pleasures." [14] But glittering and suspenseful as his production was, gigantic as was his physical image, Welles seemed to be substituting the tension of melodrama for the tragedy's true passion. The *Spectator:* "Very large, very black, very sonorous, he is nevertheless insufficiently volcanic. He does not sweep us away, he arouses sympathy rather than pity and we cannot help wondering why a man who appears to be both shrewd and self-controlled should suddenly start behaving very unreasonably." [15] And the *Times*:

Mr. Welles gives us an impressive but an unexciting Othello. He smoulders purposefully, but the repression holds to the end: the expected flame never once flashes out. So insistently quiet is Mr. Welles that almost we are made to feel that it was somehow improper to expect flame; almost, for the spell he casts soon ceases to work, and we come away muttering rebelliously that the part the actor has chosen to play is, after all, that of Othello . . . Othello has been given the cue for passion. But the cue is not taken up.[16]

A few modern Othellos have so filled out the image of the Moor by the mass of personality and technique and emotional power as to have satisfied—or nearly satisfied—critics. One gentleman-poet who had a chance to grow in the part during years of playing it, Godfrey Tearle, reached very far. In a Stratford performance, "The highest flights of passion may be lacking, but superb authority matches humanity and tenderness in a way that has not been equalled by any other actor of our time." [17] Here was the outer image of the Moor, and much of his inner life:

> . . . a first-class fighting man bred for leadership and instant decision with a simple mind cast in a noble form. He passes with a few swift leaps from a strongly masculine tenderness to disappointment and deadly rage, but Mr. Tearle holds what is savage in the Moor severely in check and when he comes to smother Desdemona compels us to the Coleridgean view that jealousy is less the point of Othello's passion than an agony that the creature whom he believed angelic should be proved impure and worthless . . . the quieter harmonies of the great speeches are unfalteringly rendered and the eye is held by a beauty of movement that seems unconscious of itself . . . Othello may be at a height of self torment; the actor is unstrained; and works on our sympathy as he will.[18]

Another Othello in this tradition was Wilfrid Walter's. He emphasized "that Othello is a stranger, and that that is the real reason of his tragic mistakes." [19] One reviewer was at first disappointed with Walter's earlier scenes, but "once he gets to the jealousy he makes a fine, wounded animal, less concerned with foaming at the mouth than with intense suffering, which is as it should be . . . the performance is piteous and notable." [20] Later, at Stratford, Walter's image was accepted wholly. He struck the keynote of a dominating nobility in his first words and kept it up throughout the first two acts, with a beautiful tenderness in the senate scene . . . His final plunge into degradation at "Set on thy wife to observe" was marked by a slight pause of hesitation and horror as the thought struck him, before he could bring himself to utter it. From this moment the barbaric element was uppermost, whether in wild rage, fierce sarcasm, or utter wretchedness, until the final return to tenderness in "It is the cause." Seldom, if ever, (have) the pity and terror of tragedy [been] so penetrated and almost swallowed up by the beauty and skill of the interpretation.[21]

Walter's passion contrasted with Tearle's restraint: He "stormed the heights of the last act in majesty and horror." [22]

The synthesis of dignity and violence developed in the image of another Stratford Othello, Anthony Quayle, was found impressive.

The nobility and the savagery of the man were equally plain; the two qualities were not allowed to cancel each other out, nor did they split the character into two incompatible halves. While the Moor was in his senses, Quayle seemed at ease in the part, developing his full strength with an unhurried assurance that held the audience, whether in the moving narrative of his wooing, in the slow, negligent reaction to Iago's first poisonous hints, or when, taking direct action, he seized his tormenter by the throat . . . the purely theatrical scene of the humiliation of Desdemona before the ambassador, so often a barren interlude before the final act, came over with rare power . . . the Moor, his back to the audience, reading the scroll that Lodovico has brought, and swinging around with it to give a savage backhanded blow to Desdemona as she comes to lay her hand in entreaty on his arm. An equally satisfying climax came with 'The pity of it, Iago'—a great, shuddering descending cry showing that the baited beast was ready for the coup de grace.[23]

Quayle's image of the Moor was classic: that of "a simple, open-hearted soldier, a child in spirit, whose agony springs not from a jealousy that is mean and vulgar but from the overwhelming feeling that the goodness which he had believed angelic in its purity had sullied itself." [24]

The best-remembered Othello of recent decades has been Paul Robeson's. By the time of the second and third of his series of performances, he had made a wide reputation for himself—though as a singer rather than actor. All agreed that here was a bodily image of Othello: "a massive creature, physically powerful, with the gentleness that often accompanies great strength . . ."; he had the physical qualities to make the greatest Othello his generation had seen.[25] And he had his great singing voice.

And he was a Negro, the first notable one since Ira Aldridge to assume the role. To some observers, this made all the difference. John Dover Wilson: "I felt I was seeing the tragedy for the first time . . . The performance convinced me . . . that a Negro Othello is essential to the full understanding of the play." [26] An American reviewer was persuaded that the "role should be played by a Negro, or none at all." [27] But others agreed the matter of color was secondary, and Robeson himself was quoted as saying, "This play is about the problem of minority groups—a blackamoor who tried to find equality among the whites." [28] This "socially conscious" meaning may well have been in his mind; and in an extended interview at the time he declared—as he did again in an interview with me—that the color difference was absorbed in the larger problem of the outsider:

> Othello is a Moor, you see, and he cannot understand why he is suddenly attacked by people who are supposed to be his friends. The father was extremely friendly, you see—up to a point. Then he turns on Othello and starts calling him names. Othello cannot understand the reason, and sets it down to the difference in their attitudes of life. He immediately becomes distrustful of their culture, and though at first he does not believe Iago he is willing to admit to himself that these people have peculiar ideas; therefore his mind is ripe for distrust. When he thinks it over he realizes that for all he knows, unfaithfulness may be

a common practice among the Venetians. He decides to bide his time and find out how Desdemona expects a wife to act. From this point onward, he is ruined. He has been unexpectedly hurt, and he is willing to believe almost anything possible.[29]

Yet apparently the color difference loomed larger to Robeson than he wanted to admit. To the critic Agate, who said Othello might as well be a white man from any English town, Robeson answered, "I had to point out the other extreme in the play of culture and jealousy—let him try to produce it in Memphis." [30] Clearly this implied a special audience mood totally unlike that of Shakespeare's time, when none of the uneasiness inherited from the master-slave relationship, or the guilt, anger, and fear of the oppressor-oppressed, would have discolored the romantic love between heroine and stranger-hero. To some reviewers of Robeson's performance, it seemed that the actor himself called attention to these sensitive contemporary relationships between white and black. Of his image in his first performance, Farjeon wrote:

> He seemed to me . . . to [lack] command. He was the under-dog from the start. The cares of "Old Man River" were still upon him. He was a member of a subject race, still dragging the chains of his ancestors. He was not noble enough. He was not stark enough. He seemed to me a very depressed Othello. The fact that he was a Negro did not assist him . . . Shakespeare wrote this part for a white man to play and Mr. Robeson is not far wrong when he says that "Shakespeare is always right." [31]

The strong sense in Robeson of his own race was also noticed by several reviewers of his latest performances. To the *New Statesman*, he seemed "to shoulder the whole dignity of the Negro race. So he plays the tragedy with a seriousness of purpose that perhaps no other could command. I'm not sure his interpretation fits exactly with what Shakespeare wrote, but he makes all others seem trivial." [32] The *Spectator* was sure this was *not* "Shake-

speare's Othello . . . He might be the son of Uncle Tom being
taught a cruel lesson by Simon Legree . . . I pitied him, but
in my pity I never felt any of that wild, guilty, apocalyptic exul-
tation at the vision of Chaos come again . . ." [33] The failure to
move to an ultimate pity and terror troubled some critics,[34] not
only in his latest performances—where he seemed handicapped
by a murky, offbeat production[35]—but also in his earlier ones.
Stark Young, who felt his being Negro was irrelevant, praised
Robeson's calm scenes as "noble, tender, and rich in scope" and
his underlying "kind of spiritual humility that is akin to grandeur." But: "In the scenes of despair he crumbles up into a
defeat far too domestic, gentle and moving though it may be
. . . [he] lacks . . . the fine tragic style." [36] The *Commonweal*
reviewer was also relatively unconcerned about the actor's
color: "What also matters (and what certainly mattered to
Shakespeare) is that this Moor is in addition a great and succes-
full warrior, although nowhere . . . are we made especially
aware of that fact. This is an 'Othello' of terrors, with no splen-
dors beyond his golden robe, and most of all, with none of the
soldier's decisiveness which must be so largely responsible for
the terrible denouement. Even the heroic 'farewell' soliloquy
seemed to lack point here . . ." [37] George Jean Nathan[38] and
Rosamund Gilder also felt a lack in the image Robeson projected.
Miss Gilder wrote: "He throws himself into the scenes of frenzy
with due energy, but the savagery is not believable, the core of
violence is lacking . . . His Othello arouses admiration and pity
but not quite the Aristotelian 'terror' that Shakespeare constantly
demands of his interpreters." [39] This is interesting because Robeson himself knew the need for this "terror." Before his first performance, he had said, "Unless I can feel that the audience is
really terrified as Iago is, unless the audience is alarmed lest I
should really leap over the footlights and come among them,
wild with rage and jealousy, I feel I am not getting across."

Few twentieth-century Othellos have quite made it across.
The ultimate passion, which dignifies as it destroys, has rarely

been reached. Good Othellos have given us the external image of the grieved Moor, and have held their own theatrically against Iago, have spoken the poetry with beauty and dignity, have held us and touched us—and all this is a great accomplishment; but we have rarely been engulfed in the true inner agony of Othello, swept with him through the fiery center of his pathos.

# 12

~~~ *Knavery's plain face is never seen ...*

## The Modern Iago

Except for a curious try by Laurence Olivier at a new, "abnormal" version of Iago's motivation, this century's theater has not experimented much with the image of the villain. Pleasant plausibility has been the great thing. He comes to us usually in the shape of a "gay" scoundrel, raising more laughter than fear, if fear at all. Occasionally he appears hard and ruthless. In either form, he has tended to dominate Othello; and so he has doubly threatened the play: partly by overbalancing it, partly because he pursues evil without purpose, and the suffering he causes seems wasteful rather than tragic. Iago still needs stature and passion to motivate his tactics and to counterpoise Othello. The ultimate complaint remains the one made of a recent villain: "There was a pettiness about this waspish Iago, his destruction of Othello an act of mere personal spite"; or of another: ". . . he never achieves grandeur." [1]

At least, by now, Iago usually seems to know he should not act like a rascal, though occasionally—as once in the 'forties— one still combined "an awkward and evasive manner with quali-

ties so deliberately serpentine that he himself is at once suspect";
or a more recent one in the old Cibber tradition had ". . . all
the tricks of a glib salesman so obviously crooked that Othello's
reiteration of his virtues begins to strike a note of farce." Iago,
above all, should be disarming, as Kenneth Tynan noted in an
incisive criticism of one who, "to coin an epithet, was profoundly arming." [2]

If he is to be a grim Iago, the villain is usually bluntly grim,
playing—as the Iago in the Welles melodrama did—with "absó-
lute hardness, the unrelenting edge, the completely unsmiling
ruthlessness." [3] Of such another Iago, called by *Punch* "just
a villain," the *Spectator* commented unhappily, "Iago takes himself so seriously that we miss the flavour of cynical gusto . . .
and the rough humour which properly belong to the part." [4]

The humorous Iago has been a favorite because he can always
entertain, even when he is failing the intent of the play. An
audience watching such a rascal's crimes will leap eagerly to
the relief of laughter; so Iago has been played almost as a comedy
figure. The danger in this was spotted as surely by modern
reviewers as by their predecessors: the play suffers because this
Iago is tempted merely to make game of Othello, but his own
character suffers even more for lack of motivation. Thus an Iago
of 1912 "tended to be impish rather than devilish . . . the real
venom . . . seldom emerged." [5] In the 'twenties, Rathbone
played him "in the tradition of Edmund Kean—gay, light-
hearted monster." Maurice Evans, in the same tradition, was
dangerously easy for an audience to like—"a dashing boon companion, a ladies' man, whose easy success as a swindler is spoilt
only by the jealousy of the servant toward his master." [6] Agate
hinted at a flaw in the jolly performance: "This was a boyish,
eager Iago, perhaps a little too light in colour." [7] *Punch* spelled
the trouble out: "Young, open of countenance, light and gay of
speech and step" as Iago was, his evil lost its point, was "too
much akin to irresponsible mischief-making." [8]

Ralph Richardson's Iago was a kind of test of how far the
villain could go in being "honest." Some applauded his almost

impenetrable show of goodness; to others his excessive decency seemed almost indecent. To the *Times* he was

A quite exceptionally honest Iago . . . where he pretends to comfort Desdemona one could hardly believe that his coarse kindness was not genuine; then suddenly it became the blackest thing about him. But . . . we have seldom seen a man smile and smile and be a villain so adequately.[9]

The *Spectator* wondered about his motivation: ". . . the bulk of the evil in Iago remained an unknown quantity, a dark power only to be guessed at, striking from behind a facade of bland normality." [10] Too bland, too normal, was one view: ". . . never more than callous and small-minded . . . The Iago of Mr. Richardson would not have exclaimed 'nor poppy nor mandragora.' " [11] Agate found his honesty overdone: "Growing more and more honest as the play proceeded, [he] convinced us that he could not hurt a fly, which was very good Richardson, but indifferent Shakespeare." [12] And Farjeon scolded him for "the most honest Iago ever exhibited on any stage," and tried to cast him out forever from the company of villains: "Mr. Richardson is too radically agreeable for any but the most sympathetic parts." [13] Whichever side was the more judicious, the impressions of the negative indicate how questionable the image of an over-honest villain could seem.

Jose Ferrer, Robeson's most notable Iago, also had trouble vindicating his evil for the critics. Nathan could be grateful that "he seems to Othello at least moderately believable and to the rest of us . . . occasionally distinguishable from the low scoundrel who used to lure little Nellie into the opium den." [14] To other reviewers, the problem was his authenticity. He was brilliant, powerful—and wrong. One writer saw in him the image of "a Renaissance gangster . . . a rat who enjoys (his) brutalities"; and Stark Young echoed this sense of undignity: "Mr. Ferrer needs first of all a more distinguished presence, more elegance." [15] This Iago seemed more concerned with action than with motivation; the play became "a conflict between these two protagonists, rather than resolving into a bloody doom prepared for the honest man by the evil one." [16] In this conflict the clever Iago was dominant, so much so that one reviewer felt the tragedy had gone from the play. "Every other character is essentially a puppet dangling on Iago's strings. There is . . . no clash of wills." [17] And motivation was obscure in this villain: ". . . a virtuoso who lays bare the workings of Iago's fiendish mind, though not the mainsprings of his enigmatic nature." [18]

What were the mainsprings of Iago's nature? A novel attempt to find and stage them absorbed Laurence Olivier. He had interpreted Hamlet as an Oedipus-complex figure, after the concept of Dr. Ernest Jones, Freud's friend, and had achieved a popular success; he now wondered if some comparable theory might shed dramatic light on *Othello*. With his director, he interviewed Jones, whose

> ideas were startlingly unconventional and as such appealed to both of them . . . to his mind the clue to the play was not Iago's hatred for Othello, but his deep affection for him. His jealousy was not because he envied Othello's position, not because he was in love with Desdemona, but because he himself possessed a subconscious affection for the Moor, the homosexual foundation of which he did not understand.

The two theater men were charmed. "The great climax in Act III, when Iago and Othello kneel together planning the death of Cassio, became virtually a love scene with Othello's 'Now art thou my lieutenant,' and Iago's reply, 'I am your own forever' taking on a new significance. Even Iago's often-repeated 'I hate the Moor' was easily explained away by the psychologist; it was simply the stubborn protestations of a man unaware of his true subconscious emotions." [19]

This interpretation was decided on, and the tragedy was produced with a notable cast—Ralph Richardson played Othello—and was a notable failure. Hardly anyone could tell what Olivier's Iago was doing and why. He seemed to be only the extreme of the "gay" villain image; he was nearly a jolly one.

Farjeon: "He started in a jaunty, humorous vein and clowned the 'put money' speech to such an extent that many of the audience decided that he was a comic character and thenceforward were prepared to laugh at anything he said." [20]

What seemed to be missing was the essential wickedness of Iago. The *London Mercury* saw him as ". . . an underbred fellow who very amusingly revels in the fertility and instant acuity of his own superior intelligence. To say that this mind was warped and evil would seem to betray a lack of humour, for Mr. Olivier comes very near to winning the kind of sympathy we commonly extend to a practical joker." "This was merely a roguish skylarker," Alan Dent observed.[21] And so once more the "gay" Iago seemed motiveless, his evil rootless. To the *Spectator*, his playing "all out for comedy, whenever possible, and in several impossible places as well" (through such puns as "abhoor the Moor") ended by making his machinations seem "the slightly malicious pranks of a young man with a grudge." [22]

What was worse for the play, the slightly malicious young man dominated his Othello—"a virtuoso toreador playing the bull"—so the audience concentrated on his attack, rather than on his victim's defeat or the interplay between them; and his attack seemed to have no motivating dimension. Only one bit of physical imagery struck the *Spectator* as disclosing inner meaning: "A most curious feature of [Iago's] performance was a sort of hysterical collapse when Othello falls in a trance—('Work on, my medicine, work!'). Presumably this was to suggest madness—a suggestion for which the text gives no warrant." [23]

Was there a clue to Iago's motivation here? Physician-playwright James Bridie thought so. In a letter to the *New Statesman* he told of sensing in Olivier's Iago a psychic source for the villain's evil: "We were shown a vital and intelligent man with a diseased and perverted sexual 'make-up.' His mental and physical forces were at odds and drove him into sadistic mischief and on to the edge of mania. His pathetic rationalizations and uncontrolled bursts of smutty talk were the expressions of his conflict. It is not necessary to accept the doctrines of neo-psychology to

recognize the type. It was drawn from a real man and the picture is horrifyingly accurate." [24] Certainly Iago is made up of
terrible impulses, but as I shall try to show in the next chapter,
his motivation cannot be narrowed to homosexuality; it is of a
more diffuse kind and springs from sources we can more easily
recognize in ourselves. Behind the surface humor of the part,
this dark smoldering must indeed erupt, as it did in the ranking
nineteenth-century Iagos—and more recently in a performance
by an American Iago, Alfred Drake, where it emerged as a
"melancholy obsessiveness and somber malice that had tragic
grandeur." [25] Iago, too, must be dignified by a terrible, familiar
passion.

*Heaven me such usage send . . .*

I will pass by the modern Desdemonas here, since their modest
contributions to the character will be considered in the chapter
comparing the heroine's theatrical and critical images.

# PART V

## Othello and the Critics

Thus the actors manifested the *Othello* images. Some failed; but the best, in spite of such handicaps as "refined" texts, so powerfully projected the intent of the characters that the most judicious critics saw in them Shakespeare's authentic designs. Here were true Othellos, Desdemonas, Iagos.

Now we can compare the actor's images with the important characterizations proposed by the critics. Here too we must deal with inevitably incomplete interpretations. However voluminous his work, the critic can only map, with words, a few selected aspects of the art of *Othello;* no amount of verbal paraphrase can encompass the live terrain of Shakespeare's tragedy. The critics' task, too, is a tremendous one. To translate the play's living characters even partly onto the still page, he must re-create *Othello* whole in the theater of his mind, must sense all the characters in their incarnate form

—must, for instance, experience imaginatively the full inner and outer manifestations of Othello's grief. This is not only demanding emotionally and intellectually; it implies a rigorous artistic discipline, for the sounding, moving imagery that goes to make up the art object "Othello" is as difficult to master as are the materials of any other art. We have seen how the best actors toiled at perceiving and "entering" the character: beyond this, they labored to find the physical means to communicate their perceptions. Thus Kean studied Othello "long and anxiously: often during half the night . . . he would act scene after scene, considering the modulation of the verse, and the fluctuations of the character." Only bit by bit, in solitary practice, in rehearsal, and in performance, can the actor discern the symbols of the art object he must personate. The critic has to do all this and more: having vicariously re-created the play, he must step outside it, to achieve an informed perspective of its meaning and value.

Here he is at a disadvantage. If the actor's insights into Othello are awry, they are exposed in performance, his audience and reviewers delight in correcting him, and he may be guided at last to an expression of Shakespeare's meaning. The critic is not so well safeguarded. He too will sometimes err, will see gestures in Shakespeare's language that are irrelevant or contradictory; but he does not have a stage on which to work out his errors, or a live audience to warn him of them. He may be the more vulnerable because by choice he lives in a world of words, and he may neglect the language of Shakespeare's physical imagery—that "soul of lively action"—without which the play is half mute. Fortunately many Shakespeareans are gifted with vivid dramatic imaginations, and their perceptions of stage meanings come easily (which may be why they became Shakespeareans in the first place). They often exercise their imagination by seeing productions of the plays they study. Some have tried to work out their conceptions by directing and acting in the plays[1]—and this is an admirable critical device, even if it only takes the form of a workshop reading. But the bulk of *Othello* commentary has not had the advantage of a theater test; I try to provide a substitute in the next four chapters by confronting critics and the stage record —not that we may battle but that we may learn from each other; and that this book may be useful to both, as any good book on Shakespeare—and any good performance of Shakespeare—should be.

Unfortunately, to a few scholars it is somehow degrading to Shakespeare to consider his intent in terms of "mere theatrical effect." Yet this was precisely the means of Shakespeare's art, his way of giving form to experience: through effect in the theater, of the theater, by the theater. Effect of thought and feeling conveyed through eye and ear. *Othello*, like Shakespeare's other "big" plays, abounds in spectacular examples of theatrical effect: the brawls, the riot, the repeated clash of swords at night; the big pageantry, as in the ducal chamber, and the arrival at Cyprus; the great storm ("drummers make thunder in the tyring house, and the twelve-penny hirelings make artificial lightning in their heavens"). But all the rest is theatrical effect too: the communication by gesture and look, the eloquent silences, the whispered, spoken, shouted language, the sound of sorrow, the color of blood, the sweetness of music, the felt anguish of betrayal and wasted love. The very organization of the play is "theatrical": Cinthio's slow narrative is compressed into a time scheme so short that if measured by the clock it is impossibly short; but given theatrical effect—the compelling illusion of immediacy in what is heard and seen and felt—no one in the theater clocks it: it seems as long as mortality. So emotion and thought are engaged, "hearts are mov'd"—so in 1610 the men at Oxford wept at the theatrical effects of Shakespeare's own company. Fortunately, most critics accept—and delight in— the stage conditions of Shakespeare's art; for to demean theatrical effect is to demean Shakespeare; to try to separate his art from theatrical effect is something like trying to separate Rembrandt's line and shape from his light and color.

This is not to say that *any* effect in the theater is good, or that the theater is always right. We have seen how terribly wrong it can be—how pretentious, awkward, dull, or merely melodramatic. It can fail Shakespeare by simply neglecting to learn the meanings of his words as these are discerned by the scholarly labor of critics. But it remains the chosen instrument of Shakespeare's art; and from the same skilled observers who describe its failures we also get details of splendid fulfillments.

Criticism at its worst is as bad as the worst theater; but it too has its fine performances, which match the fine performances of actors. Now I bring together the best learning of both—that is, the interpretations that best express the intent of the text as it can be realized in the theater for which Shakespeare designed it.

As with the actors (since I am interested in issues, not persons), I avoid identifying critics— except in the notes—unless their importance to a point of view requires it. But my gratitude goes to all of them, to those who agree and those who disagree, to the named and the unnamed, all those who, for centuries, have been winnowing through Shakespeare, trying to find new methods to illuminate his art. In turn, I hope this book may encourage a further study of the unity of Shakespeare's word-sound-action images. We cannot expect infallibility in the critic, as there is none in the actor, or the director—or in the playwright himself; but with a closer kinship between the critic and the player, the two most dedicated of Shakespeare's heirs, we may learn to synthesize as never before the secrets of his art.

I discuss the characters separately for convenience, but they must be perceived as interlocked, so that any interpretation of one must involve all. Thus, if Othello is lofty and noble, Desdemona's love and Iago's hate must be of a quality to match him; conversely, if Othello is a fool, Desdemona and Iago must be of a kind to complement his foolishness, and explain it. This interlocking is several times stipulated; but where it is not, it must be understood.

I call the next four chapters "defenses" of the characters and the play, because I have found that the debating of critical and theatrical interpretations is a useful step toward evaluating them. First, then, the character of Iago—because in his motives lies the mainspring of the play.

# 13

🌿 *Nothing can or shall content my soul . . .*

# In Defense of Iago

I should like first to defend Iago against the charge that he was a decent man—one, that is, who injured others only after he was provoked to do so.[1] This libel against Iago's wickedness is meant to provide him a motivation by apologists who see in him "an honest, charming soldier, a man of honesty and innate kindliness . . .";[2] or "A pitiful plaything of circumstance . . .";[3] or one who "might almost serve as an example of the Aristotelian hero, a good man brought, like Oedipus, to commit enormities unforseen . . ." [4] There is more to Iago than this.

On the other hand, I want to defend Iago against the charge that he was a creature of subhuman evil, malignant without *any* motivation, an embodiment of Satan. He has been called "a black angel . . . the Spirit of Evil . . . with no passions and no habitation . . .";[5] and ". . . a monster, whose wickedness should lie far deeper than anything that could be explained by a motive . . .";[6] and "a devil in the flesh . . . a fiend." [7] Again, there is much more to Iago.

Another equation of Iago with motiveless evil is urged by

imagists and symbolists. One finds serpent and devil references that identify him with Satan;[8] another, following the lead of Freud and Jekels, sees him as personifying the base side of Othello;[9] still another Freudian believes Iago is all this and homosexual too;[10] an allegorist feels that the Ancient represents ". . . unlimited, formless villainy . . . the spirit of denial . . . undefined, devisualized, inhuman . . ." [11] The impressionists are entitled to their impressions; but they fail to do justice to Iago's flesh-and-blood qualities in seeing him as a symbol; he is a better dramatic character than that.

This last is important. Some modern critics, finding neither essential humanity nor significant symbolism in him, conclude Iago is simply badly or crudely made: he is stupid and dull;[12] or poor and implausible;[13] or he is so irremediably a survival of the Vice of the old drama that Shakespeare's attempts to paste motivation on him simply failed;[14] or he is essentially only a dramatic mechanism.[15] He is very much more than any of this; the most valid theatrical and critical interpretations point to an Iago wonderfully shaped by Shakespeare into a first-rate dramatic personality, expressing in physical imagery clearly recognizable passions and frustrations—and even medical symptoms—which are so common to humanity that, in their twisted, neurotic form, they are formally classified by modern psychologists. With a great playwright's searching insight, Shakespeare was probing the roots of human wickedness to find—and to show in the theater—how a man really could smile and smile and smile and be a villain.

We can best begin by considering how unsuitable to the stage are some of the proposed solutions of Iago's character.

Iago's earliest apologist, an eighteenth-century Exeter gentleman, argued that the Ancient was respectable at first, but his promotion was neglected by Othello, and he suspected that his wife had had affairs with Othello and Cassio; largely for these two reasons he revenged himself: ". . . if vengeance can be vindicated by an accumulation of injuries, Iago's, though exorbitant, was just." [16] Massive arguments have since defended both motivations. Critics who believe in Othello's adultery with Emilia[17] observe that: Othello is a highly-sexed soldier; Emilia is quite casual about adultery (in the Willow Song scene); his calling her a "subtle whore" suggests their personal relationship —besides, why should Iago make up the affair?[18] Several apologists have seen Iago as in fact a deserving fighting soldier wrongfully passed over for a less able—and less popular—type of book soldier;* one scholar thinks this "unwise" appointment by Othello and his "love-sick" attitude would suggest to the Elizabethans that the Moor, faulty as a general, is inviting the disaster that comes.[19] Once outer motivations for Iago are accepted, he can be seen as a relatively decent man plunging for the first time into wickedness,[20] and he becomes almost lovable; thus: "Shakespeare imagined Iago a man of warm, sympathetic qualities," a kind of Falstaff who, through no real fault of his own, goes wrong.[21] This writer feels the Elizabethans would find Iago distinctly attractive; so does another, who argues that Iago, in defending his injured honor, would arouse more sympathy than Othello in many of Shakespeare's spectators because they could identify with him as one of their own class.[22]

Here is the crux of the matter. If Iago is wronged, and has cause for vengeance, then he must certainly draw warm sympathy from an audience—*through stage action*. Meanings that cannot be made apparent in visible, audible imagery on the stage are unlikely to have been intended by the playwright. Thus, if Othello had an affair with Emilia, this must be *seen* or *heard*: the Moor must be seen to engage in some sort of byplay with her —or perhaps refuse to, now that he is married. But there is no remote suggestion of this in the lines, and it seems incredible in any consistent Othello characterization. It has never even been hinted in the great performances.

Similarly with Iago's complaint about being badly treated in the matter of promotion. There must be more than his doubtful

---

* Shakespeare was using a timeless rivalry here: between the Iago, the fieldman, the Ensign, the banner bearer, and Cassio, the desk man, the "arithmetician."

word to show it; but nowhere in the lines or implied action is Othello in any way unfair to his Ancient. In fact, the visual language of the play emphasizes Othello's special respect and friendship for Iago, as in Salvini's characterization.

Again, an Iago *suddenly* turning from decency to unpleasant- ness seems impossible on the stage. His cruel exploiting of Rode- rigo is clearly a habitual thing;* thus does he *ever* make his fool his purse, and the butt of his angry wit. Even more significant, though not adequately recognized in criticism as it often is in the theater—recall Irving, for instance—is Iago's attitude toward his wife. Before others, he treats her at best with sadistic humor; alone with her, as when he tears the handkerchief from her hand and sends her about her business, he snarls orders at her as if she were an inferior being. Emilia's is no happy marriage: she resents Iago's sharp tongue, as on the Cyprus quay; she has had painfully to bear his suspicion of her adultery with Othello; she has been made by this time cynical about loyalty to husbands, as is obvious from her conversation with Desdemona in the Willow Song scene. Clearly, Iago has long been vicious by habit.

Finally, is it possible that Iago might draw compassion as a man who stumbles further into villainy than he intended? An apologist who believes so sees Iago as not meaning to rouse Othello to the final fury, and as hesitating after he sees the storm he has caused;[23] another finds Iago recoiling from his vil- lainy when Emilia, in Desdemona's chamber, guesses that "some eternal villain, some cogging, cozening slave" has made Othello jealous.[24] Considering Iago's subsequent inspired wrongdoing, it is not easy to see in him a conscience-stricken villain. On the stage, certainly, he must plunge deliberately deeper into crime, improvising new wickedness as his character builds to its climax. The absence of a real villainy in him has been severely criticized —thus Richardson was damned for too much decency. And surely Iago's lower social class could not itself make the Ancient

* The figure of a shrewd, poor soldier exploiting a gull was a familiar one; but there is a special cruelty in the way Iago does it.

attractive; there is nothing of the good common man about him: he was, as the Folio cast list unmistakably identified him, a "Villaine." Recall that in Shakespeare's own century his villainy was so palpable that it almost rubbed off on actors: "How often is the good Actor (as for instance the *Jago* in the *Moor of Venice* . . . little less than Curst for Acting an Ill Part. Such a Natural Affection and Commiseration of Innocence does Tragedy raise, and such an Abhorrence of Villainy." [25]

Was Iago *worse* than a villain? Was he the devil himself? Or perhaps the symbolic representation of what the devil stands for—of destructiveness, of nothingness, of the baser side of Othello himself?

The Satanists, who see Iago as indeed the foul fiend, face a large problem. If Iago is the Prince of Darkness, why does he seek, in his soliloquies, human motives for his evil? Why does he not sail straight ahead, passionless, doing his worst? The only answer—it is not a good one[26]—is that he is simply making up his humanity, coolly hunting about for motives. Is this valid in the theater? Is Iago to be presented on the stage as a quibbling fiend in human form? The history of the theater certainly provides no examples. I saw something of such an interpretation in a performance wherein Iago was an ugly, twisted, gnomelike creature, clinging like a dirty shadow to Othello. There was no humanity in it, no visual or aural metaphor of friendship betrayed; Iago's claims of frustration and hate sounded meaningless in a devil's mouth, and the lines about his honesty and friendliness seemed to belong to another play.

Certainly the theater record is clear on this: the more accurately the actor playing Iago expresses the image of a thwarted human being, the more powerful is the play's impression of tragic life. A great tragedy is certainly available on the betrayal of a noble man by a devil—a devil real or symbolic, Satan himself or the personified expression of the evil in the hero's character; but *Othello* is not that play as it must be lived out on the stage for which Shakespeare designed it. If it is different in the limitless imagination of a critic, it is because he transmutes Shake-

speare's work into a different art form. Consider here the in-
structive experience of Wilson Knight, a most imaginative
symbolic interpreter of the tragedy. In first studying the play,
Knight saw this: ". . . on the plane of personification . . .
Othello and Desdemona are concrete, moulded of flesh and
blood, warm. Iago contrasts with them metaphysically as well as
morally: he is unlimited, formless villainy. He is the spirit of
denial, wholly negative. He never has visual reality . . . [he]
is undefined, devisualized, inhuman."

Sometime later Knight produced *Othello*—a good procedure
for impressionist critics of Shakespeare. In Knight's next book,
there is a considerable softening of the first impressions of "ugli-
ness, hellishness, idiocy, negation"; and though he again spoke of
another level of meaning: "Othello, Desdemona, and Iago are
Man, the Divine, and the Devil . . ." he followed this with a
most significant but: "The symbolic effects are all in the poetry
. . . *But the moment any of this is allowed to interfere with the
expressly domestic and human qualities of the drama, you get
disaster.*" [27]

This makes splendid sense. The symbolism of the devil, of
denial, of the alter ego, or of whatever, may be in the poetry—
for those who, reading, find it there; but it does not fit the
imagery Shakespeare was creating for eye and ear as well as for
mind. Try to make it fit, and "you get disaster," because the
playwright was not dealing in personifications but persons of
drama, art objects communicated with such a powerful sense of
life that their reflection of troubled emotions would deeply involve watching audiences. We would not spare much pity for
the troubles of a devil, but we are strangely stirred by what we
hear and see of the familiar, passionate human malice in Iago.

For there is something curiously compelling in Iago. One reviewer noted how Iago "draws us . . . to him by a mysterious
fascination that has almost as much of admiration as of horror in
it"; Hazlitt thought his magnetism was the kind that compels
mankind to read "of dreadful fires and shocking murders . . .
[and to attend] executions and trials . . ." [28] The secret, I

think, is the wonderfully contrived projection in the Ancient of emotional drives that run deep in mankind. Shakespeare was dramatizing the deformity of personality under the intolerable pressure of these drives.

To test this, let us explore Iago afresh for the humanity most critics feel must be reflected in him, and try to synthesize it with the plausibility and motivation the best theater interpretations have provided. Shakespeare needed a villain for a play involving the betrayal of one man by another. Quite possibly Shakespeare was drawn to this story because it was one of betrayal: the theme was a favorite of his. In any event, he chose a story involving a betrayer. But from Cinthio it was only the plot function and personal image that he borrowed for Iago; the rest was his own.

Shakespeare's Iago appears in two aspects: his external appearance, as he reacts with others, and his inner life as revealed by the soliloquies. Forget the soliloquies for a moment, and examine the face that Iago turns to the world. Here is a clever, ambitious man coolly manipulating others for his own ends. The current theories of will and reason he voices belong to his character both "psychologically" and dramatically.[29] He denies the reality of loving feelings—they are only a lust of the blood, a permission of the will; he asserts the supremacy of the will and intelligence, and their power to efface emotions so that desired ends may be achieved; he idealizes the self-sufficient man—the one who knows how to love himself. This philosophy seems to have long since hardened into expert practice. Toward those he can exploit openly he is domineering and brutal. But when he is with his superiors his true emotions are hidden below the surface by his calculating will. He makes a nearly perfect pretense of being a pleasant, decent, humorous fellow: except for his treatment of his gull and his wife, almost his only *show* of passion occurs when he is so sad about Cassio's drunkenness, or when he is matching Othello's honest rage with what seems sympathetic anger of his own. So complete is his control that only in momentary slips does he show his hate of the persons about him. Without the soliloquies we get a picture of a villain who moves almost passionlessly from crime to crime.

Now this brings up an important point. Read the play through omitting the soliloquies and you discover that the soliloquies are actually not necessary to the dramatic action at all, that without them, in fact, there is an increased suspense and tightness of plot. The plans Iago reveals to Roderigo are enough to make the lurking menace clear; the apprehension is whetted by the uncertainty of what is to come, and the surprise executions of the villainy are received with more of a jolt. For instance, when Iago first gets the handkerchief, if he did not tell us how he was going to use it, the subsequent revelations of his villainy with it, as they come out in the action, would have even more impact. And the whole play would move faster.

The playwright must have been aware of this. He knew how to plant a bare hint of villainy and let the imagination of the audience work: recall, for instance, Aaron in *Titus Andronicus* hiding the bag of gold without explanation and the shock value of the trick he plays with it; or remember Richard III, after only an intimation of his intention, manipulating Hastings' doom. For that matter, how effective it is when in Act V of *Othello* Iago improvises so brilliantly to throw the blame on Bianca for Cassio's brawl. Yet Shakespeare was content to lose most of the effect of surprise by introducing Iago's anticipatory soliloquies. He did this perhaps partly because it was a tradition of his art form: inevitably traces of the traditional villain reside in Iago. However, if the traditional had been Shakespeare's aim, he could have let Iago, as a devil or man, merely outline the villainy to come and gloat over it. But the conventional was not enough for Shakespeare. It hardly needs to be said that he understood and dramatized the hidden working of the soul; generation after generation has been helped to understand its own behavior through Shakespeare's poetry. When he created Iago he was at a peak of his art, and he seems to have made deliberate use of the soliloquies to show what went on behind the surface of the kind of wicked man he chose to portray.

The outer Iago, remember, seems a cool, controlled villain, master of his feelings, who fits the characterization proposed by Bradley and Granville-Barker—of the passionless designer of tragedy in real life; or that of the gamester villain whose only passion is "mirth"; or even (*a la* the Satanists) that of a devil who of course needs no passion.[30] But there is another aspect to Iago, his inner life. A look into this tells us how little he is what he is. Once he is alone, with his mask off, all the passions hidden behind his surface suddenly boil up. Far from being passionless, this inner Iago is one great fury of passion, the more furious because so much feeling has been smothered when he is with people. Nor is this "raging torment" limited, as Kittredge suggested, to his "suspicion that Othello is Emilia's lover." [31] *Anyone* on whom his thought lingers becomes an object of some spurt of passion—hate, envy, jealousy, lust, fear. His wife and his gull demand little of his imaginative fury, because he exploits them with satisfying sadism in actual life; but the others—Othello, Cassio, and Desdemona—to whom he must outwardly turn a pleasant, social face, are, for their real or imagined superiority, intolerable to him, and he needs to crush them in his mind. When the thought of their decent or noble qualities forces itself into his awareness, it automatically evokes a counterthought of hostility: the Moor, of a free and open nature, must be led by the nose; fruitful Desdemona must have her virtue turned into pitch; Cassio, a proper man, must be overthrown. The contempt Iago shows for others is fierce and tireless; but we learn at last that behind it is a searing contempt for his own self. when the thought rises to his consciousness that Cassio

> . . . hath a daily beauty in his life
> That makes me ugly . . . (V, i, 22–23)

Mostly he defends himself from the awareness of this self-contempt with furious fantasies of his great power: he is clever—very, very clever; he is above—or below—the common sentiment and morality of those he resents and needs to despise. Not any single need frustrates Iago—the passed-over lieutenancy, the fantasied passion for Desdemona, the imagined cuckolding by Othello; it would do him no good to be satisfied on all these points—indeed, when he does get the lieutenancy, it does nothing to satisfy his hunger. What we are shown in the inner Iago is a bottomless, consuming passion that feeds on all life around him.

Is this an authentic reflection of a kind of human being? It is—not of a pleasant kind, certainly, but of one so common that it has been described as a "psychological type." Here is an abstract of a characterization—by a distinguished modern medical psychologist—of a familiar "vindictive" neurotic pattern for which Iago might have served as model:

> He believes in the omnipotence of the will, of intelligence, and reason, while denying the power of emotional forces and showing contempt for them; he has an essential disrespect for others, their dignity and their feelings, his only concern being his subordination of them; he thinks of them as people to be exploited; he is proud of his ability to exploit them, by hook or by crook, working with anything at hand—money, sexuality, feelings.[32]

What is the motive of this *vindictive* man? Why this drive— that Bradley emphasized in Iago—to "plume up his will"? The psychiatrist goes on:

> His main motivating force is his need for vindictive triumph . . . he cannot tolerate anybody who knows or achieves more than he does, wields more power, or in any way questions his superiority. Compulsively he has to drag his rival down or defeat him. Even if he subordinates himself for the sake of his career, he is scheming for ultimate triumph. Not being tied by feelings of loyalty, he easily can become treacherous . . . The drive for a triumphant mastery of life . . . with the insatiable pride that accompanies it, becomes a monster, more and more swallowing all feelings . . . [and covering] the self-hate and self-contempt that are appalling in their dimensions. Love, compassion, considerateness—all human ties—are felt as restraints on

the path to sinister glory . . . he must prove his own worth to himself. And he can prove it to his satisfaction only by arrogating to himself extraordinary attributes, the special qualities of which are determined by his particular needs . . . Having smothered positive feelings, he can rely upon only his intellect for the mastery of life. Hence his pride in his intellectual powers reaches unusual dimensions, pride in vigilance, in outwitting everybody, in foresight, in planning . . . [A] frequent outcome of [his] tendency to deprive or exploit is an anxiety that he will be cheated or exploited by others . . . He gives free range, at least in his mind, to his ample supply of bitter resentment [though the outward] expressions of vindictiveness may be checked by the considerations of prudence or expediency . . . In order to understand why his process of crushing feelings persists . . . we have to take a look [at] his vision of the future. He is and will be infinitely better than "they" [the others] are. He will become the great hero . . . or [the great] persecutor . . . These are not idle fantasies. They determine the course of his life. Driving himself from victory to victory, in large or small matters, he lives for the "day of reckoning." [33]

It is not necessary for us, as it was for the psychologist, to find in a man's childhood the conditions that make him fearful of emotion and drive him to seek omnipotence in fantasy and vindictiveness. For us, Iago had no childhood; he exists only as a more or less valid reflection of life in the dramatic art form. What is important here is that Shakespeare worked out dramatically how these things could be—how intimately related were the need for vindictive triumph and the need to deny positive feelings, how pervasive and powerful was the resulting misdirected hostility, how dangerously and poisonously it fumed beneath the surface when further compressed by the outward need to appear pleasant and subordinate.

It is no longer surprising that Shakespeare sensed complexities of human motivation that psychologists are still trying to explain. Freud long ago paid tribute to him for that. But it is interesting to see how deep his insight could go. For having shaped the true mental and emotional qualities of his "vindictive man," the playwright added a distinctive physical illness that plagued Iago savagely and one that, in his revenge fantasies, he hoped to fasten onto Othello.

The illness is common today—it is almost expected in those individuals who burn with resentment that they try to suppress. It feeds on internalized rage. In Iago it occurs when, out of the deep well of his self-contempt, he dredges up a fantasy with which to torture himself: the idea that Othello had sexual relations with Emilia.

> . . . The thought whereof,
> Doth (like a poisonous mineral) gnaw my inwards . . .
> (II, i, 329–330)

Iago does, that is, burn inwardly from a familiar, severe functional disorder that eats a man away within when his nerves flay his stomach. He resembles a recognizable type of sufferer from that abrasion of the "inwards" that leads to painful ulceration. This "type" is the person who is driven, to quote one medical study, to evolve ". . . a life pattern of being self-sufficient, independent, or the 'lone-wolf.' " This pattern is commonly accompanied by "feelings of resentment and hostility." [34] Case studies show that such persons frequently take out some of their aggressions on exploitable underlings, as an accompaniment to the aggressive fantasies they nurse toward persons they are unable to manipulate.

Iago, who is ceaselessly on fire with suppressed hostility against those he cannot openly exploit, represents the typical host for this gnawing "poisonous mineral" of an illness; if he mistakes its physiological nature, he knows well enough what causes it in him. A thought, a conceit, like his suspicion of Emilia's infidelity, is enough to set the sharp teeth biting at his gut; and it is precisely such a conceit that he hopes to feed Othello, for

> Dangerous conceits, are in their nature poisons
> Which
> . . . with a little act upon the blood,
> Burn like the mines of sulphur. (III, iii, 379 ff.)

Iago knew the feeling well. The imagery is so sharp that one wonders how well Shakespeare himself might have been acquainted with the problem. Certainly Renaissance psychologists knew its signs, little as they understood its physiology: thus, a late-sixteenth-century treatise explained: "But the envious body is constrained to bite on his bridle, to chew and to devoure his envy within himselfe and to lock up his owne miserie in the bottome of his heart, to the end it breake not foorth and shew it selfe." [35] Iago indeed chewed and devoured his envy within himself.

This characterization seems best to synthesize the critical intuitions of Iago's humanity and the interpretation of his motivation by the best actors.

Consider the theater record. The stage learned early that, in Iago's relationship with his peers, his knavery must not show, or show only by indirection. He must not be so obvious as to make Othello an idiot. So Iago the stock Cibber-type villain, not "distinguishable from the low scoundrel who used to lure Nellie into the opium den," never belonged on the stage.

As an alternative, to make his surface more plausible and entertaining, there appeared sometimes the bluff, hearty soldier, more often the engaging, humorous junior officer. But there were troubles with the "gay" Iago: light and pleasant as he was, he was too light, too pleasant. For one thing, he lacked the dignity to be a believable friend and battle companion to Othello and to be an escort—and momentarily, even an intimate confidant—for Desdemona. Cinthio's *novella*, again, probably cued Shakespeare to the character: "He was of the most handsome person (*di bellisima presenza*) . . . he cloaked with proud and valorous speech the villainy of his soul . . . he was to all outward show another Hector or Achilles." Beyond some such dignity and "honesty," great Iagos showed a solemn friendship; they were, in Cinthio's words, "very dear to the Moor" (*molto caro al Moro*):[36] thus Fechter, benignant and soothing; Forrester, tender; Booth, tenderly respectful. The friend Iago must, as

Salvini said, "express his sorrow at the offense which is inflicted on his chief, his regret that he did not himself discover it, his painful irresolution, while he shows himself honestly convinced of his suspicions, without betraying, either by gesture or word, his deception." Only the betrayal by such a sincere, trustable ally, Salvini felt, could justify the terrible passion evoked in Othello.

Another serious handicap to the "gay" Iago was his lack of meaning. A "principle," a "weight of metal," would be missing; his evil would be "too much akin to irresponsible mischief-making," or it would seem only "waspishness" or "spitefulness." This touched the core of the play. If Iago only made game of Othello, the tragedy slipped into melodrama; mere gaiety left a vacuum. Kean was criticized for this; and Kemble, because he wanted a "perturbed spirit"; and Brooke, for lacking "deep-seated malice"; and Forrest, because his Iago was "passionless." As Hazlitt noted, in the theater a motivation (not a reason) must be sensed for all this labor bringing about so much human waste, or it is pointless. The dimension of passion, of inner urgency, a "somber malice," like Alfred Drake's, "that had tragic grandeur," must supply the need, though showing in the main only in Iago's terrible, lonely moments, when he is free to reveal his troubled self. Again and again, the better villains were praised for the striking visual-aural changes between their outward show and their soliloquizing selves. Thus Fechter: "a pleasant hero of light comedy"—except for "the malice and vindictiveness of his soliloquies." Thus Booth, "persuasively frank in speech and manners," but his soliloquies spoken "in a voice of unquenchable anguish and hate." [37] Thus Irving, one of the greatest of Iagos, so full of "vindictiveness," so seemingly innocent of it. His model, Macaulay's Machiavelli, recalls the "envious body" of the Elizabethans as well as the modern psychologist's "vindictive man": "Hatred and revenge eat into his heart, yet every look is a cordial smile, every gesture a familiar caress." And thus Irving's soliloquies were not simple breast barings; the passion fumbled for rationalizations:

In "I hate the Moor!"—one of those secret, jealous, morbid broodings which belong to human nature—an admirably delivered soliloquy, he strives to find some reasonable excuse for this suggestion; "He has done my office" is merely accepted as a suitable pretext. The mode in which this was, as it were chased through the turnings of his soul; the anxious tone of search, "I know not if't be true"; the covering up of his face and the motion by which he let his hands glide, revealing an elated expression at having found what would "serve," was a perfect exhibition of the processes of thought.[38]

Iago's dual life, called chiaroscuro for its sudden stains of dark against the light, is as good theater as it is splendid characterization. His two sharply contrasting, yet complementary sides give a suspenseful unity to the role on the stage. Whether he hides behind a mask of rough honesty or polished sincerity, a constant tension underlies his humorous outward seeming. When he smothers his "raging torment" and appears without any show of hypocrisy—even to the audience—the true friend and subordinate of Othello, we know he is more than a coolly calculating pretender: he is a dangerous high explosive. So we get a glimpse of his passion when he is exploiting Roderigo, and a hint of its heat in his treatment of Emilia. Probably Shakespeare meant the mask to slip momentarily in other company too: as when—recall Booth here—Cassio kisses Emilia on the Cyprus quay, and Iago, after a flashing look of hate, covers with the line of sadistic humor aimed at his wife—his wit, Hazlitt observes, *blisters;* or when he starts to lecture Roderigo on reason and will but dwells on sexuality; or when he tells the gull about the plot to ruin Cassio and his furious envy gets away from him and he runs on and on: "Besides, the knave is handsome, young: and hath all those requisites in him, that folly and green minds look after. A pestilent complete knave, and the woman hath found him already" (II, i, 277 ff.).

Not until he is alone, however, can we look into the volcano of his emotions. Then the resentment visibly wells up, and he rages down the stage, fantasying revenge and triumph. Many emotions shake him—jealousy, envy, fear, shame, hate, self-contempt—yet, as he moves through his stormy theater life, it is always clear, from the friendship and even admiration he is seen to get from others, that the source of his torment is not outside mistreatment. His motive, as Macready showed, "was found in his own nature." The denial of positive feelings has diverted his emotions into a fountain of aggression that must escape in fantasy and scheming. To the end he tries to deceive the outer world about his inner life, as he himself is obviously deceived about his power to subdue his own emotions. Finally, when all is lost, when the others have lifted the curtain on his secret world, and he murders his wife, he immediately reasserts the rein on his emotions and tries for the last time to seal off his feelings. These mortals cannot make him speak, though his heart were in their hand.

What is compelling about this kind of Iago in the theater is the basic quality observed by the criticism that seeks motives for him—his unmistakable humanity. He evokes a terror of recognition—for he is compounded of deep human motives that may stir in any of us. We laugh too readily at his jokes, tempt him by laughter to play the comic and relieve us of the anxiety of sharing his guilt; we surprise in ourselves a kind of satisfaction in his manipulations; we listen hypnotized to his immature fantasies, his salacious plans to ruin the marriage of a noble older man and a beautiful woman. His punishment comes with relief. What he does, each of us might—would—could do. It is this uncanny echo in Iago—uncanny in the Freudian sense —that has made him so fascinating and puzzling to so many audiences and critics.

Olivier's curious attempt to homosexualize Iago may have failed because the conception was too narrow. If a repressed sexual impulse may indeed lie behind an excessive, secret hostility toward a "friend"—a much too easy generalization without supporting data[39]—then something of it may reside in Iago. There *is* sexual maladjustment in Iago's vindictiveness, as his obsessive talk certainly suggests. Unable to love, he dwells pruriently on lust: in heated, immature fantasies he fondles sex jokes, nakedness in bed, secret fornications, adulteries; he envies Cassio's sexual successes, desires Desdemona, imagines his wife in bed with Othello, with Cassio. But on a conscious level his disturbance is clearly heterosexual. Was homosexuality perhaps unconsciously expressed by Shakespeare in disguised form? Could it be made apparent in the theater? When Iago says to Othello a line like "I am your own forever," when he is "tender" or "soothing," there is an obvious hypocrisy and a veiled vindictiveness; might there also be a latent ambivalence? Yes. But could homosexuality be stipulated visually as Iago's central motivation? The six modern Othellos I questioned rejected the theory. Olivier thought it was worth a try—and it still would be for an actor who sensed such a motive in Iago strongly enough. Certainly Olivier does not now; and apparently never did. In a frank and generous comment on his experience, he reminded me that the reading was inspired by Ernest Jones, and is "not one to which I would any longer subscribe." Although Olivier can still accept a *psychological* interpretation involving homosexuality, "as it exists entirely in the subconscious, there is no object in touching on it in any detail of performance."

There was simply too much more to Iago than this, Olivier found: "When I was serving during the war I discovered that the fact of rank and its distinctions could quite frequently be found to be as justifiable a basis for Iago's bitterness as any; but he is obviously a mass of other complexes as shown in his apparently groundless suspicion of his wife, and over and above all this he certainly enjoys the sport of his machinations."

If Shakespeare's design were to be narrowed to a homosexual motivation, it must inform all Iago's encounters—with Othello, Emilia, Desdemona, Cassio, Roderigo; it must certainly emerge in the soliloquies; but as Olivier found, the lines and action do not admit of this explicit motive. A sustained visual statement of homosexuality (especially lacking, as it does, a supporting verbal statement) would distort the whole context in which Iago moves. He is incapable of—and envious of—love in *all* directions. If

Shakespeare—consciously or subconsciously—meant a homosexual drive to be latent in Iago, it would have to be felt as an unspoken symptom (as it often is in life, as Freud observed) of the much more universal paranoiac disturbance that in Iago distributes aggression not only on Othello but on all the objects —including himself—in his vicinity.

The critics who have sought to explain Iago's humanity were certainly on the right track; if their studies were incomplete—as this one may be, and as some of the actors' interpretations were—it was perhaps because they did not go far enough behind Iago's jealousy, or lust, or pride, or envy, to his broad-based affinity with mankind. The apologists have probably sought an outside provocation for Iago's wickedness because they felt that only this could justify his humanity; and perhaps this feeling also prompts those who find Iago a veritable devil—because they cannot accept as human the flood of aggression that pours from him. The devil has for a long time, either as a figure of reality or as a symbol, taken the blame for human wickedness. I think we understand by now the impulse to unload human evil on spiritual and allegorical scapegoats.

This impulse may have lain in Shakespeare's unconscious; but there is no sound evidence that he meant to find responsibility for the evil that men do anywhere but in men themselves. His greatness as a dramatist for times beyond his own lay largely in his recognizing the purely mortal forces that move men to action. In Iago, he went deep into the nature of felt life; we can try to go no less far in confirming the accuracy of his portrait.

The drives we have learned to recognize as a badge of humanity are twisted and magnified in Iago, but we cannot disown them. Man is subject to conflicting, often terrifying physical and psychical impulses; he has many desires he will not admit, and many he admits which he cannot satisfy. Even in persons we call normal, in those who learn to channel their forces into socially useful outlets, when emotional wants are frustrated, resentment rises at real and fancied wrongs, hostilities build up at obstacles in the life path. Persons living under this kind of inner tension find in the thoughts they permit to consciousness harsh wishes that harm, disease, or even death will come to rivals or enemies, while they fantasy triumph for themselves. Not a few husbands release on their wives (and children) the hostility thus accumulated—even as Iago released it. To neurotics hopelessly unsatisfied with reality—in which they are denied the endless love and power they dream of—regression to infantile wishes and glory fantasies takes on more and more importance, as these are charged with the full force of the repressed libido; sometimes the fantasies are translated recklessly into action. It is this kind of human being, when he is driven to change the form of reality to fit his immature vision of omnipotence, who makes tragedy, in life or in the drama. I believe it is this kind of human being, with his uncanny attraction for endless audiences and readers, that Shakespeare with surpassing technical skill and insight personified in Iago.

# 14

## In Defense of Othello

How could Othello be deceived by Iago? How could so noble a man turn from love to fury, and destroy his wife and his life?

Perhaps he is not really noble.

Perhaps, some critics suggest, he is meant to be an impostor, even to himself, asserting some dignity and self-command only to deceive himself, to mask a deep insecurity and predisposition to jealousy. There is in this—as in most objections to the nobility of Othello, or of the play—an echo of old Rymer. Rymer thought Othello was too ready to be jealous, in fact labored to be. This theme was refined in 1863 by the German critic Flathe, who saw an Othello motivated by enormous self-deceit. Behind his façade he has guilt feelings, partly, probably, because of his sordid sexual adventure with Emilia that provoked Iago's hatred. He is insecure, overproud, oversensitive, hungry for admiration, compulsively concerned with his appearance before the world. He is terribly fearful of humiliation: his deep inner doubt that Desdemona could love anyone as unworthy as he is makes him welcome Iago's insinuations of her disloyalty.

185

This gives him an excuse to destroy her, and to appear before the world great and self-sacrificing. At her deathbed, pretending he has acted in a righteous cause, he is at the apex of self-deceit.[1]

Modern skepticism of Othello's character has generally followed Flathe in seeing the Moor as made weak, rather than—in the Rymer (and later, Tolstoy) view—as weakly made. This "modern" interpretation was made respectable by T. S. Eliot, with his rediscovery of some of Flathe's opinions. Eliot too saw in Othello's death not the usual hero's self-perception but rather a self-deception, an attempt to avoid reality by "cheering himself up."[2] One step from this,[3] and another critic was arguing, ". . . it is plain that what we should see in Iago's prompt success is not so much Iago's diabolic intellect as Othello's readiness to respond."[4] Another step and another critic: ". . . observe how Othello cooperates with Iago, how Iago seems rather to make Othello see what corruption is within himself . . . [this] hero's flaw is his refusal to face the reality of his own nature."[5] Finally, a critic concludes that we cannot "regard Othello only as of a 'constant, loving, noble nature'" if we keep in mind all the qualities Shakespeare has given him:

> the unripeness of his sense of his own past, the flair for the picturesque and the histrionic, the stoicism of the flesh unmatched by an endurance of spirit, the capacity for occasional self-deception, the hypersensitivity to challenge, the inexperience in giving, the inclination to be irritable under responsibility and hasty in the absence of superior authority, the need to rely on position.[6]

If Othello has all these qualities, of course we cannot think of him "only as of a 'constant, loving, noble nature.'" We cannot think of him as constant, loving, or noble at all. In the brief compass of the play, these negative qualities would have to appear in Othello's action imagery—and the critic finds them appearing—at every turning point. The Othello who would emerge would be that favorite hero—or antihero—of modern drama: rootless, histrionic, weak spiritually, self-deceiving, withholding, irritable, hasty, dependent, insecure—a pathetic image who lives in a fantasy of himself and others, who shrinks from reality into a world of "pipe-dreams." This might be Richard II—but Othello?

How must such a "modern" Moor appear in the theater? Champions of the concept offer some visualizations. In the Cyprus riot, he is either upset or officious: "The God pose dissolves . . ." [7] or "the context suggests rather that he is feeling and trying to meet an intangible need to bolster himself, and that in being legalistic he is capable, as elsewhere, of the required self-deceit." [8] In the temptation scene, he is seen as ready and waiting for a chance to be jealous. Finally, before his suicide, he must give way to the last pitiful self-deception:

> On hearing the final details of the handkerchief story, Othello cries "fool! fool! fool!" His epithet reminds him only of the least of his errors. He somehow conveys the impression that his mistake was not so much murder and revenge as it was depriving himself of Desdemona; he less repudiates the violence than deplores the silly mistakes which wiped out a very nice girl. To understand the incompleteness of the self-judgment we have only to recall the stern self-appraisal of Roderigo: "O, villain that I am!" [In this view, even Iago's gull ends more honestly than the hero.] [9]

This Moor's physical imagery, as he goes to his end, is degrading: "the final Othello is not a pretty sight to watch . . . Consider his whimpering, his refusal to be himself, his uncontrolled screaming." [10]

The theater—and most criticism—flatly rejects such an Othello. There have been stage Moors less than heroic; but these were universally regarded as failures, from the great Garrick on. Even heroic Othellos who have slipped momentarily into this antiheroic mushiness have been scolded for it. This was particularly true in the crucial scenes noted by the "modernists" —who seem to miss the dramatic point of these moments. Thus, to one of these critics, stern authority on Othello's part in the Cyprus mutiny seems overdoing—after all, the wars *are* over,

Othello has "seen enough binges by military personnel . . .
How can anyone believe 'the people's hearts brimful of fear'
. . . ?" [11] The theater believes. The theater knows the visual,
aural values of a mass scene, as Shakespeare, the theater tech-
nician, did from the very beginning—remember his plaintive
stage direction in his apprentice play *Titus Andronicus* when
the conquering hero is told to enter followed by every member
of the cast the playwright can name plus "*others, as many as can
be.*" Get them all out there, he was saying, every "body" you can
lay hold of. He loved the big pageantry; the Cyprus riot gave
him a fine chance at it. In his time, such bold effects made possible Heywood's account (In *Apology for Actors*) of the Spanish
commandos who started to raid a British town one night, heard
a play in progress with its spectacular noises and lights, and were
so persuaded the town was in arms against them that they fled
to their boats. The theater has been faithful to Shakespeare in
the Cyprus riot, flooding the stage with the sound of unrest, the
movement of chaos. Has not Iago made Roderigo "cry a mutiny"? And did he not succeed—as he piously explains to
Othello?

> Myself the crying fellow did pursue,
> Lest by his clamour (as it so fell out)
> The town might fall in fright. (II, ii, 256–258)

In fright the town does fall; and we read in Stanislavski how
enthusiastically a theater seizes this chance at the imagery of
gesture: fighting natives pound at the gates; soldiers spring up;
guns are placed for defense.[12] Against such a background Othello
must come to quench dangerous disorder, dismiss Cassio. This
is a great, heroic moment, lofty without rage. Thus, Booth here
was "so simple, yet so grand." Thus Kean dismissed Cassio
"solemnly and sadly, as . . . a painful act of duty." [13] Inadequate players were scolded for showing here the very qualities
that seem to endow the "modern" Moor: Irving for being
"excited"; Fechter for being "petulant." Only unassailable dignity would do.

In the next crisis, the temptation by Iago, where the modernists see Othello hurrying toward jealousy, actors have generally won praise for their *slowness* to take fire. (Chapter 16 deals with this in detail.) And any diminution of Othello's stature in the last act's climax has also been damned, especially any descent into self-pity. Our earliest reports suggest that nothing has irritated audiences more than Othello's "whimpering." Thus Barton Booth was praised because he "never whindled, whined, or blubbered"; Pope was damned for "his vile mixture of rant and whine." Kean, urged by Hazlitt to take some of the violence from his Moor, made some softening changes, only to have the horrified critic scold him for "whining" and urge him to return to the early, intense characterization. Macready was criticized both for "whimpering" and because his "passion was irritability." This last quality, integral to the "modern" Othello, has been a sure mark of an actor fallen short of Othello's grandeur: thus Fechter was damned for his "impatient irritability," for being "loud—and weak, irritable, not passionate." Fechter, indeed, almost serves as a model of how the specious, blustering, irritable antihero Othello must fail in the theater: he becomes a "maudlin and hysterical . . . hero of French melodrama who is continually whimpering and whining about his mother."

To get living witnesses to the theater's attitude toward this and other characterizations, I have questioned six modern actors of the Moor: Earle Hyman, Anthony Quayle, Paul Robeson, Abraham Sofaer, Wilfrid Walter, and Donald Wolfit. They are British and American, young and veteran, dedicated men— and among them they have won the highest praise given to modern Othellos. Specifically, I asked them to evaluate the chief critical interpretations of Othello's yielding to Iago. First I presented the two following summaries of the "modern" Moor:

1. *Othello is flamboyant, boastful, given to high-flown language that covers an immature need for assurance as to his love and his position.*

2. *Othello, in the beginning, persuades himself he is too noble*

*for jealousy, but this is self-deception. In the final scene, after
he has succumbed to passion, he needs once more to deceive
himself, and so ennobles himself into a "honorable murderer."*

To the first concept, the reaction was unanimously, "No."
"Rubbish," was one reply. Another, "Nonsense. His flamboy-
ance and high flown language are natural to his origin, and
judged by the standards of his day he was greatly modest." A
third, "I do not agree that Othello is flamboyant. He is colourful
—which is another thing. He is not boastful; he simply tells the
truth—but not boastfully. I do not think he needs assurance of
his position; but naturally when he has given his love, the assurance that it is returned by Desdemona means more to him
than it might to a white man." A fourth, "Is Othello's speech
to the senate flamboyant, boastful, given to high flown language? Bosh!" Fifth, "I don't believe this. He is unique in a
Venetian society. He is a poet with brilliant imagination and
justly proud of his achievements." Finally: "No, no, no. Today,
traveling in the East, you can find the same exotic language." [14]
To the second interpretation—that Othello was self-deceived
—the answers were strongly negative, with one objecting that
the concept was simply meaningless to an actor. Another: "No!"
A third: "No. No. No. This is to ignore the majestic poetic
vision of the whole play." A fourth: "No. His view of how a
wife is expected to behave is an Arab view. By his own canons,
he is certainly 'an honorable murderer.' " A fifth: "I cannot see
the truth in this. I cannot see evidence that Othello 'persuades
himself that he is too noble for jealousy.' I think he genuinely
believes that he is killing Desdemona for 'The Cause' and that
what he does is entirely honorable. I cannot see where self-
deception comes into it at all." Finally: "He is not jealous, but
when all his beliefs and knowledge are shaken, what is he to
do?" [15]
Add to these the voices of Garrick, Foote, Salvini, Booth,
Tearle, Stanislavski, and the interpretations in performance of
all the others, and clearly the weight of acting intuition rejects

any interpretation centering on self-deception or pretended nobility. So does the weight of critical intuition. For indeed it is hard to imagine an effective Othello who obviously speaks better of himself than he is; who is supposed to be a great general and acknowledged commander of men, all in all sufficient, but who still scents insult in every challenge; who is irritable at resistance, hasty "in the absence of superior authority"; who faces death thinking only of himself; and who goes to his end whimpering and screaming. It is hard to conceive of such an image justifying Othello's stature in Venice, or winning Desdemona's love—or even Iago's respectful hate. Indeed, *everyone about him would have to be a fool* to justify such an Othello. Certainly he could not earn the sympathy audiences have always given him. Even the kind of pity we find for such bumbling self-deceivers as Willy Loman, O'Neill's shabby escapists, or Ibsen's Ekdal could hardly go to so pretentious a figure. The essence of Othello's finale in the theater is that he wrings from his tragic perception a renewed dignity—as Emma Lazarus saw, when she watched Salvini again and again:

> He, whose whole frame has just been quivering with affliction, "shedding tears as fast as the Arabian tree her medicinal gum," suddenly nerves himself anew, starts up with the old majesty . . . and, by the concluding six lines of the play, connects the Othello of Desdemona's love with the Othello who assassinated her . . . his Othello is not merely an embodiment of a single furious passion, but a rounded, many-sided human being, who anon compels our love, our admiration, our pity, our horror, and in the end our aching sympathy.[16]

If, as seems likely, Othello is meant to be a genuinely noble "grieved Moor," why then does he succumb to Iago? Does he have, as some critics suggest, basic insecurities because of his age or his race? Is he perhaps a noble savage—or primitive, or barbarian—whose veneer of civilization cracks under stress?

The difference between his age and Desdemona's has not been a matter of much critical concern, and the May-and-September contrast is usually not emphasized on the stage, though it offers fruitful opportunities. *Was it crucial to the character?* I asked the actors. One said simply, "No";[17] the others thought that once Othello's fears were roused, his awareness of his age contributed to them. All thought color and race—insecurities occasionally mentioned as crucial in criticism—contributed to his once-established uncertainty, though none accepted it as basic. Robeson, who was most explicit on this point, felt that race and color were only part of a larger difference that Iago exploited— a total cultural difference that separated Moor from Venetian.

Othello as a primitive or barbarian veneered by civilization, hence easily plunged into savage passion, has been a fairly popular critical interpretation. Schlegel, for instance, felt that the Moor's fiery southern blood was of the kind that made harems necessary for the protection of women in Arab countries, and that the moral man in him succumbs to the tide of this terrible passion.[18] Actors of Othello have indeed conveyed a sense of being overwhelmed by passion, but they have usually not meant it to be specifically "barbarian" or "primitive." Salvini seemed to many Anglo-Saxons to be essentially savage in his passion; but Salvini thought Othello's feeling for Desdemona was "not a sensual love; it is the pure affection of a soul which unites itself to another and without which he could no longer exist." He is forced into jealousy by his trusted friend, but Desdemona's death "is a sacrifice which he owes to society." Booth refused to admit Othello was not a gentleman.

The actors I questioned differed on this "veneered barbarian" interpretation. One thought it partly true. Another, more flatly: "Yes, of course—but that is the play." The rest disagreed. "A cheapening of the character." "Complete nonsense." "False—he is basic, fundamental, emotional—but noble—nothing of the barbarian about him." "He was more civilized than the 'whites' around him." [19] The problem seems to be partly a matter of identifying the nature of Othello's passion. All agree he has it, and theater history indicates its need to be elemental; but could not a white man's, any man's, passion be elemental? Could not

Othello even be savage—without being *a* savage? The psycho-analyst Reik writes: "I have observed the development of passionate jealousy, almost as violent as Othello's, in a white man who had as much or as little reason for his doubt as the Moor."[20] It may be that critics and actors who specify the barbarian have been unwilling to admit in themselves the forces they share with all humanity.

How universal *is* Othello's experience? I proposed this interpretation to the actors: *Othello is a larger than life projection of Everyman betrayed by a friend. His jealousy reflects the passion that might be in any of us.* "Possibly." "This is better." One, Coleridge-wise, would not admit "mere" jealousy. "No. My view is that Othello is not essentially *jealous*—but emotionally shattered by what he considers an enormous betrayal of trust." A fourth, "Betrayed not only by a friend but by himself —his passion however is indeed not foreign to any one of us." A fifth, "I would not approach the role from that point of view. All Shakespeare's characters are bigger than life. In that sense only, one can say 'these passions are human.' " Finally, "I agree that Othello's jealousy reflects the passion that might be in any of us, but he is not a larger than life projection of Everyman. He is a Very Special Man." [21]

What the last answers specified, the others imply here—by accepting the "larger than life" term—and in their other replies. Othello is no "Dodsworth in cork," as Walter Huston conceived him, and played him—unsuccessfully. Though Othello shares our passions, there is something rare and strange about him—something very special. He is not a member of an oppressed "minority group," but he is clearly a stranger, a man set apart—though more by his nobility than by his color, more by his nature than by his race. And yet this noble man is deceived by a villain. Why? I put the usual Samuel Johnson–Bradley interpretation to the actors:

*Othello is a noble, trusting, unsophisticated man unskilled in perceiving hypocrisy and evil. Hence he is easy game for Iago.*

With the essentials of this, all agreed. "Very true." "Yes—not sophisticated in *western* culture. Rich in nobility and sense of honor." Two actors emphasized that his special competence was as a soldier: "Othello has been at some pains to explain that he is a warrior." "Othello is very experienced in the ways of the world. In his dealings with men and with military matters, one must assume that he is quite experienced and competent. But in his dealings with white women he is obviously at a loss, and it is for this reason that he is easy meat for Iago." Two replies stressed that Othello was not simply foolish: "Not *easy* game, but he is all that—a great spirit tempted by the devil of jealousy." "True, but Othello is no fool. To be pure is not to be stupid." [22] This needs saying, for the Moor has been called stupid in critical opinions other than Rymer's. But as all the actors affirm and the theater has proved, Othello is not a simpleton—and must not seem so, whether by his doing or Iago's.

In extended remarks, several of the actors contributed their own interpretations, but stressed the difficulty of intellectualizing what had to be felt impulses. "My interpretation was the result of complete immersion in the events of the play and in living so far as possible inside the character." [23] "Actors feel more than analyze. They absorb the text into their veins and into their bloodstream, rather than reason it out in their heads. For only in this way can they hope to *be* the character, rather than give a dissertation on the character. Also, every actor is bound to use his own personality to a very large extent in presenting dramatic character, and this is a mystery which the actor himself is the last to analyse." [24]

Nevertheless, several actors contributed valuable insights. Hyman saw Othello as a rounded man:

> Othello is a Negro, an alien in a "super-subtle" Venetian society. He is straightforward, honest, uncomplicated, a man of extraordinary dignity—and hence a little uncomfortable in a decadent, hypocritical, overly "civilized" civilization. He is a brilliant military leader—clear thinking, expeditious—but he is a deeply emotional man, a "heart" man, a "poet," and he *knows* this about himself and has built up a rigid sense of discipline

and control over his emotions that is almost perfect. In that *almost* lies the rub. He is not a jealous man. The tragedy is that of a man whose life is shattered when he finds that all he has believed of life is proven false by the "infidelity" of Desdemona.

Robeson, himself highly conscious of racial divisions, stressed Othello's cultural pride and sensitivity:

Shakespeare meant Othello to be a "black moor" from Africa, an African of the highest nobility of heritage. From Kean on, he was made a light-skinned Moor because Western Europe had made Africa a slave center, and the African was seen as a slave. English critics seeing a black Othello—like my Othello—were likely to take a colonial point of view and regard him offhand as low and ignoble. But the color is essentially secondary—except as it emphasizes the difference in *culture*. This is the important thing. Suppose a white American boy, a soldier, married a Japanese girl in Japan. It wouldn't take much for a Japanese Iago to mislead him with stories of secret Japanese sophistication he could never understand. Shakespeare's Othello has learned to live in a strange society, but he is not *of* it—as an easterner today might pick up western manners and not be western. Othello's personal, racial dignity is involved in his love. He might have been much slower to suspicion if his wife had been of the same background. But he is intensely proud of his color and culture; in the end, even as he kills, his honor is at stake, not simply as a human being and as a lover, but as Othello. The honor of his whole culture is involved. "It is the cause . . ."

Sofaer, on the other hand, saw a gentlemanly Arab:

Othello is not a "coloured" man in the American sense of the word, but a noble Arab—probably a Christianized Spanish Arab who found employment as a military man in Venice after the fall of the Spanish-Arab Empire. . . . The keynote of his character is his nobility and trustfulness, as a contrast to the "sophistication" and guile of the Italians around him.
He is quite incredulous at first when Iago insinuates his sus-

picion of Desdemona, but his complete trust in his Ancient
leads him to consider it . . . Othello decides that Desdemona is
evil and must be put away. Because he is noble he cannot at
first get himself to confront her with his doubts; but when suspicion becomes fact in his mind at last, he rails at her in one
of the most magically poetic scenes in the play, and Desdemona's
innocent confusion only seems to make him more certain of her
guilt. He kills her, sacrificially.

There is nothing low or gross about Othello. His portrayal
should elicit a superb "maleness" with great beauty and charm
of thought and utterance. There is only one moment when
Othello goes berserk, and that is when he suspects Iago might
be imposing on him—

Villain, be sure thou prove my love a whore . . .

But he recovers control. He has great anguish but no savagery,
and the tragedy is quite inevitable when you consider his way of
thinking.

Quayle emphasized Othello's passion:

Othello is a man in whom a volcano continually rages, but who
has imposed on himself a prodigious control. His life has been a
harsh, cruel and hazardous one; and it is a miracle to him, after
all the adventures he has been through, that he should be alive
at all. He has a great sense of destiny, and it seems to him that
the culmination of his extraordinary destiny is that he should
love and be loved in return by Desdemona. He can't deal at all
in a dry, legal manner with such a vast emotion. This is the
crown of his life, and when he thinks that the crown is cracked
and besmirched, the volcano in him erupts and nothing but
death can wipe out the dishonour.

I think the important thing for an actor at the very outset
of the part, is to have this sense of destiny, the feeling that the
sun, moon and stars in their spheres have all moved so as to preserve his life and to set this ecstatic crown of love upon it. In
all of his expression of this he is certainly colourful, but never
boastful, and, in fact, always speaking with a certain restraint.

From what stage history and the actors have told us of Othello, there must clearly be many shadings in the theater's Moor, as there are in the Moor of the critics; put together the best of the two, and something of a composite image emerges with four main components (and note that sight and sound are as essential to the communication of this dramatic art object as words):

First, Othello is an outsider, a splendidly talented professional employed by a sophisticated society to which he can never belong. He is a big man (or must *look* big), a warrior, romantic, urgent, commanding, from the "antres vast and deserts idle"; the Venetians are town men, who hire warriors. He wears the dress of his profession, a soldier's dress—usually one unmistakably "foreign," of a grand simplicity; they are robed in ornate city garb. His speech, issuing in a voice that is deep, musical, and sure—until emotion roils it, and its melody grows wild and anguished—is touched with the strangeness and vastness of his birthplace; theirs, though often poetic, is domesticated. He is accustomed to life among fighting men; they are an effete society, a court society, with polished tactics of manners that are to him opaque and mysterious—and dangerous, when he feels threatened by their secrecy. To the eye, to the ear, to the heart, to the mind, he is a man apart. Yet his very apartness reflects a kinship with us: who has not known isolation in the midst of many? He is the authentic hero, the splendid soul that no man knows.

In this apartness there was perhaps also reflected a repeated dramatic theme of Shakespeare's time: the fate of the romantic or blunt general who is unappreciated by society in spite of his greatness.[25] There may even have been a direct echo of the unfortunate Earl of Essex—Shakespeare had much admired this dashing captain, and was indirectly involved in his rebellion.[26] (And was there something in Othello of the artist-playwright himself, the hired professional who served a glittering court but stood apart from it? Some of the great actors of the role seemed to feel keenly this aspect of it. It is worth noting that in Cinthio no age difference is stipulated between the Moor and

Disdemona; but in the play, Othello is much older, "declin'd into the vale of years"—that is, he had lived more than half of the proverbial threescore and ten. So had Shakespeare at the time he wrote the play.)

The shade of Othello's stranger skin was part of his apartness. Was it more? To a symbolist, his skin can seem a sign of darkness, hence be regarded as a visual emblem of evil. (But see Chapter 17.) To Paul Robeson—and others—the matter of Othello's being *Negro* is important. The actor mentioned how much tension would be roused if a Negro tried to play Othello to a white Desdemona in Memphis; but, as he acknowledged, Memphis represents a special social mold, stemming from a Western enslavement of Negroes long after Othello was written. Historical evidence indicates that African Negroes were hardly known in Shakespeare's England; but for many years Englishmen had read about, traded with, worked and mercenaried in Barbary (Chaucer's Knight, among others, had fought there). In Shakespeare's time, Morocco still had exotic, "barbarous" connotations, but by 1604 its remoteness and mystery had a kind of familiarity. Many Britons at the time enjoyed meeting and working for the current Moorish king, whom Captain John Smith found "everie way noble, kind, and friendly." [27] After the Battle of El Ksar el Kebir (Alcazarquivir) in 1578, in which the Moors annihilated the Portuguese army and upset the balance of power in Europe, their fame as fighters had spread in the West and made them especially interesting to England, for the two shared a favorite enemy: Spain. Queen Elizabeth, having sent an ambassador to Morocco, was visited in turn by a Moorish diplomat—"a Captaine and a Gentleman" [28]—who, the Foreign Office informs me, came from his king to offer "men, money, supplies, and the use of [Moroccan] ports" against the Spanish.[29] In 1600, not long before *Othello*, London played host for months to Moorish emissaries, the chief of whom seems from his portrait to have been very like the Prince of Morocco in *The Merchant of Venice:* "a tawny Moor all in white" (II, i). Some Englishmen resented this am-

bassador for being "uncharitable";[30] if he was, he left no preju-
dice behind, for other envoys would come to be lavishly and
enthusiastically welcomed by cannon salutes, by cheering, street-
packing crowds, and by king and court.[31] In the decade after
the first performance of *Othello*, when a great London parade
was held in honor of the city's Fishmongers, the emblem chosen
to represent their quality and generosity was "the King of
Moores, gallantly mounted on a golden Leopard, he hurling
gold and silver every way about him." [32]

In the drama of the time, there was no stereotype of a Moor.
Thus Aaron in *Titus Andronicus* and Eleazar in *Lust's Dominion*
are thoroughly wicked; in *The Merchant of Venice* the Moroc-
can Prince, if not lovable, is lofty and dignified: "Mislike me not
for my complexion,/ The shadowed livery of the burning sun
. . . I do in birth deserve her, and in fortunes,/ In graces and
in quality of breeding . . ." (II, i; II, vii); in Peele's *The Battle
of Alcazar*, "good" Moors defeat a "bad" one allied to the Christian Portugese in much the same way that one side defeated another in English historical drama. In *The Fair Maid of the West*,
Moorish King Mullisheg is a reasonable, gracious monarch, of
poetic speech, whom good English Bess is happy to salute with
a kiss; and though, for purposes of plot, passion momentarily
sways him to scheme against his English rival, he is essentially
gallant and generous. In Greene's romantic *Orlando Furioso*,
and more especially in Webster's *The Thracian Wonder*, the
Moorish kings are noble men of the most honorable and generous
language and spirit.

An appealing, exotic aura had long been associated with Moors
in England. As early as 1547, elaborately costumed Moorish
masques were fashionable at court. Edward VI himself dressed
in black to dance in one. In 1585, a parade in honor of London's
Lord Mayor was headed by a "Moor," riding on a lynx and
singing the praises of the city:

> behold I come,
> A stranger, strangely mounted.[33]

To come closer to our own study: in 1604, so fond was Queen Anne of the familiarly strange wonder of the Moors that she asked Ben Jonson to write her a masque especially about them[34] —to be given the same winter season in which *Othello* was presented, in the same palace theater. (Had Shakespeare known of the queen's whim? Had it cued his mind to his next play, as other royal whims are rumored to have done?)[35] Though the queen was pregnant, and immediately afterward had to go to Greenwich to "lay down her great belly," [36] she insisted on dancing in this gorgeous *Masque of Blackness,* appearing "strangely mounted"—"in a great concave shell, like mother of pearl, curiously made to move on [the] waters and rise with the billow"—and made up, with her ladies, in the exotic, darkened skin of a Moor.[37]

This does not tell us how the Jacobeans would respond to a dark Othello. Nothing but actual evidence of their reactions, as it confirms our own experience of the play, can do that. But it does suggest that the playwright was not limited by any rigid notion of a dark-skinned Moor as a national stereotype or symbol; he was free to play on the connotations of darkness and racial difference to strengthen action and character and still preserve the design of a grieved stranger-hero rich in dignity and honor. Probably Burbage played Othello black, rather than tawny, for this was the theater tradition that survived unbroken —as Shakespearean traditions usually did, unless an important social or theatrical development intervened—until widespread Negro slavery. Othello changed to "tawny" in the 1800's to free the role from the unfortunate connotations borne by that growing social evil, and to preserve the vision of a gallant, high-hearted man whose lineage, though strange, is in no way inferior to that of his hosts, nor is thought so by them. His apartness is a badge, not a shame.

Second, Othello is essentially noble—as a general, as a friend, as a lover. He has a gracious natural dignity that surrounds him even in his desperate moments. Before the crisis, it sits lightly and surely on him. In his first brush with Brabantio, he is unruffled, his self-assurance complete: "Keep up your bright swords, for the dew will rust them," spoken easily, but with absolute command. Thus Keats saw and heard Kean: ". . . we feel that his throat had commanded where swords were as thick as reeds." Forrest touched the speech with "humorous playfulness," Salvini with "gallant laughter." The theater has been intolerant of any blustering, any anxiety here; or before the ducal council, where the true Moor's warm, generous unfolding—never arrogant, never pleading—would clearly win all other daughters, too. To Desdemona, his love—whether it has the force of a Salvini or the gentleness of a Booth—is absolute, the fully committed passion of a resolved maturity. It has no trace of Irving's "uxoriousness" or the foolish "lovesickness" the unbalanced, blind infatuation some critics see;[38] yet it is sometimes, as on the Cyprus quay, lighted with the bright, endearing boyishness of a man who never loved before. Great Othellos have thus been playful in their love, emphasizing a quality of innocence in the Moor's nobility. The simplicity Bradley finds in him the theater also found: remember what failures the clever, the feline, the brainy Othellos have been. So Booth called him "simple-hearted gentleman." But he is not *stupid*—neither the stage nor our consulted actors would tolerate that; his is a serenity untinged by the caution of shrewdness.

Only once, before the temptation scene, is he disturbed: at the Cyprus riot. He finds his trusted lieutenant, responsible for keeping order, is fighting drunk and has himself set afoot a riot in a

> town of war,
> Yet wild . . . (II, ii, 238)

As we have seen, he acts decisively; and in a moment, by the authority of his voice and presence, the fighting is stopped, the dreadful bell silenced—in almost a whisper, by Forrest—and he questions the rioters. He is angry at being denied and deceived, and the dangerous power that is leashed in him is revealed; but no great theater Othello lost self-control here: the scene has usually been a triumph of personal assurance, of "commanding dignity," as with Barry, clear of hysteria or malice. He must make his friend Cassio an example; but the next morning he is ready to forgive and would have forgiven, if Iago had not intervened.

Like all Shakespeare's tragic heroes, Othello is self-aware, speaks freely of the image of his person that he carries in his mind; and in the first acts the theater has insisted that there must be no discrepancy between the mental image and the physical one: his "parts, his title, and his perfect soul" *do* "manifest him rightly." Up to the temptation scene, his is as lofty an image of a hero as Shakespeare could produce, and so the great actors have made him, giving him their best. He is not simply a good, noble man—he is one of the finest, one of the noblest of men.

But to be the best of men is still to be frail, to be subject to vanity, pride, insecurity, credulity, and the other marks of mortality. So Othello is no sugar hero of romance. He errs terribly. But the artistic design does not require from him an early "sin" to bring on retribution; his tragic flaw is that he is human. He succumbs at last to a passion that runs in all men; but as the character—the art object—is giant size, his reactions are hero size, and so his catastrophe is titanic.

This is a third constant in the Othello image: a passion so elemental, so entire that once roused it seizes and dominates the man. It was no less essential in the "refined" eighteenth century, and in the "repressed" nineteenth, than it is in the "uninhibited" twentieth. It does not emerge at once; again and again it is flung back by reason, by remembrance, by love. So all the best Othellos were praised for the wrenching torment of their seesaw battle with passion. Finally it rises nakedly, savagely from the uncensored depths of Othello's psyche, but in its very absoluteness there is heroism: this is mortality. And it must be absolute: whether it blazes, as in Salvini, or is a shimmering flame, as in Booth, it must *consume*; the theater has forgiven least a passion that is inadequate, calculating, malformed. A sheer physical torment, moving to watch and to listen to, is part of the imagery of the character; so staggering is Othello's burden that he must weep, often, and we must see "the muscles stiffening, the veins distending, the red blood boiling through his dark skin"—until a point is reached when for a while he can no longer bear what he knows and consciousness gives way. As the bloody passion shakes his very frame, as his psyche begins to dissociate under the strain, and the psychic censor abdicates, there must emerge in the noble man images, thoughts, intents that are stained and dark—but they are the common property of humanity: even poor innocent Ophelia, in her agony, sings her little share of them. In Othello they are never pretty or romantic; speech and action are soiled, ugly; but they are not tuned to the crude animalism of a Rossi: in their size and truth there must be art, in the violence there must be a quality of heroic anguish, in the very wildness of the voice there must be, as with Barry, the "wildest harmony." Swept up in a passion like Othello's, any man might lose his "self," and seek refuge in a more savage, more instinctual one. The best of men might.

But if he is to be the best of men, there must be an irresistible cause for his fall. What could subvert such nobility? And betray it into murder? Only—and this, I believe, is a fourth essential element in the characterization, and one perhaps least appreciated—betrayal by a friend so close, so trusted, that Othello has no choice but to listen to him. Our outsider-hero is also a husband, vulnerable to an age-old anxiety: a doubt of his mate. In a world of strangers she is a pledge that two mortals can know each other all. When communication with her is made to break down—as by Shakespeare's contrivance it is—Othello's only resource is the old battle companion who seems to have linked arms with him against an alien society. The visualization of this relationship between Othello and Iago may be hard for the reader who learns the depths of the Ancient's villainy in the play's opening scene as he schemes with Roderigo. But imagine, instead, that Iago first appears in scene ii, with Othello: that he is seen first earnestly telling how he could have "yerk'd" Othello's enemy under the ribs, with a sincerity so complete that neither the audience nor the Moor could possibly doubt him— as they could not when Booth played Iago. Picture him physically not as the shabby subaltern his villainy may seem to make him, but once more as the officer Shakespeare may have copied from Cinthio: ". . . a man of the most handsome person . . . *very dear to the Moor* . . . he cloaked with proud and valorous speech . . . the villainy of his soul with such art that he was to all outward show another Hector or Achilles." Picture him with the Booth-Iago's "grave, sympathetic, respectful, troubled face." "A man he is of honesty and trust," Othello says, and unhesitatingly names Iago as the escort for his dearest treasure, his beloved wife. "Honest Iago . . . honest, honest Iago." "Good Iago," says Desdemona. "I never knew a Florentine more kind and honest," says Cassio. To Othello, Iago's friendship is "benignant," "soothing" (as with Fechter): even "tender" (as with Forrester and Booth). Othello and Iago had fought together, shared dangers, perhaps more. Stanislavski, trying to re-create Othello's background so he could give meaning to the Moor's relationships in performance, muses:

> Othello greatly values Iago's astuteness and cleverness and his advice which more than once proved its worth in battle. In a campaign Iago was not only a help but a good friend. Othello used to confide his sorrows, doubts, and hopes to him. Iago slept in his tent. He was Othello's servant, even his doctor . . . In the morning, while Othello dresses, Iago may have entertained him with stories and jokes, while Othello was communicating to him his inmost secrets. . . .[39]

Othello often speaks his heart to Iago:

> On thy love, I charge thee . . . If thou dost love me, show me thy thought . . . and for I know thour't full of love, and honesty . . . I greet thy love . . .

Iago reciprocates:

> My lord, you know I love you . . . Now I shall have reason to show the love and duty that I bear you . . . I humbly do be-

seech you of your pardon for too much loving you . . . I hope
you will consider what is spoke came from my love . . .

Salvini, who realized that so terrible a violence as Othello's
could be understood only after so great a betrayal, expected his
Iago to grieve with him in his agony, and in return he took care
to emphasize Othello's reciprocal trust and affection. Thus, in
the council scene, as Desdemona defends her love to the Duke,
"Othello turns to Iago with a smile, seeking his sympathy. This
indication of the warmth of Othello's nature and of his affectionate confidence in Iago, as his 'heart's friend,' is very strongly and
beautifully emphasized throughout this scene." [40]
Once we have seen and reluctantly accepted this bond between them, we can only sit in helpless dismay at the temptation scene, hoping the "grieved" Moor will not, but knowing he
must, listen to his "honest" friend. A good man may do a terrible
thing. There may be no escape, even for the best of men, from
betrayal without, from passion within.

# 15

## In Defense of Desdemona

It may seem something of an insult to Desdemona to offer to defend her; yet this loveliest of heroines needs a champion, not only against the criticism of her detractors, but also against the dangerous praise of some of her friends.

Rymer's first attack was a horrible example of her enemies' twisted method. He was infuriated when he could find no poetic justice in her downfall, so he pretended to see it in the loss of her handkerchief: "This [play] may be a warning to all good Wives that they look well to their Linnen." When Desdemona's beauty of character eluded him, he tried to get a cheap revenge by ridiculing her. He pointed to one of her most touching moments, the plea to Iago to reunite her with Othello:

> O good Iago,
> What shall I do to win my Lord again?
> (IV, ii, 177–178)

"No woman bred out of a pig-stye cou'd talk so meanly," Rymer cried. He lavished insults: ". . . the silly Woman his Wife . . .

the poor Chicken, his wife . . . Fool . . . there is nothing in the noble *Desdemona* that is not below any Countrey Chambermaid with us." [1]

History does not suffer asses gladly: his meanness only rebounded, and he lives in our books as Rymer the foolish. Fortunately, few critics since have dared to measure Desdemona by Rymer's perverse standards, but some have been as extreme in their own directions. On purely moral and social grounds, heavy assaults have been leveled against her since the early nineteenth century. It was thought by stern minds then that utter perfection of character was possible in man—and even in woman. Alas for this theory, Desdemona was too excellently designed by Shakespeare to be perfect. Her little flaws were seized on and declared to be her essential qualities, and she was damned for them. The comprehensive case for her damnation was argued by no less a personage than the sixth president of the United States, John Quincy Adams. Wrote that upright New Englander:

> . . . The Lady is little less than a wanton . . . Who can sympathize with *Desdemona?* . . . She falls in love and makes a runaway match with a blackamoor, for no better reason than that he has told her a braggart story . . . For this she not only violates her duties to her father, her family, her sex, and her country, but she makes the first advances . . . *Desdemona* has been false to the purity and delicacy of her sex and condition when she married [Othello] . . . while compassionating her melancholy fate, we cannot forget the vice of her character . . . Who, in real life, would have her for a sister, daughter, or wife?
>
> [Her] character . . . is admirably drawn and faithfully preserved throughout the play. It is always deficient in delicacy. Her conversations with Emilia indicate unsettled principles, even with regard to the obligations of the nuptial tie, and she allows Iago, almost unrebuked, to banter with her very coarsely upon women. This character takes from us so much of the sympathetic interest in her sufferings, that when *Othello* smothers

her in bed, the terror and the pity subside immediately into the sentiment that she has her deserts.[2]

Adams's stern indictment has been embroidered in detail, in his century and in our own time. One critic spoke of the "strumpet-like resolution" with which Desdemona determined to restore Cassio; one found her, in pleading to the Duke, as cold and calculating as Shylock.[3] A whole school of Continental commentators were shocked at her shameful filial misbehavior in deceiving and eluding Brabantio, and found in it the poetically just cause of her catastrophe.[4] She has been charged with a habit of lying: "In word, deed, thought, she must have been guilty of falsehood; and, virtuous as she otherwise is, we find . . . she has a habit of fibbing . . . Practically, too, she dallies with falsehood: 'I am not merry, but I do beguile the thing I am by seeming otherwise' . . . To *seem otherwise* than she is, in order to obtain her end, is at all times lawful in her estimation . . ." [5] To another critic, she seemed a "moral coward" when faced with severity;[6] and recently one noted "Her characteristic lack of self-respect, her tendency toward concealing truth by prevarication." [7] Adams's claim of something indeed unnatural in her love has also been repeated,[8] most recently in an essay published in France which asserts that to understand this play properly one really needs to be French.[9]

Perhaps the most unkindest cut of all has been the suggestion that Desdemona is weak not so much personally as dramatically. Even by partisans she has been called too gentle and too passive;[10] more recently a basic contradiction has been seen in her, supposed to involve a British softness and modesty and an unassimilated Italianate sophistication and aggressiveness.[11]

So much for her critics. At the other extreme, among her friends, Desdemona has been in grave danger of being canonized. She has been called "angelic," [12] and "an earthly paragon," [13] and "ardent with the courage and idealism of a saint." [14] Recent critics who are sensitive to extra levels of meaning in Shakespeare have tended to see her as the pure, white complement to the dark passion in the play,[15] or as the heavenly contrast to Iago's diabolism, a representation of divinity.[16]

It seems to me as dangerous to rob Desdemona of her human frailty as it is to steal her essential goodness from her. Fortunately for the long life of Shakespeare's play, she no more personifies divinity than deceit. If she were not much more than either, we would not care what she was. But we care intensely for this young, passionate woman who ran away secretly from her father's house to the arms of her lover, who has a healthy desire to be with her husband on her wedding night, who cries when she is struck, and who fears death terribly. Divinity is beyond our pity; but we weep for the mortal woman who was Desdemona.

To come away from her tragic experience remembering her as either a saint or sinner is to abstract from the complex weave of the character a few small threads of behavior, meaningless out of the pattern, and find in them the design of the whole. Desdemona indeed tells a lie, as Othello commits a murder; but we never think of Othello as an assassin—it is Shakespeare's art to make us feel Othello is a good man driven to kill, as he meant us to feel Desdemona is a fine woman, a fair woman, a sweet woman driven by fear and love to untruth.

This, certainly, is the interpretation that best unites the prevailing critical perception of her essential goodness with the franker humanity that great actresses have brought to her. Both aspects contribute to a central character purpose in the living theater. Here, in the play's natural home, where meanings are determined by what reaches the brain and emotions through the eye and ear, where the bits and pieces of Desdemona's behavior are absorbed into a total, tangible artistic image, we first see her as a young, still playful, utterly devoted wife, whose character is being changed and shaped by her love for her husband. We see this love urge her rebellion against her father, her hazardous trip to Cyprus, her lies, her dying attempt to save Othello. We see it mature her, as it kills her. Our *seeing* is of the utmost importance: the way she looks always toward Othello, the way she surrounds him with her affection, her unspoken happiness in his presence. Her love, like her honor, must be always apparent, for it defines her.

In reports of well-played performances the dominant characteristic singled out is the heroine's "tenderness." This essential quality in Desdemona triumphed even over such awful majesty as that of the great Mrs. Siddons. As we saw, when this commanding matron, who seemed born to play Lady Macbeth, agreed to take on Desdemona, to the surprise of the judicious Desdemona won. One critic, unable to identify the players for lack of a handbill, exclaimed, as he saw the part acted with "violet-like sweetness," "*This soft, sweet creature cannot be Siddons!*" By some miracle, the mighty actress somehow even looked smaller in the part. She herself, somewhat surprised at what she had done, wrote to a friend, "You have no idea how the innocence and playful simplicity of my Desdemona have laid hold on the hearts of the people." [17] On less majestic players, Desdemona's womanliness sat quite naturally; and on them, when they captured her intrinsic quality, reviewers lavished the softest adjectives: "delicate sensibility . . . lovely gentleness . . . pearl-like." [18] Ellen Terry, perhaps the most famous Desdemona, was "gentle, tender, and most pathetic";[19] "no living actress could have invested the character with more tenderness." [20] One review spoke of her "seeming simple tenderness and grace, these 'tears of the voice' as the French say . . . this charm . . . this rare and delicate quality." [21]

The only serious complaint against Miss Terry was for a single moment of too much tenderness—but this turned out to be a special instance. It was during the famous productions of *Othello* in London when Booth and Irving alternated as Iago and the Moor. Where Desdemona pleads with Iago to show her how to win her lord again, Miss Terry went so far as to throw herself weeping on the villain's breast. This seemed overdoing softness, and critics said so. It was soon observed, however, that Miss Terry was so ardent only when Irving was Iago, not when Booth was; and since she was known to have private reasons for

liking to rest on Irving's bosom, this seemed to be a matter less
of the actress's characterization than of her character.

Still, the criticism of the business was sound. Desdemona was
not meant to have a spineless tenderness, though her partisans
have sometimes charged her with it. Thus Mrs. Jameson: "Desdemona displays at times a transient energy, arising from the
power of affection; but gentleness gives the prevailing tone to
her character—gentleness in its excess—gentleness verging on
passiveness—gentleness which not only cannot resent, but cannot
resist." [22] And Bradley:

> Desdemona is helplessly passive. She can do nothing whatever.
> She cannot retaliate even in speech; no, not even in silent feel-
> ing. And the chief reason of her helplessness only makes the
> sight of her suffering more exquisitely painful. She is helpless
> because her nature is infinitely sweet and her love absolute.[23]

Absolute in love, yes; but actresses discovered that this devoted heroine was no helpless passive "ninny"—to use Ellen
Terry's word—but a passionate, lively woman, with a fine
womanly strength behind her softness. Reviewers agreed: they
have been critical of acting that missed this and that made her
flabby or mewly. Thus, all-yielding Desdemonas have been
scolded for being "puerile," [24] or "merely meek," [25] or like "a
shrinking maiden." [26] On the other hand, the hard-finished Desdemonas, who suggested sophistication or cleverness or casual
emotion were similarly dealt with: one was scolded for a "sort
of brittle pertness which makes it impossible to feel sorry for her
as we should";[27] another was damned beyond hope with the curt
judgment that she "lacked breeding." [28] But simple goodness was
not enough to save the heroine: an over-angelic one was reproved for "the embodiment of a radiant innocence which too
effectively makes Othello's jealousy repulsive";[29] and another
was dismissed for playing "with pathos and charm the traditional
gentle misused lady of melodrama." Clearly more was needed,
as another critic suggested: "The only positive element she

brings to the scene is her fair fragility, but Desdemona is much more than fair and frail." [30]

↗  The reviewers were grateful for signs of courage and strength and womanly passion: thus one observed "with relief that . . . Desdemona is more spirited than the usual wilting lily." [31] Another actress was praised for her "ardent and courageous girl," and for "a fresh performance, chin-up in happiness and chin-up in defiance." [32] So, long ago, Mrs. Cibber was applauded for the "uncommon energy with which she declared her innocence."

These comments pretty well circumscribe the Desdemona image as it must appear on the stage for which Shakespeare meant it. The characterization, in terms of emotional material, is compounded of equal parts of softness, passion, and strength; it does not tolerate deviations from a warmly human appeal. The crucial test of stage action shows how unsuitable to the dramatic form are some of the abstractions imputed to Desdemona. Consider that first confrontation in the ducal chamber, the night of the elopement, when we are asked to find in her traces of deceptiveness, or calculation, or irreverence. Even before her appearance, audience sympathy has been drawn to her, hearts have been pledged to her beauty, her femininity, her daring to love. Half the first act becomes a prelude to her entrance—one of the most dramatic Shakespeare has contrived—which follows like an exclamation point Othello's eloquent story of their courtship and the sudden hush as he senses her approach:

Here comes the lady: let her witness it. (I, iii, 193)

Her confession, read silently, may seem to have about it what her attackers have seen: a certain smooth guile, a confident casualness, as if her deception of her father was an easy and innocent thing. But in the physical imagery to which Shakespeare mated his poetry, her honesty and her feelings of strain and regret are unmistakable. Often, when she first enters, the Othello gives her his hand; but then he retires, to scotch any suspicion of "witchcraft," and she is left alone, before all these important, busy men. She begins hesitantly, with a troubled bow to her father, whose answering sternness troubles her the more. There is nothing remotely hard or demanding about her. But when she comes to her declaration of love, it is firm and forthright, for she is not a passive doll and will not now take refuge in deception. The effort takes something out of her: thus in one performance she was "distraught under her composure. A great effort of self-control is necessary to carry her through the situation. At this point she stretches back her hand, as if for moral support, to Othello . . ." [33] A moment later her unwillingness to live with her father may be voiced, as one stage version has it, "with sad resignation." [34] And when the crisis is over and the broken Brabantio turns to leave, she is often directed to kneel to him for a blessing, and his rejection is another shock to her. Two modern scholars ask us to believe that this girl seemed highly blameworthy and unsympathetic to many Elizabethans for following her true love without her father's consent.[35] Can there indeed have been so much change in the human heart in a few centuries? Surely Shakespeare's audiences cherished runaway sweethearts as much as we do—or how could the playwright have risked his treatment of the theme so often? Surely then, as now, audiences felt that Desdemona had reluctantly given up one relationship because this was the only way to a much deeper one: the central fact in her life. And her new love must seem natural and good to us. Thus a reviewer praised one performance because "It is perfectly clear before the first act is over that Desdemona *wasn't* a queer girl for loving a black man; if she were, we might say, serve her right—which would be fatal." [36]

It is Shakespeare's triumph that we never think, "serve her right," but are led always, from what we see and hear, to know that this tender woman could have done nothing else and love as she did. Even in the moments on the Cyprus quay, when she tries lightly to keep up the company's morale, we must watch her worried eyes return always to the stormy bay and, lest we have any doubt, must hear her say that she is most unmerry. Always her husband and marriage are meant to show as uppermost in her mind, and we must see her trying to save them even when her frailty seems to destroy them.

The plot turns on this—on the moment when she might tell the truth and admit the handkerchief is lost. But as the scene develops, such a confession is impossible. It is not simply her physical terror of Othello, though this is great; the passionate Moor is already at the point of violence, and in some stage versions stops short only because the presence of Emilia brings him to his senses. Desdemona is suddenly afraid of him—he speaks so startlingly and rash; but she is more afraid for her marriage. For what if the handkerchief *were* lost, she asks quickly, and his fierce answer, coming after his ominous tale of the Sybil's curse, tells her that then there would be an end to love.

By this point the cumulative image she has communicated to eye and ear has prepared us for what lies ahead. As Prior wisely insisted, the characters in *Othello* are not fixed entities, but dynamic personalities developing in relation to new action.[37] By the crucial fourth act we have seen and heard enough to be prepared for what Desdemona will do to save her marriage, and her yielding action now only entraps us further into pity for her. Later, as we watch her scold Othello to herself for his cruel blow and then scold herself for scolding him, our pity grows.

Yet by now we know too that she is not all-gentle and passive, giving before every wind. She is not a sentimental figure; she earns all the sympathy we give her, and much of it for her valiant firmness and resolution in the face of stern masculine opposition. We know this quality from her plea to the Duke. Later, determined to save Cassio's friendship for her husband, she goes about her task resolutely, without shrewdness or deceit. "If I do vow a friendship, I'll perform it, to the last article"—and especially this one, since as she tells Othello, it is really no more than a wife's duty: "Why, this is not a boon. 'Tis as I should entreat you wear your gloves. . . ." Most of all here, in this stumble toward catastrophe, there must be about Desdemona nothing of the pale transparency of divinity. It is as a mortal, mistaken

wife that she must blunder so stubbornly to her death. So one
actress was praised for making Desdemona's "tactlessness an integral and rather endearing part of her character." [38] One of the
most touching ironies of the tragedy is that she must destroy the
marriage for which she risked so much when she is trying hardest to save it.

Desdemona's delicate, difficult characterization is often not
realized in the theater—and the fault has not always been with
the actresses. The two male leads hugely overshadow Desdemona; hers has not usually been a highly regarded role for the
stage, and in repertory companies, according to Godfrey Tearle,
was likely to fall to the "blonde, simpering girl" who
acted Ophelia on other nights.[39] The part was often played for
its soft surfaces only, and this may have contributed to the critical doubts about Desdemona's depth. But actresses who saw into
the organic center of the characterization knew better. Recall
Helen Faucit's conception—"in all things worthy to be a hero's
bride." Any young woman ready to face a ducal council and
go off to the wars with her husband needed to be played with
spirit and valor, Miss Faucit felt; and her interpretation "bal-
anced" the play "by giving [Desdemona's] character its due
weight in the action." [40] So Ellen Terry too felt Desdemona was
not a "ninny," to be played by "an actress of the dolly type, a
pretty young thing with a vapid expression . . . a great tragic
actress . . . is far better suited to it, for Desdemona is strong,
not weak." [41]

Unfortunately the force of the character was often diluted
in the theater by the textual cuts. During much of its stage history, it has been robbed of some of the richest and most meaningful bits: in particular of the Willow Song scene, with its
touching insights into Desdemona's still half-maiden mind—a
scene made to draw tears and carry a crescendo of sympathy
toward the final crisis. Another brutal cut was Othello's tender
reminiscence in Act IV, ending in "O, the pity of it, Iago," in
which he recalls the sweet loveliness of his wife, and so rounds
out the playwright's eye-ear image for the audience. Recently

these lost scenes have usually been restored, though the Willow Song has suffered sometimes from a Desdemona who sings the mournful ballad in a highly trained, operatic voice and destroys the almost heartbreaking intimacy of the young wife's sorrow. It is a song to be sung as Sarah Bernhardt did it: "avec une inexprimable poésie de langueur mélancolique." [42]

On the stage, the roundness of Desdemona's image has frequently been threatened too by Othello's superior theatrical importance. Paired with a Macready who was not above putting a headlock on an actress to keep her out of the way while he declaimed, the heroine had to fight simply for a chance to be heroine. Against Salvini's savage manhandling, an actress had to defend herself as well as the role. At the other extreme, the Desdemona to as poetic a Moor as Edwin Booth had to resist his idealization of her into a sacrificial lamb or a mere accessory in pity: recall how an ardent admirer of Booth could write of the actor's "proud, beautiful face," "Desdemona was not worthy of it." [43]

The crisis in her stage relation with Othello comes in the final chamber scene. This heroine's character requires that she not let life go easily, that once alive to her danger she resist with all her woman's strength, her human fear, and her wife's pride in innocence. Thus Miss Faucit who was so very "hard to kill." How could it be otherwise? she asked. "*I would not* die dishonored in Othello's esteem." [44] But for Othello's sake as much as for Desdemona's, the violent action imagery in the killing must not be merely ugly violence. Too often in performances the scene's ruling motive has been the leading man's impulse to tear a passion to rags: thus Othellos have chased Desdemona around the stage, wrestled her to a fall—no holds barred—and even dragged her about by the hair, to the hisses of the audience. We all know how wrong this last is. There must be terror in the killing, as well as pity: this *is* a terrible murder, and Shakespeare would have been pleased to hear Pepys tell how the pretty lady cried out to see Desdemona smothered; but surely we are meant to weep at the death while we shudder. Men have wept, beginning with the playwright's own time—as happily we know from the report of the Oxford *Othello*.

Tears are Desdemona's due if, in the theater or on the stage of the mind, she is seen to meet her death with the same brave love that has brought her to it. Her speaking after we thought her already dead is close to grotesque and can be grotesque when badly done or wrongly visualized—when, for instance, she is seen suddenly to rise, Lazarus-like, utter two sentences, and collapse. But when it is rightly done, when we are aware, after the second strangling, of some flutter of life, and the few words come as a final, supreme effort, they seem the inevitable reprise with which the design of her part in this tapestry of pity and terror must be completed. As she had shielded Othello from her father's wrath, from the loss of a friend, even from her own anger at him, so now Desdemona tries for the last time to protect him from the penalty of his violence to her. Her world is not well lost; but in both its strength and its softness, it is indeed all for love.

# 16

*⟡ O, the pity of it!*

## In Defense of the Play: I

Critics of the form and meaning of *Othello* who go astray do so in two general directions. Some try to load the tragedy with symbolic, allegorical, or moral implications that threaten its integrity as a work of dramatic art. At the other extreme are the "skeptics" who by reducing it to a patchwork of theatrical conventions deny the play the meaning it does have. I shall consider the latter first.

The dean of the "skeptical" critics, E. E. Stoll, is a direct heir of old Rymer; and indeed Stoll, feeling himself linked with that foolish critic's arguments, pleads, "Surely the editor of the *Foedora* was not altogether an ass . . ."[1] No, not when he edited the *Foedora*, an intelligent clerk's collection of public records; nor even in some of his earlier criticism; but when he turned to *Othello*, he proved himself the very king of asses, achieving a blunder that few fools have since been able to equal. As Rymer's own incomparably awkward, unplayable play[2] indicates, he had no feeling for the theater's best creativity—which moves in free rhythms that he could not even dimly perceive;

and he was impervious to staged human emotion unless capsuled in prescribed forms. His clerk's mind submitted readily to the then current pigeonhole theory, perverted from Horace, of dramatic types: stage soldiers must be honest, generals and their ladies must speak only in specified, decorous fashion, and so on. With this bludgeon he assaulted *Othello*. But this was not the worst. Other neoclassicists similarly misused Horace's premises to misjudge literature; if Rymer, frustrated by the freedom of Shakespeare's tragedy, had stopped with calling *Othello* a "Bloody Farce," he could merely have been consigned to oblivion. But embittered by the rejection of his own rule-made play, envious that "from all the tragedies acted on our English stage, *Othello* is said to bear the bell away," he put such fury in his brays that they still resound, and criticism has never been able to forget him decently. A man who writes of Shakespeare's language for the Moor, "There is not a Monkey but understands Nature better, nor a Pug in Barbary that has not a truer taste of things . . ." or, of Desdemona, "No woman bred out of a Pig-stye could talk so meanly"—such a man obviously bears an immortally foolish grudge as well as an insensitivity to the tenderest art of the theater.

Nor is the spirit of Rymer dead in the land—which is why we must pause to deal with it now. So important a modern critic as T. S. Eliot once—in his "early" period [3]—regarded it kindly, and wrote, "I have never, by the way, seen a cogent refutation of Thomas Rymer's objections to *Othello*"—as if one could argue with a deaf man that he ought to have heard. Although Eliot, before his own stage experience, frankly shared some of Rymer's antitheatrical notions of drama, Stoll seemed to lead from a more promising stance. "Great actors," he once said, "are likely to be nearer the spirit of Shakespeare than the critics." [4] Admirable—except that, like Rymer, Stoll was never able to share the actor's kinship with the playwright, and does not seem to have tried. He almost never refers to actors' interpretations of *Othello;* he reveals no understanding of its stage problem,[5] even as a spectator, and his rare visualizations of the drama are incompatible with the acted play. Indeed, sometimes his criticism seems hardly to apply to the *Othello* Shakespeare wrote for the theater.

Stoll has chiefly argued that the Moor's jealousy is utterly inconsistent psychologically. Othello, he says, is at first utterly noble, not at all a man to become jealous. Shakespeare simply advances the plot with a *convention:* the "in itself improbable complication of a generous hero causelessly in a jealous rage." [6] The second Othello succeeds the first, does not emerge from him. This rigid position, although securing some acceptance,[7] has involved Stoll in controversy[8] with critics willing to suppose Othello a recognizable reflection of humanity, with the usual latent frailties, and that he could quite consistently sink into jealousy under the pressure of the insecurity Shakespeare contrived for him. Stoll, distrustful of modern psychological interpretations,[9] seems to hold to a psychology that classifies people into types, acting in typical ways.[10] Thus: "No man not *jealous by nature* [italics mine] was ever thus put into a jealousy without process of proof or show of reason . . ." [11] What is involved here is a kind of Rymer-like "decorum" [12] that sees people as endowed with fixed, inborn emotional characteristics, and obliged to act accordingly, independent of environmental stress. Anyone believing this must of course resist the idea that a tragic hero can change from one "nature" to another—though, as Prior points out, *Othello* in fact deals in character change. Plausible character change. To quote the psychoanalyst Reik again: "I have observed the development of passionate jealousy, almost as violent as Othello's, in a white man who had as much or little reason for his doubt as the Moor." [13]

Stoll's psychological perceptions of *Othello* are related to his misunderstanding of the art form—the theater—for which the play was created. Here is the heart of the matter. It is much less important that Othello's emotions duplicate those of real men than that Shakespeare communicated an artist's reflection of experience so recognizable and powerful that it stirs deeply moved audiences to sympathy and empathy.[14] If *Othello* does this when properly presented on the stage—as Stoll admits it does—that should be enough. For Stoll it is not enough. He wants the play to be more than a play.

Thus he quotes from Archer: " 'Othello, when we look into it, succumbs with incredible facility to Iago's poisoned pinpricks; but no audience dreams of looking into it; and there lies the proof of Shakespeare's technical mastery.' " Stoll goes on: ". . . we observe that he says 'audience,' and *is thinking of Shakespeare's undoubted success in attaining his temporary end* [italics mine] . . . technical mastery would be proved only by Othello's succumbing *credibly* [italics Stoll's]." [15]

But the credibility Shakespeare aimed at was *only* to be achieved through the genius of the theater's compound of word, thought, audible speech, and visual action. Any attempt to be more credible in a nondramatic logical sense, to satisfy the Stolls and Rymers, might have diminished the play's power for the stage. "Shakespeare's undoubted success in attaining his temporary end" in the theater is the *only* success that counts, the *only* sure mark of "technical mastery" as a playwright. Even if *Othello* seemed madly improbable to readers, the measure of its greatness would be that it goes on being credible—and powerful—in its proper medium.

This is not to say, as J. M. Robertson would have it in one of his furious thrusts at J. Dover Wilson, that for *Othello* "the impercipience of the audience is the guarantee of dramatic merit." [16] We do not damn as impercipient the man who admires the wild bumblebee's flight and fails to observe that aerodynamically the thing is impossible. Properly stimulated, an audience is absorbed into *Othello*, empathizes, shares the emotional experience. Not that the intelligence is dormant; if it is not challenged by the content of language and action, or if it is offended by anything implausible, stupid, or artistically inept, it wilfully shatters empathy. But if it is satisfied by the force and meaning of the experience, it "suspends disbelief," willingly agrees to sense the context as the characters themselves sense it. This has happened to centuries of audiences at *Othello*. But not to Stoll. He stands apart from the life of the drama. Thus he writes of Cassio's leaving Desdemona hastily when Othello and Iago approach: "Why should he not steal away, being degraded and disgraced? His friend Othello . . . should think of this at once and suspect . . . the generosity of Iago." And of the temptation scene itself; "How questionable, moreover, are the aspersions now cast upon Othello's dearest friend's honor . . . proceeding out of the mouth of the man who had just supplanted him in the lieutenancy—whose testimony had been the cause of his supplanting." [17] This is simply meaningless to a spectator at the play, who, having accepted the dramatic context, is aware that Othello trusts Iago absolutely, even with his wife, that he shares troubles with him—and the more so by Act III, because now Iago is his only dependable friend left, Cassio having failed him. The *only* trouble Iago has given came when at the night riot he was so obviously *reluctant* to say anything against Cassio, had almost to be forced to; and even in the temptation scene he only yields "involuntary confidences" (Booth). Given Shakespeare's context, with Othello's many indications (as with Salvini) of his "affectionate confidence in Iago, as his 'heart's friend,'" given Iago's "grave, sympathetic, respectful, troubled face," Othello could not possibly suspect his Ancient of malice —nor could the usual spectator expect him to. Of course even the stage cannot overcome an impenetrable shell of skepticism, a resolute unwillingness such as Stoll's to participate in the illusion of dramatic action. Given a rigid enough decorum, of course a different Othello should (as Rymer and Stoll say) have looked more thoroughly into things—and so should all erring heroes who did not see beyond the context in which they were placed.

A curious example of the application of such a decorum—political, in this instance—appeared not long ago in the press. A dispatch from Hungary told how a Communist-oriented critic would have made Othello's behavior rational. Instead of the deception,

Shakespeare would find that such tragic blundering was impossible where typical Communist efficiency prevailed. At the first hint of violence Communist authorities . . . would race to the rescue and uncover Iago's villainous plot. Since Othello then would have no compulsion to commit either murder or suicide, the drama's climax instead would be the final glorification of the party leadership.[18]

For crucial evidence of Stoll's resistance to the illusion of the theater, consider his exaggerated impression of the speed of Othello's fall. In one of his very rare—and very revealing—visualizations of Othello's physical imagery, he thus describes the beginning of the temptation scene: "In a moment [Othello] is hanging upon the Ancient's lips, his eye fixed on the baleful, mesmeric orbs, on the waving, wizard hands, and to every suggestion he responds with little better than a groan or a sob." And in a note: "To me a careful reading of the text seems to show that at once he is on tenterhooks and all agog." [19] This visualization seems to be the keystone of Stoll's criticism of the "psychology" of the play. He could imagine no transition in Othello's "soul-states," so of course it could not be there for him.

Let us test this. Stoll has written that great actors are likely to be closest in spirit to Shakespeare. Did the great ones begin "in a moment" to "groan or sob" at Iago's every suggestion? No. As we have seen, they were likely to begin the vital scene busy at something, with half a mind still on the lovely, departing Desdemona, and rather annoyed to be bothered by Iago. In the Cumberland acting edition of 1829, one of the first to record stage business, Othello is directed to enter in the crucial scene "reading a paper." Cumberland was no innovator; the business, probably traditional, gives Othello a reason to be pleasantly exasperated by Desdemona's pertinacity, before he sends the "excellent wretch" away, and it serves as a focus of attention from which Iago could very slowly distract him. Thus Stanislavski tells how relaxed Salvini was here:

How he disliked to occupy himself with his affairs and part from Desdemona. How long were their farewells, and how their

eyes talked for them and they made mysterious cabalistic signs
to each other that expressed their hidden secrets. And then,
when Desdemona left him, Othello still followed her with his
gaze so that poor Iago found it hard faring to distract the attention of the general from his young wife and concentrate it
upon himself. It seemed that today Iago would reach no results
with Othello, who was too much in love with Desdemona.
Looking sidewise at his papers of business, idly playing with
a goose-feather pen, Othello was in too good spirits to enter
with his soul into tiresome affairs. . . . Iago's first hints about
Desdemona only amused Salvini.[20]

Mason more prosaically describes the same business: "Upon
Iago's saying, 'My noble lord,' Othello pauses in his writing,
expressing annoyance that he could be again interrupted in his
work. This manner he continues throughout Iago's following
four speeches: he is bothered, bored, teased . . . and impatient
of this interruption . . ." [21] Fechter's instructions between
these speeches describe Othello as "throwing aside some of his
papers, and signing others" and "still busy with his papers." [22]

The lines here are beautifully designed to allow a slow,
mounting development, Othello's resistance intensifying the
suspense established by Iago's known course of action (which,
as we have seen, is *not* put into operation with "baleful, mesmeric orbs").* In the Edwin Booth version, deep in the scene
at line 193 when Iago says, "O, beware my lord of jealousy . . ." and Othello answers, "O, misery!" the stage direction is: "(Spoken without reference to himself)." Iago continues in the same vein, ending, ". . . the soul of all my tribe
defend from jealousy." Booth's stage direction: "A pause.
Spoken slowly and with significance. Othello now, for the first
time, begins to be conscious of a doubt—which, however, he
immediately shakes off, and he turns to Iago with a clear
front." [23] Salvini's mind too was still free here.[24] When these

* Except by a Cibber who ". . . shrugs up his Shoulders, shakes his Noddle,
and, with a fawning Motion in his Hands, drawls out" his villainy (*Gentleman's
Magazine*, November, 1734). This archetype of the worst theater Iago, who
inevitably made Othello seem a fool, is apparently what Stoll visualizes here.

actors—and others—were praised for their portrayal of Othello's fury, the emphasis was almost always on their slow, skillful development of the passion, while hasty jealousy has regularly been condemned.[25]

The abrupt character alteration Stoll visualizes, which supports his theory that Shakespeare "takes a leap as he passes from one 'soul-state' to another" is as stoutly denied by modern Othellos as by most past ones. I proposed to my six actor-consultants Stoll's "convention of the calumniator credited":

*The early Othello has no relation to the later Othello. His becoming jealous is a dramatic convention, and cannot be explained by his character. Shakespeare was not trying to be psychologically consistent here.*

The replies were almost passionately negative. There were two blunt "No's," and one "I don't agree at all," and one "This is rubbish. Most actors find Othello a great and consistent piece of character drawing from beginning to end." Another, "Shakespeare was creating a great character in a great play." Finally, the rationale of the change: "A man driven mad with jealousy may be considered a 'changed man'—see daily murder reports."[26]

Stoll fails to visualize the slow process of Othello's jealousy, because when he attends to what he calls "the inelusive language of the stage," he seems to mean only words; he slights the aural, visual elements that are so eloquent a part of Shakespeare's tripartite imagery. Hence his remark: "Of that undertow of passion and predilection which sweeps us—considering and debating, choosing or refusing—imperceptibly but irresistibly on to our purpose, Shakespeare . . . could have known nothing at all." [27] This could be said only by someone unable to hear the agony, and see the irresolution, in the sound and movement of Shakespeare's troubled heroes. Stoll seems to share this insensitivity with other critics of his school. Thus M. C. Bradbrook, once accepting him absolutely, wrote, "The Othello of the first act is no more than a magnificent study in poise, judgement, and *savoir faire* . . . It is impossible logically that he should ever become horn-mad; neither predisposition to jealousy, racial differences, nor the devilish skill of Iago is adequate to explain his taking the word of a subordinate against his wife and his best friend." [28] A few years later Miss Bradbrook allowed Shakespeare more art. "Here, if anywhere, slander is made credible, and the movement of the hero's mind from security to doubt to conviction by slander is adequately shown." But then she pigeonholed Othello again as the same "type" as Claudio and Posthumous, and "the fixed type made . . . reversals of character the only possible form of character development: each type was like a mask which could only be replaced by another mask and not modified in itself." So even in *Othello* "there is a moment at which Shakespeare deliberately underlines the arbitrary nature of Othello's belief." [29] Yet the moment which Miss Bradbrook picks as "arbitrary" is exactly that one which precedes Othello's plunge into the most terrible torment of doubt. It is in III, iii.

> Now do I see 'tis true. Look here, Iago,
> All my fond hope thus do I blow to Heaven.
> 'Tis gone.
> Arise, black vengeance from the hollow hell . . . (507–509)

Here the man thinks—not arbitrarily, but after long, bitter pressure—"*now* I do see 'tis true," and believes once and for all he can hate what he once loved. But he cannot wear this new mask even though he would, as his physical imagery makes so clear. His face rejects this grim mockery of his nature, it looks torture instead, until, in IV, i, he sinks, in the undertow of his passion, into a "trance." And even then, though he has "seen the handkerchief in Cassio's hand," though the case seems ironbound, complete, he cannot tear himself loose from himself: "Oh, the pity of it . . ." Iago's sharp, uneasy reactions suggest how doubtful the outcome still may be. Enough so that in the audience there is a momentary hope—an urgency that seeks out Othello: "Yes, yes—remember her as she is! It's not too late!"

... This way, that way, he swings ... (my gaps in the text suggest the pauses of indecision):

*Iago:*    Did you perceive how he laughed at his vice?
*Othello:* O Iago.
*Iago:*    And did you see the handkerchief?
*Othello:* Was that mine?
*Iago:*    Yours, by this hand ...
*Othello:* I would have him nine years a killing:   A fine woman, a fair woman, a sweet woman?
*Iago:*    Nay, you must forget that.
*Othello:* Ay, let her rot and perish, and be damned tonight, for she shall not live.  No, my heart has turned to stone; I strike it, and it hurts my hand.  O, the world hath not a sweeter creature: she might lie by an emperor's side and command him tasks.
*Iago:*    Nay, that's not your way.
*Othello:* Hang her, I do but say what she is: so delicate with her needle: an admirable musician.  O, she will sing the savageness out of a bear: of so high and plenteous wit and invention?
*Iago:*    She's the worse for all this.
*Othello:* O, a thousand, a thousand times: And then of so gentle a condition?
*Iago:*    Ay, too gentle.
*Othello:* Nay that's certain: But yet the pity of it, Iago: O Iago, the pity of it Iago.
                                        (IV, i, 188 ff.)

Then, under Iago's taunts, he tries indeed to fix on the new mask ... but still it slips, it slips, to the very end.

It would be easy enough to cite more evidence here, but we are at a level of perception where argument will not count. We see what we are ready to see. Stoll is not wrong; he is Stoll. Certainly he has made large contributions to the knowledge in his field; he has been a stalwart axeman chopping away at sentimental or unrealistic interpretations of Shakespearean characters as quasi-real people; and he has enlivened the area of

Shakespeare controversy with his hard-headed scepticism. But scepticism can overreach itself, and, in refusing to see unreal values, fall t'other, and blind itself to real values, too. If Stoll knew the theater better, if he perhaps tried to recreate in stage action the characters he criticized, he might have learned to yield to their humanity. As it is, his private visualizations of the drama, his reluctance to recognize in Shakespeare's characters the deep, familiar human insecurities which others so readily find, to their great enrichment—these lead invariably to his first conclusion on *Othello:* ". . . the play as a whole, is a feat of the imagination merely and of a cunning pen. What great play is more?" [30] *Othello* is nothing more to those who will find nothing more in it. To others, it is a glimpse into their own souls, an experience of mortality.

That such an effect may be wrought does not mean, as Stoll would have it, that the play must be "not the product of art at all [but] the record of an oracle, the vision of a seer." [31] To the extent that the playwright opened to us a vision of the potentialities and limits of humanity, he was indeed part oracle, part seer; but being an artist too, his inspiration was subordinated to his aesthetic purpose. Shakespeare *designed* the involvements of his audience in the passions of his characters. While his creative intuition struck off images of language, sound, and movement that would kidnap spectators into the fictive experience, his craftsmanship manipulated the plot to strengthen his grip on sympathy and empathy. The whole action served this central purpose, to the very end. The critic, unhappy about Desdemona's dying, who claimed that all the final deaths were unnecessarily copied from Cinthio—"his live characters had to be unnaturally forced to behave as the Italian puppets behaved" [32]—failed to see that the killings specifically served the artist's goal of drawing most deeply on the emotional resources of the audience. So he killed Cordelia, and Lear who did not die in the earlier *Lear* play, and so in *Othello* he killed Emilia, who lived to tell the tale in Cinthio. The poet-craftsman, having bonded his audience to his lovers, having at the same time evoked subterranean identification with the hostile impulses let loose, ennobles the first involvement and cleanses the second with an annealing catastrophe rich in compassion. Old Sophocles was practising the same craft when Oedipus, after his *pathos*, comes blinded and stumbling to find a little comfort in the arms of his baby daughters. First the violence that shakes body and spirit with a genuine terror; then the grace of pity. Shakespeare knew there were few theater moments more moving than the wasted deaths of those whose guilts and hopes we partly share; so we weep for Lear and Cordelia, dying; we weep for Hamlet, dying; and so we weep for Desdemona and Othello. We weep for ourselves.

# 17

~ *Thou dost mean something . . .*

# In Defense of the Play:  II

The light and dark playing against each other in *Othello* give a special molding to the tensions of action and character: the black or tawny Moor in the white robe; the dark lover, the white bride; shadowy evening, full of passion, conflict, or violence, closing in on the day. The playwright was using darkness often now, in the great tragedies, so *Othello* is dappled with the imagery of night scenes that complement the dark-light of the felt life. Torches bob on murky streets, in the shadows plots are made; Venetians brawl at night, on Cyprus soldiers carouse and islanders riot; and in a dim, candle-lit chamber, a woman is killed. There is love, too, at night: an elopement, a nuptial embrace, an assignation. At the Globe, of an afternoon, it took a word and the flicker of a torch or candle to make darkness of daylight in the minds of an audience; but in indoor theaters, and in the Globe at night,[1] there was perhaps already some use of ambient darkness to shadow the play's emotional conflicts.

To some critics, Othello's brilliant dark-light imagery has

230

been a frustrating puzzle. Clear and functional as it is, they have looked for secrets in it, for something more than the play's ardent humanity. Not all succeeded. As devoted a Shakespearean as Bradley finally threw up his hands at ". . . the comparative confinement of the imaginative atmosphere. *Othello* has not (equally with *Macbeth, Hamlet,* and *Lear*) the power of dilating the imagination by vague suggestions of universal powers working in a world of individual fate and passion. It is, in a sense, less 'symbolic.' " [2] But some rushed in where Bradley would not tread. Imagists, symbolists, allegorists, moralists found patterns of meaning in *Othello* overriding the human drama. Victor Hugo long ago equated the tragedy's dark-light contrast with good-evil—as if the play were a microcosmic reflection of an opposition between brooding universal forces.[3] Some modern impressionists found it easy to follow this track: though as they tried to work out the color-morality contrast in detail, they inevitably met trouble, for they had to see Othello, a visual form of "dark," of "blackness," as a symbol of evil. This has been done;[4] but it obviously outrages every normal response Othello evokes. The trouble lies in dependence on purely verbal meanings. Of course darkness could connote wrong in Shakespeare's time; it could also connote other things: in the Christian vocabulary, blackness of skin could mean an afflicted state, blackness as in Christ's hair could mean "spiritual inward beauty and strength." [5] As we saw, a dark Moor might be a villain in one play, but in another a noble monarch; as a figure of pleasant, romantic strangeness he might be personated in masques by a king or queen; he could lead a London parade as a symbol of generosity. But in a play his dark strangeness need not suggest any of these things, or it might have dim echoes of any or all of them. The artist determined the effect of his imagery by his treatment of it in the context of his total design. In one *Gestalt,* for instance, black night could be made hard and threatening; in another, soft, magical, kind. In *Othello*'s context, even before Othello appears, clearly he is much respected by all but an evil schemer—a "bad" man—who is trying to destroy him; at

Othello's first entrance there is no doubt at once who the "good" man is. Standing next to Iago (now doubly evil for his hypocritical display of friendship) is a lofty Moor—a figure of romantic interest—heroic in stance, word, and gesture, surrounded by respect and even awe, not only from his officers and Brabantio's brawlers, but also, in a moment, from the highest dignitaries of the state, and then from one of the loveliest of women. Clearly this dark man is a "hero"—with all the nobility, and frailty that heroism involves.

Hugo manipulated his black-white interpretation by suggesting, in a fluid interchange of symbol and idea, that Othello became the ally of the evil (hence dark) Iago; modern followers have generally met the problem by leaving Othello's color out of the symbolic scheme, by equating darkness with hell and evil and identifying these with Iago. Here Othello is a kind of neutral "Adam" between Iago's blackness and Desdemona's white. If Shakespeare had thought to design Othello a swarthy Latin, Iago a Moor, and Desdemona a Dane, he would have left things much easier for the symbolists; but, indeed, in making Othello black and Desdemona imperfect, the playwright seemed almost deliberately to be negating this symbolism. He seems to have made Othello a Moor because Cinthio's dark-skinned hero's splendid strangeness served his total artistic purpose. He used dark-light images and symbols to accent moments of mood, character, and action with connotative overtones; but there is no evidence that this imagery was intended to govern the human tragedy.

The same seems true of the symbolism that sees Othello between the Iago-devil and Desdemona-divinity. This can be conceived only if the special human qualities of the characters are explained away. An assiduous symbolist can do this. Thus:

> Desdemona, beguiling her anxiety for Othello by pretending to be merry, listens smilingly to Iago's double entendres and, frightened by Othello's violence, tells him a lie; she is, however . . . a Christ figure.[6]

This seems a rather promiscuous attribution of divinity in any event; but here it is worse than that, because it attempts to muffle the essential humanity of Desdemona with the swathing of a symbol. Shakespeare dealt in mortality; in men and women who, living, changed with life, bending to some pressures, resisting some, ending differently than they began. Such characters cannot be harnessed to symbols or circumscribed by image patterns or concepts. They are not the creatures of symbolic language; the language issues from their character, changes when they change. Shakespeare deliberately wrote too much humanity into Desdemona for her to masquerade as white purity or divinity; too much in Iago for him to stand merely for evil. "Good-bad-dark-light" do not begin to comprehend the mortal shadings of *Othello*.

It is not hard to understand how the enthusiasts for this symbolism—and for other extradramatic interpretations we shall consider—were prompted to their convictions. Shakespeare the poet used widely connotative language to reach common chords in us—familial, social, religious—that vibrate fiercely at the initial stroke and reverberate long after. To intensify his characterizations—of Iago's vindictiveness, say, of Desdemona's loveliness, or Othello's grandeur—he used magnificently the tradition of the poetic figure that he was born and bred to; he levied on almost the whole range of human experience—on theology, social organization, astronomy, animal life, plant life, color, sound, touch, smell, sea, storm, stones. Actors would marvel at how this wealth of language grew from character and dramatic destiny, which were ever changing, ever demanding changes in word and gesture. In this tragedy of spiritual pursuit and torment, the dominant imagery came easily from animals "in action, preying upon one another, mischievous, lascivious, cruel, or suffering," [7] but other character involvements demanded other images that splashed out in linked metaphor. Because there was so much of war, in surface and inner action, military figures abounded. In the dramatization of motivation toward good and evil, theories of passion, reason, and will were echoed, and many references were made to the Christian ethic, with all the haunting overtones of its punishment-reward system, of hell and heaven, of devil and divinity. There were shadows of pagan magic and morality, too, to enhance the apartness of the stranger hero: the suspicion of witchcraft, the men whose heads grew beneath their shoulders, the occult handkerchief, shielded by a curse—and such dark mysteries were far from wholly fanciful in 1604.[8] The heavily erotic atmosphere of the play emerged in both verbal and visual statements of character and action: the pervasive, prurient sexual talk of Iago; Othello's early love lyrics, and then his heated fantasies of copulation; Desdemona's involvement in Iago's bawdy talk at Cyprus, and later, when Emilia evaluates adultery to her, and when Othello charges her with whoredom—these are complemented by the sights and sounds of passion: Desdemona roused by the Cyprus riot from her bridal bed—which was fixed in our minds by Iago's coarse jests a few moments before; her long undressing with Emilia; her last scene, when she invites her husband to her bed; and on another level, Cassio's dalliance with Bianca, who is a very sign of yielding sex. The fruitful abundance of *Othello*'s connotative poetry has been given much deserved study[9] (though the erotic imagery is usually ignored in favor of the more "symbolic" elements); but such study will be more useful when it recognizes that Shakespeare's verbal image was created partner to a visual-aural image, and needs to be considered as one element in a dynamic dramatic action, not as determining the pattern of a static verbal tapestry; that the language is stillborn without that actual or imagined realization in voice, body, and spirit that Hazlitt so brilliantly called the "obstetric" art of the theater.

Critics who ignore this art, those who look for the playwright's meanings in the words alone, are in danger. We saw how one of them found in Othello the extreme "modern" Moor; irritable, hypersensitive, withholding, hasty. This study represented much intensive, talented work; but conducted as it was apart from the living context of the play, it led to an aborted Othello. If such a critic would conduct—or observe—the play through rehearsals to performance, and then apply his special sensitivity to the organic whole, we might have a truly valuable study of the reciprocation of the playwright's verbal and physical imagery.

The same is true of another excursion into the implications—or "ambiguities"—of Othello's language by a critic who scents something "queer" in the tragedy's use of the word "honest." He proposes that when it describes Iago, the word carries not the usual denotation of trustworthiness but rather a "covert assertion that the man who accepts the natural desires, who does not live by principle, will be fit for such warm uses of *honest* as imply 'generous' and 'faithful to friends.'" But when the critic tries to relate his verbal subtlety to stage action, the disharmony is obvious. To give one example: "Everybody calls Iago honest once or twice, but with Othello it becomes an obsession; at the crucial moment just before Emilia exposes Iago he keeps howling the word out." [10] The critic may have some overtone concealed in "obsession" and "keeps howling"; but certainly there is nothing in their normal—or clinical, or dramatic—usage to justify his concept of the action. In the mentioned scene with Emilia, Othello uses "honest" in just two speeches:

> *Emilia:* My husband?
> *Othello:* Ay, 'twas he that told me first,
> An honest man he is, and hates the slime
> That sticks on filthy deeds.
> *Emilia:* My husband . . .
> *Othello:*                        He woman.
> I say thy husband. Dost understand the word?
> My friend, thy husband; honest, honest Iago.
> (V, ii, 182 ff.)

For Othello to *keep* howling a word he says only these three times defies meaning; and we do not see him obsessed with it, nor hear him *howl* it: stage history suggests, and common theater sense confirms, that the hero, with desperate seriousness, is intent, after the orgasm of the murder, on justifying himself. Nor is there anything remotely covert in "honest" here; it is used honestly, as it was from the very beginning, when Othello, putting his life's dearest treasure—his wife—into Iago's hands, says to the Duke "A man he is of honesty and trust." * Shakespeare applied the word to Iago chiefly in two ways: as others say it about him, and as he says it about himself. Each time someone calls him honest honestly, there is a sharper lance of irony because Iago, in his references to himself, can be seen to twist the word into a mask for dishonesty. The clarity of the irony depends upon the opposition of the two uses of the word, as it chimes out again and again. Let the critic but direct the play, and try to get a corrupt inflection of "honest" into the mouth of Othello, and his experience may lead him to really useful syntheses of the indivisible verbal-visual-aural implications of Shakespeare's art.

Another danger of studying language apart from the accompanying eye-ear image is that the verbal imagery is taken not as imagery but as data. The symbol becomes a sign. Thus: Iago speaks of hell's power, and others call him a devil—hence he is one. He is even seen admitting it,[11] in V, ii, at:

> Othello:   I look down towards his feet—but that's a
> fable. If that thou be'st a devil, I
> cannot kill thee.
>       [*Wounds Iago*]
> Lodovico: Wrench his sword from him.
>       [*Othello is disarmed*]
> Iago:      I bleed sir, but not kill'd. (351–354)

Supposedly Iago is in fact saying he *is* a devil here. (A *bleeding* devil?) Then what must happen on the stage? Surely the men surrounding Iago must react with some violent kind of fear,

---

*Othello himself insists on the strict meaning of the word:
> *Oth*. Is he [Cassio] not honest?
> *Iago* Honest, my lord?
> *Oth*. Honest? Aye honest. (III, iii, 120 ff.)

perhaps flight—*a devil in their midst!* They do no such thing; they go about the matter-of-fact preparation for a wounded man's punishment. Lodovico calls him "hellish villain," and "slave," and prepares to torture his mortal flesh. Are we not here clearly dealing with supportive imagery? As we are when Othello growls at Iago, "Thou hads't better have been born a dog," and Roderigo cries "O inhuman dog," and Lodovico, "O Spartan dog." Iago is not a dog; but certain low "dog" associations are made to him. The same is obviously true of the devil imagery; but there is more of it because Shakespeare is saying, as clearly as symbolic language will let him: here is a man who acts as wickedly as our archetypal image of wickedness—the devil; never, here is a devil who acts like a man. Shakespeare's imagery serves action and character, they do not serve it; he freely varied it to keep in continuing focus his *Othello* Gestalt: the dynamic working out of a tragic relationship among three fearfully human figures, each with a distinctive stature, a distinctive passion. As they change, the imagery follows them. As the theater knows, any blurring, isolation, or rigidity of their personalities to fit a pattern threatens the whole dynamic design. There is not a shred of direct testimony from Shakespeare's time, in all the collected allusions, to support any theory that *Othello* was seen in symbolic or allegorical terms. The evidence of the play's reception indicates that it was enjoyed only as a *play*. Thus that learned Oxonian who saw the tragedy in 1610 had no thought of Desdemona as a Christ figure, or divinity, or "the traditional sacrament of the altar," or—in one suggested political allegory—Venice;[12] he wept for the representation of a woman killed by her husband, as succeeding generations of playgoers would.

Whenever the critics look for subtleties in *Othello* beyond the clear demands of the theater, they inevitably diminish the humanity of the tragedy. Such a gambit is the perception of Iago and Othello—and even Desdemona, too—as facets of a single character. This split-ego concept, originally exploited by

Freud [13] to explain Macbeth and his lady as complementary halves, is an appealing notion that could probably be applied to almost any pair—*conflicting or harmonious—in life as well as in art*. Partly, we are all members of each other. But we are also independent sovereignties that often fail—sometimes tragically, as did Othello and Desdemona—at communication. A symbolic play might certainly be designed in which a man and his friend—and/or wife—are specifically made parts of a single entity; but *Othello* is not so designed. To minimize Iago—or Iago and Desdemona—into parts of a unity with Othello is to fit them into a limited context that ignores the fierce insistence of their individualities throughout the tragedy. The Iago who gulls Roderigo, traps Cassio, harasses Emilia, soothes Desdemona, and tortures himself cannot be reduced to a segment of Othello's character without throwing both him and the play out of focus; and neither can the Desdemona who dares the Council, who jests on the Cyprus quay, who debates adultery with Emilia, and fights for her life. Othello, Desdemona, and Iago are each total personalities; and the play's tension comes when the clearly defined mortal edges of one threatens the borders of another.

A case study in the hazards of seeking more in *Othello* than the play can communicate in the theater is provided by G. Wilson Knight. (I criticize his first approach to *Othello* the more freely here because elsewhere I so readily applaud his experimental production of the play, and his adjustment of his views.) Knight seemed to be driven by a kind of missionary persistence, not unusual in impressionists, to search for extra-dramatic meanings. Thus, in his first study, he wrote:

> Interpretation here is not easy, nor wholly satisfactory. As all within *Othello*—save the Iago theme—is separated, differentiated, solidified, so the play itself seems at first to be divorced from wider issues, a lone thing of meaningless beauty in the Shakespearean universe . . . It is unapproachable, yields itself to no easy mating with our minds. Its thought does not mesh readily with our thought.[14]

Its thought does not mesh readily with *his* thought, that is—but he would continue the attack. Surely this play cannot be merely about the passions of people; there must be more. He persists, and at last the play "*yields to a mating with his mind*" (a curious image, that seems to whisper "*assault*"). He evolves the concept of Iago as "undefined, devisualized, inhuman," which "alone, if no other reason existed, would force the necessity of an intellectual interpretation. Thus we see the Iago-spirit gnawing at the root of all the Othello-values, the Othello beauties; he eats into the core and heart of this romantic world . . . Once this is clear, the whole play begins to have meaning."

Was there really no meaning before? Is there really more meaning now? Or less? When Knight and like critics seek beyond the limits of the art form for symbolisms intolerable to it, what inevitably results, as Knight found when he produced the play, is disastrous "*if allowed to interfere with the expressly domestic and human qualities of the drama*"—as of course it must so interfere. Then how can Iago be "undefined, devisualized, inhuman," a "devil," if this must not emerge—as indeed it never could—on the stage for which Shakespeare designed it? *How can this illuminate the work of art?* In fact, it can only cloud it. The extratheatrical abstractions that may clarify other literary forms and some modes of symbolic drama only veil in Shakespeare the essential outlines of his mortal roles. Iago is a man, defined by speech and action as well as by thought and passion, terribly visual and human. The devil is a convenient projection of our experience of guilt and evil. A ready-made stage devil—a jocular Iago, for instance—can be laughed at, laughed off; but not so the wicked man whose passions belong to us, whose impulses to hate and destroy are our impulses. So Shakespeare shows us in Iago not Satan, or any other "universal power," *but that within ourselves which made us conceive Hell and the devil*—and other "universal" projections of evil. The very mortality of Iago's badness is what draws us so powerfully to him. Blunt the hard cutting edge of his humanity—the play's humanity—with symbol and, Knight learned, you get disaster.

Here is a lesson the theater is ever ready to teach: you cannot force into the drama a level of meaning it does not have without lowering the level of meaning it does have.

The search for more than humanity in *Othello's* characters sometimes springs from the urge to tie Shakespeare to some theological or philosophical system. Champions of all systems claim him—and in their counterclaims, dispose of each other's arguments. When they do not, Shakespeare does. We are sometimes referred, as if to Shakespearean gospel, to Ulysses' speech in *Troilus and Cressida* stating the need of a firm, hierarchical order in society and universe:

> The heavens themselves, the planets, and this centre
> Observe degree, priority, and place . . .
> Take but degree away, untune that string,
> And hark what discord follows. . . .

In fact, the play itself—like all the tragedies—is a star-shower of humanity in its inevitable disorder, almost as if the playwright were mocking the pontifications of the speaker—as indeed he counters any of his characters who pretend to discover formulas for behavior beyond man's own uncertainty. Gloucester, in despair, sees himself a fly in the hands of gods like wanton boys: but is there ever any doubt that all the cruelty, suffering—and perception—in *Lear* belong to men? Is not this the heart of the tragedy? In Shakespeare, there is no evil worse than that which men and women do to each other. They need no gods to cue them, praise, or punish them; and though nature may storm at them, or witches lead them on, all must in the end acknowledge " 'Tis in ourselves that we are thus and thus."

This troubles moral-conscious critics of *Othello*. Their need to find something beyond its own profound human values in the tragedy seems grounded on a fear that its catastrophe lacks poetic or moral justice. This objection, which like most others originated with Rymer, was dodged, as we saw, by those interpreters who were able to see Desdemona and Othello as deservingly punished for her filial disobedience or for his "lovesickness." But most modern critics, looking for morality, could not swallow this. They knew that if ever we were meant to sympathize with parent-defying lovers, it was here in *Othello*; and they were troubled by the warm acceptance we extend to Desdemona and particularly to Othello. It seemed somehow wrong that he is not more utterly damned; that he could, at the end, if not "cheer himself up," at least pause to explain himself before giving himself to divine judgment. The conclusion: that the playwright expressed no "Christian" or "moral" vision in this play.[15]

Shakespeare's view of life was certainly religious, but in the widest, least doctrinal sense. Whether he dealt with gods pagan, Roman, or Christian, he was for good and against evil—though with an enormous compassion for the wrongdoer; he was for the approved, timeless values of our society and against their destroyers. Shaw can fairly complain that Shakespeare was no original thinker, but we are content because he could powerfully explicate common beliefs—in drama so compelling that the beliefs were absorbed in the drama, subordinated to the character and movement, so that they became a voice of life instead of a comment on it. His refractive mind saw and dramatized tragic experience, not as it should be, but as it might be. This seems to be the hardest fact for the teleological critics to accept: that instead of declaring "Life is ———" and filling in the blank with the word for a closed world ("Christian," "just," "Stoic"), the playwright could simply say, "Humanity is." But disinterested critics must at last accept this; and an example of poetic justice for them is Haydn, whose large study of the "Counter-Renaissance"—the conflicting forces that made Shakespeare's time—led to a final chapter in which he expected to estimate the playwright's own moral order. Haydn tried earnestly to find a pigeonhole for it: humanism, Stoicism, Christianity, naturalism. Failing here, he looked for combinations: "Hamlet's semi- (or wholly) Christian-Stoic providence." Finally he gave up: no hyphenations even would enclose Shakespeare's compassion for humanity:

If then, his final position is unquestionably humanistic, it is not so in any prescribed narrow sense. If it is Christian humanism, it is his own loose variety. If it is naturalistic humanism, the same is true . . .

And at last Haydn made the inevitable confession of his failure:

Finally, then, I am admitting the traditional defeat. I can establish Shakespeare's awareness of the intellectual conflicts of his time, his use of Counter-Renaissance ideas and themes. And I can indicate the consistent elements in his point of view, as he expressed it in his major tragedies. Yet, when that is done, it is little enough. The man escapes me, as he escapes everyone else. There are all the other plays to contradict me; other scholars' material findings to suggest other influences than those I have cited; and other directions. Most of all, there is the man's insistent interest in life as spectacle, rather than argument, and the incredible range of his creative sympathies.[16]

Life was spectacle to him, and more. He penetrated beyond the show into the core of living and conveyed it to audiences. His moral purpose was an artist's: to apprehend (and share) the human sources of good and evil. This is primal morality: it is the essential experience that must lie behind any explicit statement of ethics. The teleological critics want not the art, but the explicit statement, the intellectualization of experience: good should—must—will conquer evil. Shakespeare does not indulge us in such an easy retribution fantasy. His morality is a far deeper thing. He draws us into the web of dramatic experience, involves us personally in the impulses which drive his characters to disaster, so we must share with the best of men— and the worst—those common passions and urges which are usually repressed, but which clamor for understanding and release. We must play out these roles to their authentic, agonizing ends. From this vicarious life we experience what moralists try to abstract: the nature and the needs of mortality. When we have been Othello, Iago, Desdemona, we need no one to tell us what humanity ought to be. We know what it is: what we are.

*If more thou dost perceive, let me know more . . .*

# Appendix

*Reputation oft lost without deserving*

# A Kind Word for Bowdler

Among the refiners who chipped away at Shakespeare's erotic imagery in *Othello*, one of the least offensive, strangely enough, was Thomas Bowdler. We libel him when we let his name stand for the first and worst in the censorship of Shakespeare. He was neither. He does not deserve our ugly "bowdlerize," with its suggestion of a monstrous old-maidism, of a prurient delight in hunting down literature's "indelicacies" for their own sake. An examination of his place in the history of *Othello* "refinement" will do him some justice.

It was not even Bowdler's idea to publish the expurgated *Family Edition* (1818) that brought him so much infamy. According to a family memoir,[1] the first, smaller 1807 version of the edition (20 plays), which appeared without an editor's name, was initiated by an unidentified near relative. This was perhaps Bowdler's sister, who would go unnamed out of sheer delicacy: how would it look for a proper woman to be expurgating literature that had to be expurgated precisely because no proper woman would read it in the original? For that was the com-

244

pelling motive behind the *Family Edition*: to protect the purity
of British womanhood from rape by indecent language.

How foolish it sounds now; but in Bowdler's day, society
agreed that many of Shakespeare's words were simply too potent
to be trusted with a lady. They had a raw, assaulting maleness
safe only in the company of men—if there. Of course, Victorians of all classes often ignored this—and their other—professed conventions; a society with rigid taboos always has a less
inhibited subculture, and an unwritten vocabulary that deals
frankly with the forbidden. Our own has. But to Bowdler, as
to many of the Brahmins of his time, the tyranny of words was
absolute. It was a hard fact that Shakespeare was soiled with
rapacious indecencies.

Still, Bowdler wanted Shakespeare widely read: "the transcendent beauties ought to be accessible to every person who
possesses a single spark of poetic taste. But [Shakespeare's writ-
ings] are, nevertheless, stained with words and expressions of so
indecent a nature that no parent would chuse to submit them
in an uncorrected form to the eye or ear of a daughter . . ." [2]
So Bowdler gladly completed the *Family Edition*, and offered
England a Shakespeare that "a father could read aloud to his
children, a brother to his sister, or a gentleman to a lady." This
was important; reading aloud was a basic form of social activity
in that primitive pre–movies-radio-television era. Parents commonly read to families of an evening; the illiterate joined tea
clubs, where they heard novels by the chapter; even in the
sweatshops a girl would be chosen to read to her fellows at work.
*Gentlemen read to ladies!* Bowdler provided a Shakespeare that
a decent British female could listen to without being despoiled.

It was an honorable purpose, but of course honorable purposes are not enough. If Bowdler had twisted Shakespeare's plot
lines to make the plays morally palatable; or if he had translated
profound passages into simpler, baser language for the sake of
baby comprehension; or if he had so slashed out indecencies in
the plays that the central fabrics were torn and unrecognizable,
his good intentions would have been worth nothing: he would

have been paving the highway to an artistic hell. There was a great temptation to do this in Bowdler's generation, and others succumbed to it; Bowdler did his best not to.

I do not mean to apologize for the least of Bowdler's expurgations. Censorship is always a dangerous social act; where it involves the pruning of Shakespeare's language, it is artistically dangerous as well, for the playwright frequently used profanity and sexual allusion to strengthen character and mood and to intensify action, and these suffer when the language is meddled with. But censors we have always with us. We have seen how, beginning in Shakespeare's own lifetime—when a ban on stage profanity forced changes in the language of *Othello*—the play was persistently "refined" long before Bowdler laid a hand on it. British literature generally was "Victorian" years before Victoria was crowned and gave her name to a repressive way of life; and Bowdler's expurgation of *Othello* came only after many years of other Shakespeare bowdlerizations—I use the word, *faute de mieux*, until I propose a better one in a moment—that were generally *worse* than his.

These early expurgations were the already discussed editions of *Othello* "as acted" on the London stages. These "theater" versions were for the general public reading and not exclusively for actors, as might be supposed. Thus Bell's (Francis Gentleman's) "refined" Shakespeare of 1773–1774, the first of the collected theater versions, was the most popular edition of Shakespeare to that time. Eight hundred sets were sold the first week[3]—an impressive record then. The plays in Bell's edition were also available separately, as were literally dozens of other theater editions in the late eighteenth century. Almost all were printed in the cleaned-up acting form. I say almost all; there was one experiment in which the complete text of a play was published, with the acting lines in normal type and the parts that were eliminated in the theater set off in italics. This did not catch on; the acting editions that continued popular were those with the theatrical text alone. Clearly a large public wanted only to read those parts of the plays that were regarded as decent enough to be spoken in the theater.

Bowdler's *Family Edition* gave Victorians their Shakespeare nearly entire, and they were very happy to have it. The edition went into many printings and was generally well received both by the people of his era—even Swinburne was to praise it— and by the press. The one paper that hit hard enough to provoke a reply, the *British Critic*, attacked, on principle, all editors who changed a single word, even for sense, in the original text, and it put Bowdler in good company: "They have purged and castrated Shakespeare, tattooed and beplaistered him, and cauterized and phlebotomized him . . . Here ran Johnson's dagger through, 'see what a rent an envious Pope has made,' and 'here the well beloved Bowdler stabbed . . .' " [4]

Bowdler was shocked. The writer had obviously ". . . paid but little attention to some words in the original which are so indecent, that if the Reviewer should dare to read them aloud in the company of virtuous women, he would be (or he would deserve to be) immediately ordered to quit the apartment." [5]

Bowdler was particularly concerned with words relating to the love act:

> I have been told, that at the first performance of the lately-revived play of the "Two Gentlemen of Verona," some indelicate words of Lance, respecting his dog, were very properly marked with the disapprobation of the audience and omitted at the second representation of the play. This surely was very proper; yet these words, though much better omitted, were far less objectionable than the [sexual] speeches which I have mentioned. [6]

Hence his guiding axiom:

> If any word or expression is of such a nature, that the first impression which it excites is an impression of [sexual] obscenity, that word ought not to be spoken or written or printed: and if printed, it ought to be erased. [7]

There is no denying Bowdler's raw sensitivity to "indelicacy." To protect womanhood from seduction by language, he wanted to edit out not only

> . . . words which are in themselves indecent, but those which, though naturally innocent, are rendered otherwise by the context. No word can be more harmless than the short words *to do;* yet in the mouths of Pandarus and Cressida [when he has arranged her assignation with Troilus] these words are unfit to be repeated.

>> [*Cres:* . . . you naughty, mocking uncle!
>>           you bring me to do—and then you flout me, too.
>> *Pan:*  To do what? To do what? let her say what:
>>           what have I brought you to do?]

> I observe in one pretty edition of Shakespeare . . . the reader is informed in a note that the words *to do* are to be understood in a wanton sense. If this be true, and I think that no person who reads the passage can possibly doubt it, I assert that . . . it would be better to omit them than to explain them.

Bowdler did not want to "blot his pages" with many examples, but he warned parents against such speeches as Hamlet's in the mousetrap scene, and that remarkably bawdy English lesson the French princess gets in *Henry V*, if they valued "the purity of their daughter's mind." [8] A modern psychologist would find much food for thought in Bowdler's still harping on his daughter, in his anxiety to protect her from sexual allusions that would be meaningless unless she already understood them.

This was Bowdler at his worst, the complete child of his culture. Still, he could rise above it when he had to; his anxiety about the assaulting power of language could not destroy his fidelity to his author's art. He was able to convince himself, usually, that the indelicacies he deleted were superfluous "excrescences . . . one might almost be led to consider them as interpolations, as if the wretched taste of the age had compelled Shakespeare, after he had finished those beautiful plays, to write something of a ludicrous cast. . . ." [9] If this was rationalization, weightier critics than Bowdler shared it. The mighty *Edinburgh Review* declared, "It has in general been found easy to extirpate the offensive expressions . . . without any visible scar . . . in the composition—the work generally appears more natural and harmonious without them." [10] But Bowdler himself could not always swallow this. He recognized that some plays—*Othello* particularly—could not be "refined" and keep their integrity— and he refused to refine them. For his courage here we can look more kindly at his other work.

*Othello* was his severest test. Its elements of adultery and sexual jealousy carried echoes of all the guilty thoughts that underlay the Victorian taboo system. It includes a prostitute, a wife cynical about fidelity, and a bedroom scene. Its language deals often and unmistakably with the sexual act. If the playwright had deliberately set out to shock poor Bowdler's sensitivity, he could hardly have done better.

And yet, although the censor in Bowdler was affronted, the man recognized the greatness of the play and yielded to it. His preface observed: "This tragedy is justly considered as one of the noblest efforts of dramatic genius . . . but the subject is unfortunately little suited to family reading. The arguments which are urged and the facts which are adduced as proofs of adultery are necessarily of such a nature as cannot be expressed in terms of perfect delicacy; yet neither the argument nor the facts can be omitted. . . ."

So Bowdler tried only lightly to clean up the play's surface; he protected the core

From the multitude of indecent expressions which abound in the speeches of the inferior characters, I have endeavored to clear the play; but I cannot erase all the bitter terms of reproach and execration with which the transports of jealousy and revenge are expressed by the Moor, without altering his character, losing sight of the horror of those passions, and, in fact, destroying the tragedy. I find myself, therefore, reduced to the alternative of either departing from the principle on which this publication is undertaken, or materially injuring a most valuable exertion of the genius of Shakespeare. I have adopted the former alternative.

Compare the stage version of *Othello* with Bowdler's. At this time many British publishers were publishing, and the two royal theaters were playing, the John Philip Kemble cutting of the tragedy. As we know, many lines of the original had been slashed away, partly to reduce the playing time, but mainly to appease the social dread of certain words and ideas. Hence the deletions in Iago's sensuality, the elimination of Bianca, of the Willow Song scene, of Othello's trance, and other bits of "offensive" action and language. It would seem that even the sternest nineteenth-century Puritan might have been satisfied with this refined stage *Othello* of Kemble's; and yet there was the *Monthly Mirror* comment on it in 1808: ". . . we contend that it can never be played without committing such a violence on the modesty and decency of the house as is altogether intolerable." [11]

Against this background, we can appreciate what Bowdler did—and did not do. He left the play basically untouched, cutting only the language and action he could not bear. Could he have read without blushing Iago's taunts to Brabantio about the old black ram tupping his white ewe, and the two-backed beast? Images of this kind must have struck his fearful imagination like an electric shock. Where he could, he kept the sense but blurred the image: the beast figure became "your daughter and the Moor are now together." The ram was obliterated—as it had been on the stage. In two instances, to weaken Shakespeare's imagery, Bowdler used language more explicit than the playwright's: thus, where Iago, in soliloquies, voices his suspicion that Othello has "done my office," and "leaped into my seat," Bowdler has, "in my bed has done me wrong," and "hath wrong'd me in my bed." Some taboo words bore images that were intolerable to Bowdler; thus, from Othello's phrase, "lest

her body and beauty unprovide my mind," the offending "body"
is removed. He cut briefly in the temptation scene.

> I have reduced two lines and a half to two, in a speech of Iago,
> (in the third scene of the third act) which begins "And may,
> but," etc. Perhaps some persons may blame me for omitting so
> much; but I think that even the British Critic, if he were to
> retain the half line, could not object to the substitution of the
> word "crime" in the place of the last word of the speech.
> [Would you, the supervisor behold her topped], a word which,
> whether it be written in the old or in the modern way, [tupped]
> is equally impossible to be pronounced in the company of vir-
> tuous women.

Even here Bowdler deserves some credit; the sentence he ends
in "crime" had been stricken entirely from the earlier *Family
Edition*. He dared to restore the sense of it, as he restored a few
other lines previously cut.

True to his principles, Bowdler hounded out the simple words
that were sinister in context. Thus, Iago tantalizes Othello with
the thought that the lovers would hardly allow him to "see them
bolster." Bowdler observes that "bolster . . . is as innocent a
word as any in our language . . . but so employed as to assume a meaning so grossly improper that no gentleman could
venture to read it to a lady." Bowdler substituted "to see their
guilt."

Inevitably, in this kind of censorship, the poetry of the play
sometimes suffered; and thus "the bawdy wind that kisses all it
meets" becomes merely "the very wind." But Bowdler did no
more of this than he thought he had to do; he kept almost all the
"inflammatory" visual action—for example, the Act II scene,
where Desdemona comes to the Cyprus riot flushed from
bed and is led back to it by Othello. Bianca is preserved with her
full part. The hot fourth act is refined a little, but only a little.
Words like "naked" and a few others must be removed of
course; but the nature of the images that torment Othello to the

point of his trance is unmistakable. The moment in which his mind keeps wandering back to the loveliness of Desdemona is preserved. So is the Willow Song scene; Bowdler takes from the ballad itself only the couplet with "If I court more women you'll couch with more men." Emilia's earthy talk is reduced only by a few words and a couple of sentences, including her gag about adultery: "Nor I neither by this heavenly light. I might do it as well in the dark." In the fifth act hardly a word is changed. The characters go to their doom in Shakespeare's language.

Bowdler might have done much, much worse for his readers; and to see how much, consider the crime committed on the play by another nineteenth-century censor, the Reverend James Plumptre. Some years *before* Bowdler's *Family Edition*, Plumptre published a savagely refined version of eighteenth-century plays titled *The English Drama Purified*. In addition to his fashionable fear of the sight and sound of words that suggested physical love and physical function, and his fastidious aversion to language of violence, Plumptre was also infected by a Rymer-like passion for poetic justice. He liked the kind of happy ending Tate had grafted onto *Lear*. Plumptre wanted to do at least as much for *Othello*.[12]

He wrote in his preface: "The object . . . has been to do away with the prodigality of death . . . and to clear injured virtue in preserving the life of Desdemona, and, with that, the life of Othello, and to expose and punish the villainy of Iago . . . It seems surprising that it did not occur . . . to any other manager or author . . . to give a happy termination to the play."

Plumptre was not content with merely bettering the plot line; he generously offered to improve Shakespeare's characterization too. "Another object has been to soften some of the less amiable features of Othello's character, his concern with his own disgrace at the supposed infidelity of his wife, more than for the sin which she is laying upon her soul . . . It seemed desirable, too, to make Emilia's character less doubtful, and to save her life likewise."

The resulting playscript has all the worst excesses of the gutted theater versions, plus much of Plumptre's own mortal verse. Bianca and the clown are of course out, with all the other major and minor stage cuts. The fourth act is dismembered as usual. The Willow Song is lifted bodily from this act and put into a new context in the fifth act. This opens on Desdemona in her bedchamber and with another character Shakespeare never dreamt of seeing there, a maid, Barbara. Plumptre has Desdemona say:

> I pray thee, Barbara, stay with me yet.
> I feel unwillingness to go to bed.
> I will but in my night clothes lay me down,
> Until Othello comes. You have a song
> Of Willow; an old thing it is; tonight
> That song will not go from my mind.

Barbara explains, in Plumptre's mighty weak lines, that her sister sang the song when her love proved false. Then, urged by Desdemona, she begins to sing a Plumptre ballad. The changes from the original emphasize the baseness of what the editor has added. Thus the original:

> The fresh streams ran by her and murmured her moans,
> The salt tears fell from her and softened the stones . . .

becomes in Plumptre:

> The cold streams ran by her, her eyes wept apace,
> The salt tears fell from her, which drowned her face.

The song goes on in Plumptre's weak vein for many lines more, and ends

> Farewell, O false-hearted: plaints end with my breath!
> Thou loaths't me, I love thee, Tho' cause of my death!

But by the time it gets this far, Desdemona is in bed, asleep—
or at least she is pretending to be, so Barbara will stop. Barbara
goes. The fifth act then proceeds pretty much as in the stage
version, until Othello first strangles Desdemona. He does not
try to administer the *coup de grâce*; and when Emilia enters,
Desdemona gives herself away by moaning. There are large
cuts in the moving poetry of this scene, as Plumptre rushes it to
climax. Iago comes in; but instead of wounding his wife, he is
stabbed by Othello. Emilia revives Desdemona, and cries:

> My mistress' fame is clear'd: her innocence
> Is pure and spotless as the driven snow.
> Oth.: O my much injur'd, dearest Desdemona,
>            How can I dare to look thee in the face,
>            How hope forgiveness ever can be mine?

How indeed, with these lines?
     Desdemona, now fully recovered, leaps across the stage, and
they embrace. She says:

> The storm is over-past—The sky is clear.
> And heavenly sunshine is again our own.

Plumptre now garbles Othello's last speeches, joining four lines
beginning "Here is my journey's end," with a dozen of those
that follow the final "Soft you, a word or two before you go."
However, when Othello gets to the final, tragic "Set you down
this . . ." instead of going on to the suicide planned by Shakespeare, he finds himself interrupted by his wife—a rather ominous sign, too, for the poor man, who will surely spend the rest
of his life repenting under the thumb of this amazingly resilient
woman who can spring up from a strangulation to finish his
speeches for him. Where, indeed, can this poor Othello go now?

What a parody of the tragedy, as the triumphant Desdemona brings down the curtain with these lines to Lodovico:

> Say thou, moreover, when, unto the state,
> Thou shalt, with heavy heart, these deeds relate,
> With Desdemona all is clear and bright—
> Iago was the black—Othello white.

This is Plumptre's *Othello*—an infantile fantasy. Surely his kind of work earns itself a special title in the language of literature. If we need a word to describe prudish, Philistine assaults on great writing, would it not be fairer to give Bowdler back his patronym and make my proposed new word from the name of this literary butcher: "plumptrization"?

Can we read Plumptre's rape of the noble play with the mean adulterations visited on it and not feel a little kindly toward Bowdler, with his limited refinements, and his careful preservation of the basic character of the tragedy? True, when Bowdler finished his editing of *Othello*, he wrote uneasily, ". . . if . . . it shall still be thought that this inimitable tragedy is not sufficiently correct for family reading, I would advise the transferring it from the parlour to the cabinet, where the perusal will not only delight the poetic taste, but convey useful and important instruction to the heart and the understanding of the reader." Perhaps Bowdler would not dare to risk his own daughter's virtue with the passionate language of Shakespeare that he saved; but the play is there, in his edition, along with all the others, for those who did dare. Probably Bowdler's edition assured the Victorian family circle the oral reading of a good deal more Shakespeare than is provided in these enlightened days by most parents. Certainly it offered more Shakespeare than adolescents get today from some of the plumptrized versions of the plays used in school or on radio and television.

I like to think of Bowdler, after his labors, sitting in the midst of his family and reading from his edition the most nearly authentic Shakespeare virtuous females were then likely to hear.

I like to think of him, too, after the reading of one of the comedies in the parlor, withdrawing, as was his male privilege, to his cabinet to enjoy privately the *Othello*—even if perhaps he first hid it inside the covers of a larger book, lest his wife pop suddenly in. After the best fashion he knew, Bowdler was faithful to his author.

# Notes

## PART I
### The Beginning
(Pages 1–4)

[1] Until fairly recently, the general acceptance of a November, 1604, date for an *Othello* performance has depended upon the faith of the critical world in a scribbled memo by the great Shakespeare scholar Malone. The original evidence for the date was offered by one Peter Cunningham, who claimed he had discovered it in a lost document of the Master of the Revels. Among other entries was supposed to be this one: "Hallamas Day being the first of Nouembar/A play in the Banketinge house att Whithall called the Moor of Venis." After an "exposure" of these Revels data by Richard Grant White, they were commonly regarded as forgeries. But a note in Malone's papers with these same data, and his statement in his Variorum (1821), "we know it (*Othello*) was acted in 1604, and I have therefore placed it in that year," carried such weight that Shakespeareans have usually assumed Malone's prior verification and have taken the date for granted.

The date has stood partly because no other suggestion has been substantiated. Formerly, because of its excellence, the play was thought to be a late one. But the Warburton guess of 1611, based mainly on the allusion to heraldry ("hearts, not hands") has been denied by evidence of the play's performance the year before. At the other extreme, Collier's "discovery" of a paper referring to the play's performance before Elizabeth in 1602 was almost certainly a fraud. Some consideration has been given to a 1602 date on the grounds of lines remotely like some of *Othello*'s in *Hamlet*. (See Alfred Hart, "The Date of *Othello*," *Times Literary Supplement*, Oct. 10, 1935, p. 631.) The proposed parallels are such lines as "but to my unfolding lend thy listening ear" and "to my unfolding lend your prosperous ears." These lines are of the nondistinctive kind Shakespeare the craftsman not infrequently repeated; and in any event there is no evidence of *Othello*'s priority or proximity in time. An allusion in Dekker's *The Honest Whore*, written early in 1604, that might refer to *Othello*, seemed to Kittredge (*Othello*, New York, 1941) to confirm his belief—and Malone's and C. H. Herford's (Arden edition, New York, 1924) and Chambers (*William Shakespeare*, Oxford, 1930, vol. I, p. 462)—that the play belongs to 1604. However, I don't see how the Dekker phrase can be linked to *Othello*. Hippolito is accused of being "more sauvage than a barbarous Moore." This seems to refer to

257

a—that is, *a typical*—savage foreigner. In Peele's *Battle of Alcazar*, where there are Moors both good and bad, the phrase refers to "bad" ones. If it refers to any specific figure in Shakespearean drama, this might be the cruel Aaron of the popular *Titus Andronicus* (who is twice in the play referred to by this very phrase: "barbarous Moor"); that it should take Othello as a model of a barbarous tribe seems unthinkable. This man of grace and dignity would much more likely be remembered, as he is in the Burbage elegies, as the "grieved" Moor.

Some concrete support of the Malone-Revels document dating has appeared in recent times with the reassertion of the validity of the Cunningham papers. A. E. Stamp, Deputy Keeper of the Public Records in England, undertook this position with technical and persuasive arguments (*The Disputed Revels Documents*, Oxford, 1930). His book, partly an answer to a new attack on the documents by Samuel Tannenbaum, has an impressive collection of greatly enlarged photographs of the Revels papers. In some of the pictures the nap of the old paper seems to stand as high as a meadow. Technical details about the ink on the sheets is supposed to demonstrate the authenticity of the documents. The pictorial evidence seems scientific, although not easy for the layman to evaluate.

Even if the documents are to be accepted as indisputably valid, however, they still help only to indicate that one performance of *Othello* was given in November, 1604. Is there any reason to suppose that this was the *first* appearance of the play? Is it only an interesting coincidence that for the same 1604 winter season when *Othello* was performed, and for the same palace theater, the queen had asked Ben Jonson to prepare a gorgeous masque—and had expressly desired that it be about Moors? See the discussion in chap. 17.

[2] G. E. Bentley, after a critical examination of the seventeeth-century allusions to Shakespeare, finds references to *Othello* leading the rest of the tragedies; it is topped only in the canon by *The Tempest*. He adds: "The popularity of the *Tempest* . . . is a somewhat dubious measure of Shakespeare's appeal. The *Othello* allusions are based on much more solidly Shakespearean material, and are more evenly distributed through the century. Indeed, in the allusions through 1680, *Othello* is Shakespeare's most popular play." (*Shakespeare and Jonson, Their Reputations in the Seventeenth Century Compared*, Chicago, 1945, p. 113.)

We cannot be certain, of course, that allusions are a fair measure of popularity, but we may suppose that the favorite plays were most widely talked and written about. We may recall here Dekker's note about the popular plays that "every punck and her squire can rand out by heart they are so stale."

Leonard Digges' poem for the Folio said of the playwright's works:

> . . . of how the audience
> Were ravish'd, with what wonder they went thence
> When some new day they would not brook a line

Of tedious (though well laboured) Catiline;
Sejanus too was irksome, they prized more
Honest Iago, or the jealous Moor.

According to Bentley's comparison of allusions by number, both
*Catiline* and *Sejanus* rank above *Othello*. That the former play of Jonson's ranked with *Othello* as the twin classics of the time is suggested
by a reference, dated 1651, by Samuel Sheppard, in a verse on Davenant's
*Albovine:*

Shakespeare's *Othello*, Johnson's *Cataline*
Would lose their luster were thy *Albovine*
Placed betwixt them.

(*Shakespeare Allusion Book,* Vol. II, p. 10).
It would be pleasant if we could refer to the commercial returns of
the King's Company men, play by play, but unfortunately they did not
have their Henslowe. One reference to financial gains from *Othello*
survives by a fortunate accident. Sir Henry Herbert, Master of the
Revels to James I, Charles I, and Charles II, records that the King's
Company agreed to give him two benefit days in the year: one in summer, one in winter. He lists nine of the resultant benefits between May,
1628, and November, 1632 (the tenth was lost because the plague made
playing impossible). Four comedies listed drew appreciably more than the
"Moor of Venise," suggesting that the seventeenth-century British, like
Chaucer's knight and our own times, preferred the happier fictions. But
*Othello* outearned *Richard II* almost two to one, did better than *The
Prophetess*, and much better than two plays Sir Henry left unnamed.
The average return on the benefits was 8 pounds, 19 shillings, 4 pence.
*Othello* was the only tragedy above the average with 9 pounds, 16
shillings. (See *The Dramatic Records of Sir Henry Herbert*, ed. J. Q.
Adams, New Haven, 1917, pp. 43–44). Thomas Rymer, *Othello's*
greatest enemy at the latter end of the century, acknowledged, "from
all the tragedies on our English stage, *Othello* is said to bear the bell
away."
[3] E. C. Mason, "Satire on Woman and Sex in Elizabethan Tragedy,"
*English Studies*, XXXI (Feb., 1950), 1.
[4] Alfred Harbage, *Shakespeare and the Rival Traditions* (New York,
1952), p. 208.
[5] See A. D. Beach Langston, "Tudor Books of Consolation," unpublished dissertation (University of North Carolina, 1940), pp. 107 ff; Don
Cameron Allen, "The Degeneration of Man and Renaissance Pessimism,"
*Studies in Philology*, XXXV (1938), 202–227; and Arnold Williams, "A
Note on Pessimism in the Renaissance," *Studies in Philology*, XXXVI
(1939), 243–247.
[6] For discussions of the yeasting new forces in British culture, see
E. M. W. Tillyard, *The Elizabethan World Picture* (London, 1944);
Douglas Bush, *The Renaissance and English Humanism* (London,

1939); F. P. Wilson, *Elizabethans and Jacobeans* (Oxford, 1945); Hiram Haydn, *The Counter-Renaissance* (New York, 1950).

[7] Harbage, *op.cit.*, p. 252, prefers the latter term.

[8] James was not a bad man; if he had stayed in Scotland, he would probably have ended a better one. The Scots had kept him to the mark, as he wrote to Cecil: "It is a more barbarous and stiff-nekkit people that I rule over. Saint George surely rides upon a towardlie ryding horse, quhaire I am daylie burstin in dauntin a wylde unreulie colte." He came south for the easier ride, and it spoiled him, spoiled England, and set the country on the road to civil war. He stood blindly for absolute monarchy at a time when the middle class and its parliament had to rise. He was repressively anti-Puritan, and drove English Puritans into colonies abroad or toward civil war at home. He joined in subverting national policy to effect his unpopular dream of a marriage with Spain. He spent the nation's wealth heedlessly ( £ 92,000 went for jewels alone in the first four years) on his queen, on himself, and on his favorites, to whom—Buckingham in particular—he gave dangerous power they did not know how to use. As for his notorious conduct with his favorites, Sir John Oglander wrote: "I never yet saw any fond husband make so much or so great dalliance over his beautiful spouse as I have seen King James over his favourites, especially the Duke of Buckingham." His behavior fostered dissipation; on some public occasions he drank so much he could not walk.

James had moments of good humor, of openness of mind, of concern for his subjects; and he had the sense to authorize—and give his name to —the Bible translation proposed by the Puritans he hated. But on balance he was a reactionary, corrupting force; perhaps his best excuse for occupying history was that he did provide Shakespeare with royal patronage and a royal theater.

[9] As Harbage points out, *op. cit.*

[10] The playwright was moving toward the "tragic frontier"—in Willard Farnham's fine phrase—of his last great plays, where he chose deeply flawed men as heroes.

## Chapter 1
### THE ACTOR'S SHARE
(Pages 5–15)

[1] From a Latin letter quoted in Geoffrey Tillotson, "*Othello* and *The Alchemist* at Oxford," *Times Literary Supplement*, July 20, 1933, p. 494.

[2] See B. L. Joseph, *Elizabethan Acting* (London, 1951), for a synthesis of the formalist view.

[3] *Op. cit.*, pp. 151–152, 153.

[4] Alfred Harbage was willing to call them puppets, "Elizabethan Actors," *PMLA*, LIV (Sept., 1939), 703. Harbage has since altered some

of his beliefs about Elizabethan acting (See a review in *Shakespeare Quarterly*, II, Oct., 1951, 360–361). His 1939 arguments for formal acting are explored hereafter only when they represent opinions not known to be altered or when they are representative of the formalist case generally. Harbage's willingness to reconsider evidence is altogether admirable—and a good example to us all.

[5] See M. C. Bradbrook, *Elizabethan Stage Conditions* (Cambridge, 1932), p. 113; Harbage, *op. cit.*, pp. 702–703; Robert H. Bowers, "Gesticulation in Elizabethan Acting," *Southern Folklore Quarterly*, XII (Dec., 1948), 270; Ronald Watkins, *On Producing Shakespeare* (New York, 1950), pp. 168–169; S. L. Bethell, "Shakespeare's Actors," *Review of English Studies*, I (July, 1950), 205.

[6] Thomas W. Baldwin, *The Organization and Personnel of the Shakespearean Company* (Princeton, 1937), p. 36. They had been with Beeston at the Cockpit in 1621, and the usual starting age, according to Baldwin, was from ten to fourteen.

[7] *Apology for the Life of Colley Cibber* (New York, n.d.), p. 67.

[8] Thomas Jordan, in *Royal Arbor of Loyal Poesie* (1664), pp. 24–25.

[9] Pepys's diary, January 8, 1661.

[10] *Roscius Anglicanus* (London, 1708), ed. Montague Summers (London, 1927), p. 19.

[11] Miss Bradbrook quotes several such satirical passages to support her formalist view. M. C. Bradbrook, *Themes and Conventions of Elizabethan Tragedy* (Cambridge, 1935), pp. 21 ff.

[12] *Theatre Book of the Year 1943–44* (New York, 1944), p. 27.

[13] *Themes and Conventions*, p. 22.

[14] No genuine acting manual survives to indicate puppetlike training of Elizabethan actors. The nearest thing to it is a find, in manuscript, of an obscure play dated sometime after 1633 giving such instructions as "in a sorrowful parte, ye head must hang downe; in a proud, the head must bee lofty; in an amorous, closed eies, hanging downe looks, and crossed arms . . ." Harbage, the discoverer, refused with scholarly honesty to admit this evidence for the case he was then making for formal acting. He noted it might easily have been an amateur's work; and he found, as have others, that through the nineteenth century other stereotyped acting manuals appeared while players were acting individualistically. It has also been argued that actors were probably trained to puppet patterns because they were occasionally likened to orators, who presumably exemplified stereotyped techniques. But the evidence, when examined, turns back on the formalists. One piece cited is a 1644 manual of rhetorical delivery by John Bulwer, a teacher of the deaf and dumb, who tried to show how the hand, arm, and fingers might be used in certain fairly universal gestures. But a contemptuous phrase suggests how differently he himself regarded actors and orators. Of the striking of the forehead with the hand: "my Author concurs in the opinion with Quintilian and adjudgeth it worthy of banishment from the Hand of an Oratour, and to be confined to the Theater, and the ridiculous Hands of

Mimicks." There is no evidence that Bulwer's kind of stereotype conditioned the artists of the Elizabethan stage.

Other formalists bring up testimony that turns out, in fact, to support the concept of a very individualistic, very "modern" approach to the inner meaning of dramatic character. Thus Joseph quotes Richard Flecknoe's statement (1664) that Burbage "had all the parts of an excellent orator." But left unquoted is the description of Burbage as "a delightful *Proteus* . . . wholly transforming himself in to his Part . . ." Is this not an earlier Stanislavski—"wholly transforming himself in to his Part"?

[15] This is from Heywood's *Apology for Actors* (1612), in the Scholar's Facsimiles and Reprints edition (New York, 1941). This work has been cited to show that Heywood, a theater veteran, believed "rhetorical acting could provide the audience with an experience as intense as anything we are likely to know today"—and this is quoted: "To turne to our domesticke hystories, what English blood seeing the person of any bold English man presented and doth not hugge his fame . . . offers to him in his hart all prosperous performance, as if the Personator were the man Personated, so bewitching a thing is lively and spirited action, that it hath power to new mold the harts of the spectators and fashion them to the shape of any noble and notable attempt."

Neither here nor anywhere else does Heywood even countenance "rhetorical" acting. The key phrase is "as if the Personator were the man Personated"—again a "modern" theater concept. It is true that Heywood elsewhere speaks of acting and rhetoric together, but only for tactical reasons. "Moved by the sundry exclamations of many seditious sectists in this age," Heywood was using every argument he could think of to appease the attackers. He would have claimed the stage cured the pox, if he could have made out even a remote case. As it was, he solemnly demonstrated the theater's power for good by telling how plays had at various times brought two women spectators to confess the murders of their husbands, and of the night performance that helped a British coastal community drive off a surprise attack by Spanish raiders. Heywood seized on rhetoric because it was respectable; and by relating it to acting, he could borrow some of that respectability. But then he went on to say how much more valuable acting was than oratory—which was, in comparison, a mere "speaking picture." What really brought history and morality to life was the stage, where only could be seen "a soldier, shap'd like a soldier, walke, speake, act like a soldier."

[16] Though we are told that the nature of Shakespeare's theater demanded formal acting, ". . . to maintain attention it would be necessary to exaggerate movement or statuesqueness, to use inflated delivery and conventional posture" (Bradbrook, *Themes and Conventions* . . . , p. 21). Why? The indoor theaters were not large; the great Globe had an outside diameter of no more than 85 feet. The very farthest spectator could be no more than 75 feet away from the rear wall of the inner stage; most of the audience would be proportionately much closer to the action,

and nearly surrounding it. The Globe would not be unlike an abbreviated theater in the round today; if Hotson's guess is sound, the palace theaters even more closely approximated this format. In central staging, as we know, players need not shout or resemble statuary; in fact it is probably a safe generalization that as audiences approach more closely to actors, the acting must be more and more subtle, less and less "inflated and conventional." Once more recall the *Othello* at Oxford, probably played to an intimate audience; there the actor clearly relied on an expressive face to communicate Shakespeare's effect. Why should he not count on as much in the Globe?

[17] For this quotation, I am indebted to David Klein, who published a note in *PMLA*, LXXI (March, 1956), supporting my paper on acting, *PMLA*, LXIX (Sept., 1954), 915–927.

[18] *Elizabethan Essays* (New York, 1934), p. 15.

[19] The modern "Epic Theater" actor theoretically stands apart from his character and comments on it; yet what this seems to mean in practice is the same kind of "interpretation" that is traditional in the theater.

[20] Richard Flecknoe, *Loves Kingdom, With a Short Treatise on the English Stage* (London, 1664).

[21] For "Greued Moor," see *Ingleby's Centurie of Praise*, p. 131, quoted in Furness, *Variorum*, p. 396. The "Grieved Moor" verse, it should be noted, is a Collier Manuscript "find" (*History of English Dramatic Poetry*, 2d ed., vol. III, p. 299). See *Variorum, loc. cit.*

[22] *The New English Dictionary* gives as the meaning for "grieved" since Shakespeare's time (1586–1896): "Affected with grief; vexed, afflicted, troubled, or distressed in mind."

[23] From *A Defence of Dramatick Poetry: Being a Review of Mr. Collier's View of the Immorality and Profaneness of the Stage* (1698), p. 72; in G. E. Bentley, *Shakespeare and Jonson* (Chicago, 1945), vol. II, p. 13.

[24] A rumor about the comedy in Iago turned up near the end of *Othello*'s first century. "I'm assur'd, from very good hands, that the person that acted Iago was in much esteem of a comedian which made Shakespeare put several words and expressions into his part, perhaps not so agreeable to his character, to make the audience laugh, who had not yet learnt to endure to be serious a whole play." This last is a rather patronizing look at the past, and suggests the growing neoclassical distrust of the Elizabethan barbarians who dared mix comedy and tragedy types. (Charles Gildon, *Reflections of Rymer's Short View of Tragedy*, 1694, in *Variorum*, p. 397.)

## Chapter 2

### OTHELLO IN THE RESTORATION
(Pages 16–28)

[1] Aphra Behn, *Works* (London, 1915), vol. III, p. 186, preface to "The Lucky Chance, or an Alderman's Bargain."

[2] See the *Apology for the Life of Colley Cibber* (New York, n.d.), p. 52. Cibber personally knew the value of "real, beautiful women" in that theater.

[3] See J. P. Collier, *History of English Dramatick Poetry*, 2d ed., vol. I, pp. 452–453, for a letter telling how shocked London was to see women actors in 1629.

[4] Thomas Jordan, *Royal Arbor of Loyal Poesie* (1664), pp. 24–25. See J. H. Wilson's book, noted below, for a discussion of the identity of this Desdemona.

[5] John Harold Wilson, who generously corresponded with me on this subject, agreed with my "general analysis of the acting styles of the Restoration," specifically "the constant emphasis on impudicity and lascivious behavior." See his *All the King's Ladies* (Chicago, 1958) for descriptions of physical display.

[6] See John Downes, *Roscius Anglicanus* (London, 1708), p. 21, for a story suggesting that Davenant passed on Shakespeare's concepts to Betterton.

[7] The evidence on Restoration acting style is not conclusive. The excellent synthesis by Arthur Colby Sprague of the information on Betterton's manner (*Shakespearian Players and Performances*, Cambridge, 1953) suggests that though there was some convention in the acting, and some declamation, Betterton's chief aim was to convey the essence of character. To later generations the "ranting" style now developing would become old-fashioned, and actors like Macklin and Garrick would "naturalize" it; but this seems to be a continuous process, each age "correcting" the excesses of its predecessor. For further evidence that Restoration acting had both "natural" and "formal" aspects, see Wilson, *op. cit.*, and Lucyle Hook's excellent "Shakespeare Improv'd, or a Case for the Affirmative," (*Shakespeare Quarterly*, IV [July, 1953], 289–299). The specific information on the Restoration acting of *Othello* amounts to little more than bits and pieces of data on the casts: see, for contemporary accounts, James Wright, *Historia Histrionica*, Downes, *op. cit.*; and for modern summaries Allardyce Nicoll, *Restoration Drama*, 1660–1700 (London, 1928), Hazleton Spencer, *Shakespeare Improved* (Cambridge, 1927), and Wilson, *op. cit.*

[8] See John Dryden, preface to *Troilus and Cressida*.

[9] See Anthony Aston, "A Brief Supplement to Colley Cibber, Esq.," in Watson Nicholson, *Anthony Aston* (South Haven, Michigan, 1920), p. 72.

[10] Famous British Othellos played Smock Alley; the tragedy was popular there. (See La Tourette Stockwell, *Dublin Theatres and Theatre Customs*, 1938). A later Irish acting version duplicates British ones, and we may probably assume identity here. Unfortunately, there are no genuine London acting editions of the period, unless the text was played untouched. The so-called "as acted" versions published in the Restoration were simply uncut copies of early texts. Jaggard's bibliography lists eight quartos between 1670 and 1705 of *Othello*, usually ". . . as it hath been

divers times acted at the Globe and at the Black-Friers: And now at the Theater-Royal . . ." According to Jaggard, these were "edited" or "altered" by John Dryden; actually, four cannot be found, and the others are clearly copies from Jacobean texts except for minor matters like misprints. There is certainly no evidence of any work by Dryden.

Smock Alley's markings on a Third Folio text are preserved except for six pages missing between II, i, and III, iii; and one at the end, after Othello's death on a kiss. The text markings indicate Towne for the opening scenes of the play; Presence, for the Duke's council; Palace, for outside Cyprus Scenes; Court, Chamber, Anti-Chamber, Bedchamber for the inner scenes. One scenic direction, for the beginning of Act II, suggests something unusual in the way of backdrop or property—"Ye Shipps," either instead of, or as well as, Castle. In other surviving Smock Alley Shakespeare texts, the same stock scenes are used, suggesting a convenient, mechanical stage technique, using a minimum of time.

My conclusions are based on my own study of the Smock Alley *Othello*, but it depends upon the earlier study and verification of the text as authentic by others. I am particularly grateful to G. B. Evans, whose study will be of special value to scholars in the field; and to R. C. Bald, "Shakespeare on the Stage in Restoration Dublin," *PMLA*, LVI (June, 1941), 369–378; William Van Lennep, "The Smock Alley Players of Dublin," *English Literary History* (1946), XIII, 219–220; and Allan Stevenson, "The Case of the Decapitated Cast or the *Night-Walker* at Smock Alley," *Shakespeare Quarterly*, V (Summer, 1955), 275–296.

[11] This may later have come back in. See next note.

[12] This may have been restored after a first cut; a later "stet" is marked on the page, but it seems to me to refer to cutting "nor from mine own weak merits . . ."

[13] John Evelyn, *Diary*, January 24, 1682.

## PART II
The Eighteenth Century
(Pages 29-33)

[1] Oliver Goldsmith, "The Good Natured Man," *Works* (New York, 1908), vol. II, p. 6, warned against the "too much refinement." (See also "An Enquiry into the Present State of Polite Learning in Europe," *Works*, vol. VI, p. 81). William Cooke, *The Elements of Dramatic Criticism* (London, 1775), p. 142, argued that now a "feeble commonplace morality" shamed the drama. For more on contemporary taste, see James J. Lynch's excellent *Box, Pit and Gallery* (Berkeley and Los Angeles, 1953), Chapters 14, 15; and Harry W. Pedicord, *The Theatrical Public in the Time of Garrick* (New York, 1954), Chapter V.

[2] See Donald J. Rulfs, "Reception of the Elizabethan Playwrights on the London Stage, 1776-1833," *Studies in Philology*, XLVI (1949), 69:

"As a result of the increasing pride of the age in the greatly improved moral condition of the stage, the old plays were of course altered to eliminate much of the Elizabethan directness."

[3] See George C. Branam, *Eighteenth-Century Adaptations of Shakespearean Tragedy* (Berkeley and Los Angeles, 1956), p. 127. Branam, a strong friend of the century, describes some of the "flattening" effects of the Shakespeare adaptations.

Freud, and after him many modern psychologists, have speculated on the function of formal literary patterns in providing an order for minds troubled by doubt and fear of uncertainty.

[4] There were, of course, other reasons for cuts. As before, some material that merely seemed dull, awkward, or obscure was cut; and some to make time for the voracious stage spectacle, now growing so important in the theater. An amusing snarl at this appears in Fielding's *Tumble-Down Dick*, in a dialogue between Mr. Prompter, the theater manager, and his temperamental "machinist," the stage designer. (I am indebted to Charles Woods for calling this to my attention):

> Mach[ine] . . . But, Mr. Prompter, I must insist that you cut out a great deal of Othello, if my Pantomime is perform'd with it, or the audience will be pall'd before the entertainment begins.
> Promp. We'll cut out the fifth act, Sir, if you please.
> Mach. Sir, that's not enough, I'll have the first cut out too.
> Fust[ian]. Death and the devil! Can I bear this? Shall Shakespeare be mangled to introduce this trumpery?
> Promp. Sir, this gentleman brings more money to the house, than all the poets put together.
> Mach. Pugh, pugh, Shakespeare!———

But most of the cutting reflected the increasing "sensibility" of audiences. For a detailed account of the cutting—a general description will be given in the next chapter—see Marvin Rosenberg, "The 'Refinement' of *Othello* in the Eighteenth Century British Theatre," *Studies in Philology*, LI (Jan., 1954), 75–94.

[5] *Theatrical Review; or New Companion to the Playhouse* . . . 1, 310.

[6] *Blackwood's Magazine* (Sept., 1825), 299. See also Dutton Cook, " 'Othello' in Paris," the *Theatre*, 11 (Oct. 1, 1880), 209–214.

[7] I am indebted to Professor Alois M. Nagler for this reference. See his "German Audiences in the Eighteenth Century," *The Theatre Annual* VIII (1950), 34–55.

## Chapter 3
### THE EIGHTEENTH-CENTURY ACTORS
(Pages 34–53)

[1] Sir John Perceval, quoted by Hazelton Spencer, *Shakespeare Improved* (Cambridge, 1927), p. 26.

2 For a detailed account of the cutting of the text, see Marvin Rosenberg, "The 'Refinement' of *Othello* in the Eighteenth Century British Theatre," *Studies in Philology*, LI (Jan., 1954), 75–94. Cuts discussed in this chapter are dealt with in detail in that essay.

3 George Granville, who resented the criticism of the swooning of his own tragic hero (*Heroick Love: A Tragedy*, London, 1698), protested: "Hitherto [heroes] have pass'd for Men, and by consequence subject to humane Infirmities." Othello's trance was apparently eliminated at least as early as 1712. See the complaint about this in *Original and Genuine Letters sent to the Tatler and Spectator*, ed. Charles Lillie (London, 1725), vol. I, pp. 255–256.

4 See *Othello . . . as performed at the Theatre Royal, Drury Lane, Regulated from the Prompt-Book . . . By Mr. Hopkins, Prompter. An introduction, and notes critical and illustrative by the authors of The Dramatic Censor* [Francis Gentleman], London, Printed for John Bell . . . and C. Etherington, at York, 1773, p. 210. (This is part of Bell's bound volume, with page numbers beginning at 151; the edition also appeared separately.) Gentleman's notes to this edition will be referred to in the text. Further comments of the same general kind appear in his *The Dramatic Censor* (London, 1770), vol. I, pp. 131 ff.

Whether Gentleman was sincere in expressing as his own the contemporary moral attitudes, or was only opportunistically "echoing back the publick voice" to win favor with readers, has been considered at some length: see the unpublished dissertation (University of North Carolina, 1950) by Philip Henry Highfill, Jr., "A Study of Francis Gentleman's *The Dramatic Censor* (1770)." Highfill concludes ". . . it is my contention that Gentleman's moral criticism, as all-pervading as it seems to the modern reader, is probably based ultimately on a desire for critical success . . ." (p. 129). With Foote's comedies, Gentleman cut his morality to fit bawdry. He happened to share certain social prejudices with Foote, and had motives to propitiate the satirist; hence he professed to find realism and significant satire in material much more "indecent" than the Shakespearean lines he found so shocking. Highfill finds some extenuation for his hypocrisy, but not much (pp. 288–289).

5 Gentleman, *op. cit.*, p. 230.

6 Benjamin Victor, *History of the Theatres of London and Dublin* (London, 1761), vol. II, pp. 13, 8–9. Italics for stage directions are mine.

7 Benjamin Victor, *Memoirs of the Life of Barton Booth* (London, 1733), p. 29; Theophilus Cibber, *The Lives and Characters of the Most Eminent Actors and Actresses of Great Britain and Ireland, from Shakespeare to the Present Time, Interspersed with a General History of the Stage* (London, 1753), p. 50.

8 See Gabriel Harrison, *Edwin Forrest* (Brooklyn, 1889), p. 53. Thomas Davies declared he "could neither express the tender nor violent emotions of the heart" (*Life of Garrick*, Boston, 1818), vol. I, p. 3. See also Genest, *History of the Drama and Stage in England from 1660 to 1830* (Bath, 1832), vol. IV, p. 375.

[9] Samuel Foote, *A Treatise on the Passions So far as they regard the Stage; with a critical Enquiry into the THEATRICAL MERIT of Mr. G — K, Mr. Q— N, and Mr. B — Y. The first considered in the part of Lear, the two last opposed in Othello* (London, 1747). See also Davies, *op. cit.*

[10] *Gentleman's Magazine*, Nov., 1734.

[11] *The Poetical Works of Charles Churchill* (London, 1844), vol. I, p. 99. Macklin wrote that if he had tried the trance scene, the audience would have laughed at him.

[12] Foote, *op. cit.* Victor agreed that he was virtually without feeling. Benjamin Victor, *Original Letters* (London, 1776), pp. 97 ff.

[13] William Cooke, *Memoirs of the Life of Charles Macklin* (London, 1804), p. 13.

[14] George Colman and Bonnell Thornton, the *Connoisseur*, no. 34 (Sept. 19, 1754), written on the heels of Quin's retirement. See *British Essayists* (London, 1823), vol. XXVI, pp. 172–173.

[15] Percy Fitzgerald, *Life of Garrick*, p. 53; Victor, *History, op. cit.*, vol. III, p. 86.

[16] Frank Hedgcock, *A Cosmopolitan Actor: David Garrick and His French Friends* (London, 1912), p. 341 *n.*

[17] James T. Kirkman, *Memoirs of the Life of Charles Macklin* (London, 1799), vol. II, pp. 260–261. That letter writer to the *Spectator* mourned the elimination of this scene by 1711–1712, but his voice was lost in the tide of refinement. To him, it had seemed "a thing not strain'd, but very natural, which once did give great satisfaction."

[18] See Kirkman, *op. cit.*; W. Clark Russell, *Representative Actors* (London, n.d.), p. 119; G. W. Stone, Jr., unpublished dissertation, "Garrick's Treatment of Shakespeare's Plays" (Harvard, 1940), p. 123.

[19] Victor, *Original Letters, op. cit.*

[20] Aston pretended to pass on the opinions of a third party. Protected by this time-honored dodge, he criticized freely. (*The Private Correspondence of David Garrick. With the Most Celebrated Persons of His Time*, London, 1881, p. 30.)

[21] Cooke, *op. cit.*, p. 113.

[22] Aaron Hill, *Works* (London, 1753), vol. I, pp. 217–218.

[23] H. W. Baker, *John Philip Kemble* (Cambridge, 1942), p. 250, speaks of the "chill grace" of his style.

[24] Arthur Colby Sprague, *Shakespearian Players and Performances* (Cambridge, 1953), Chapter III. All workers in theater research are indebted to Sprague for this and his other volumes.

[25] *The Thespiad* (London, 1809), pp. 16–18, quoted in Alan Downer's "Nature to Advantage Dressed: 18th Century Acting," *PMLA*, LVIII (Dec., 1943), 1002–1037. I am obliged to Downer for valuable insights into the acting of the time.

[26] James Boaden, *Memoirs of the Life of John Philip Kemble, Including a History of the Stage from the Time of Garrick* (London, 1825), vol. I, p. 292.

27 See *The Attic: or Characteristic Mirror of Men and Things* (London, 1789), vol. 1, p. 88, in Downer, *op. cit.*, p. 1018, for a lampoon of Kemble's declamatory manner in the Senate speech. The *Morning Herald* (Sept., 1783) said cruelly that his whole interpretation "was contending at once against Nature."

28 Percy Fitzgerald, *The Kembles* (1917), vol. II, p. 336.

29 W. C. Macready, *Reminiscences* (New York, 1875), p. 88.

30 Hazlitt, *Works,* Centenary edition, ed. P. P. Howe (London, 1930), vol. V, p. 338.

31 Baker, *op. cit.*, p. 125.

32 *Life of Kemble*, pp. 256–257.

33 Thomas Davies, *op. cit.*, vol. II, pp. 176–177.

34 See the *Dramatic Censor*, vol. I, pp. 150–151. The need for sheer physical reserves in Othello was pointed out by John Hill (*The Actor* [London, 1755], p. 46): ". . . tis an invariable rule that the coldest representation is the most defective. The principal thing the actor has to observe, when the circumstances of his part make it necessary that he should be vehement, is that he does not strain his voice, so as to render it incapable of carrying him thro' the rest of the piece . . . There are some peculiar characters on the English stage, and those of the very first consequence, in which a caution of this kind is very necessary to the actor . . . among the principal of these . . . Othello."

35 See John Bernard, *Retrospections of the Stage* (London, 1830), pp. 26–30.

36 Cooke, *op. cit.*, pp. 180 ff.

37 *London Chronicle*, March 5–8, 1757, p. 231.

38 Quoted by William Winter, *Shakespeare on the Stage* (New York, 1911), p. 247. Winter gives no source, and is no scholar; but this phrase seemed too good for him to make up, and it seemed consistent with contemporary reports of Barry's action here. Thus The *Daily Advertiser* (October 7, 1746) said the address had the "Diffidence of one unused to speak in such Assemblies . . . it had a fine Effect, and certainly more in Nature than a mouthing Vociferation . . . which has been the practice of celebrated actors . . ."

39 Cooke, *op. cit.* For other praise of the amazing flexibility and beauty of this Othello's voice, see the *Craftsman*, Jan. 25, 1777; the *Theatrical Review, or Annals of the Drama* (London, 1763), pp. 227–228; *Candid and Impartial Observations of the Principal Performers Belonging to the two Theatres Royal* . . . (London, 1774), p. 3.

40 Bernard, *op. cit.*

41 Cooke, *op. cit.*

42 Bernard, *op. cit.*, p. 28. This was "the terrible at its utmost height"— *The Theatrical Review for the Year 1757* . . . (London, 1758).

43 These paragraphs on Barry come from John Hill, Bernard, Cooke, and Foote, *loc. cit.* and from the *Theatrical Review*, Jan., 1772, pp. 8 ff., and the *London Magazine*, July, 1767.

[44] *Gentleman's Magazine*, Nov., 1734; Thomas Davies, *Dramatic Miscellanies* (London, 1784), vol. III, p. 440.

[45] Johnson, *Works* (London, 1810), vol. II, p. 144; Gentleman, *op. cit.*, p. 155.

[46] Though Booth would obscure it by deleting " 'Twixt my sheets." See *The Shakespearean Plays of Edwin Booth*, ed. William Winter, (Philadelphia, 1899), p. 32.

[47] Gentleman, *op. cit.*, p. 175.

[48] *Ibid.*, p. 203.

[49] *Ibid.*, p. 205.

[50] Cooke, *op. cit.*, p. 407. Kirkman, *op. cit.* (vol. I, pp. 301–303), speaks of his "distant, artful manner," his "hypocritical diffidence," the "subtle affectation of chagrin" at Othello's angry suspicion.

[51] *The Actor*, p. 274; and see B. Matthews and L. Hutton, *Actors and Actresses of Great Britain and the United States* (New York, 1886), vol. I, p. 9.

[52] Edward A. Parry, *Charles Macklin* (London, 1891), pp. 28–29. He was praised for the "silent eloquence of his gestures, looks, pauses."

[53] *London Chronicle*, LXII (Oct. 11–13, 1787), p. 359.

[54] *Monthly Mirror*, N. S. III (Jan., 1808), 51–52; Irving quoted in Matthews and Hutton, *op. cit.*, vol. II, p. 6.

[55] *European Magazine*, Sept., 1783, Dec., 1829; James Boaden, *Memoirs of Mrs. Siddons* (London, 1893), p. 245. Similarly, Kirkman, *op. cit.*, vol. I, p. 329, criticized Ryan: "In his plausibility and ease he was very commendable; but he appeared very deficient in design."

[56] *Monthly Mirror*, *op. cit.*

[57] Foote, *op. cit.*, p. 36.

[58] Boaden, *Mrs. Siddons*, p. 320.

[59] Boaden, *Kemble*, pp. 258 ff. Here the offending critic (*European Magazine*, March, 1775) was quoting from a comment on "modern" acting. But of a later Siddons Desdemona the same year, the magazine commented (Sept.), "Never, perhaps, did this great actress appear with more effect."

[60] *Mrs. Siddons*, p. 321; *Kemble*, pp. 259–260.

[61] Gentleman, *op. cit.*, p. 210.

[62] *Mrs. Siddons*, pp. 321–322.


# PART III
The Nineteenth Century
(Pages 55–60)

[1] *Monthly Mirror*, N. S. III (Jan., 1808), 51.

[2] See William Jaggard, *Shakespeare Bibliography* (Stratford, 1911), p. 504.

[3] *Hinds English Stage* (London, 1938).

4 *Letters* (Bloomsbury, 1938), vol. I, p. 8.

5 Cyril Pearl, *The Girl With the Swansdown Seat* (New York, 1956), pp. 235–237. Pearl's book is a popular history of proud Victorian whoredom.

## Chapter 4
KEAN
(Pages 61–69)

1 See Julian Charles Young, *A Memoir of Charles Mayne Young* (London, 1871), p. 57.

2 See Barry Cornwall, *The Life of Edmund Kean* (London, 1835), pp. 79–80; and the *Theatrical Inquisitor and Monthly Mirror*, April, 1814, 306, which summed up the criticism by observing that Kean was "deficient in that quality which among painters is called keeping."

3 Cornwall, *Life, op. cit.*, pp. 83–85: ". . . the son of a burning soil, transplanted into the camp, and tamed."

4 See *ibid.*, pp. 85–86, and W. R. Alger, *Life of Edwin Forrest* (New York, 1877), vol. I, p. 142.

5 See *Life*, vol. II, pp. 165 ff, on his performance with Junius Brutus Booth. (Subsequently, Booth left England for America. His Othello was impressive but not first rank, and I felt a discussion of it in detail was not needed in this book. A full description will be found in T. R. Gould, *The Tragedian*, Cambridge, 1868). See also, later, the account of Kean's performance with Macready.

6 See Hazlitt, *London Magazine* (Jan., 1820), in *Works*, vol. 18, p. 278.

7 *Ibid.* (Sept., 1820), *Works*, vol. 18, p. 332.

8 G. H. Lewes, *On Actors and the Art of Acting* (New York, 1956), p. 18.

9 Lord Granville Leveson Gower, *Private Correspondence 1781 to 1821*, ed. Castalia Countess Granville (London, 1916), vol. I, p. 457; quoted in A. C. Sprague's valuable *Shakespearian Players and Performances* (Cambridge, 1953), p. 79. Sprague has an excellent chapter on Kean's Othello in this book.

10 "On Edmund Kean as a Shakespearean Actor," *Works*, vol. V, p. 230. However, Sprague (*op. cit.*, p. 79) notes that another observer felt Kean strove too much for effect here.

11 Lewes, *op. cit.*, p. 17. Lewes disapproved of this kind of sudden transitional "point."

12 F. H. Hawkins, *Life of Edmund Kean* (London, 1869), vol. II, p. 382; Henry Ottley, *Fechter's Version of Othello Critically Analyzed* (London, 1861), pp. 19–20.

13 Frances Anne Butler, *Journal* (Philadelphia, 1835), vol. I, p. 147; see Sprague, *op. cit.*, p. 81, quoting John Finlay, *Miscellanies*.

14 Hawkins, *op. cit.*, p. 209; Sprague, *op. cit.*, p. 82.

[15] Charles Durang, "History of the Philadelphia Stage," series 1, chapter LXXII, quoted from Sprague, *op. cit.*, p. 6.

[16] *Times*, May 14, 1814. The *Times* was the more impressed because this was an early Kean Othello.

[17] Matthews and Hutton, *Actors and Actresses* . . . (New York, 1886), vol. III, p. 7. Crabb Robinson almost wept; it reminded him of a lover's farewell to his mistress. *Diary, Reminiscences and Correspondence* . . . (London, 1869), vol. I, p. 430.

[18] Keats, *op. cit.*

[19] Leigh Hunt, *Dramatic Criticism* (New York, 1949), ed. L. H. and C. W. Houtchens, pp. 201–202.

[20] Hawkins, *op. cit.*, vol. I, p. 229.

[21] Henry Ottley, *Fechter's Version of Othello Critically Analyzed* (London, 1861), p. 32. Hawkins (*op. cit.*, vol. I, pp. 229–230) reports, "he repeated the word, quickly, and almost inarticulately, and with a half-smile of wonder at his incredible stupidity in having been such a fool."

[22] Leigh Hunt, *Dramatic Essays* (London, 1894), p. 229; Hawkins *op. cit.*, vol. I, p. 231; the *Theatre*, 11, 209–214 (October 1, 1880).

[23] *Examiner* (Jan. 7, 1816), in *Works*, vol. V, p. 271; and *Times* (Oct. 27, 1817), in *Works*, vol. XVIII, p. 263. His only objection here was the "virulence" of the last line.

[24] *London Magazine* (Sept., 1820), in *Works*, vol. XVIII, pp. 362–363.

[25] Lewes, *op. cit.*, p. 19.

[26] Fanny Kemble wrote, "When not in action, he was comparatively insignificant." "Salvini's Othello," *Temple Bar*, 71 (July, 1884), 368–378.

[27] Hazlitt, *Works*, vol. XVIII, p. 262.

[28] Thomas Colley Grattan, quoted in Nigel Playfair, *Kean* (London, 1950), p. 166.

[29] *Ibid.*, pp. 241, 243.

[30] Lewes, quoted, *ibid.*, p. 312. *The Court Journal* was rather more aware of Kean's infirmities (Dec. 1, 1832), 794; *The Theatrical Observer* (Nov. 27, 1832) thought Macready "surpassed himself" in playing up to Kean.

[31] *Life, op. cit.*, pp. 239–241. Kean did not die that night, but now death was only a matter of time; his acting career was over.


Chapter 5
MACREADY, FECHTER, IRVING
(Pages 70–79)

[1] ". . . he had scarcely a friend in the profession, at any rate of the masculine gender. Coldly ceremonious when in a good temper, fiercely abusive when in a bad one, always on the watch for slights, and morbidly alert to conjure up affronts, his existence in the theatre was little better than a long-drawn ordeal to himself and a frequent source of exaspera-

tion to his colleagues." William Toynbee, ed., *Diaries of William Charles Macready* (New York, 1912), preface.

² See J. C. Trewin, *Mr. Macready* (London, 1955), p. 205. Forster and the Pollocks, for instance, could be counted on for high praise; but their eulogies, and the occasional paeans by others, were not substantiated by comment that seemed to me more reliable. Where their praise *is* substantiated, as in the case of Macready's Iago, I accept them. For a large collection of Macready materials, see *William Charles Macready, A Memorial*, ed. Sir Frederick Pollock, Bart. (Comprising *Macready's Reminiscences*, interleaved with playbills, reviews, and so on).

³ John Coleman, *Players and Playwrights I Have Known* (London, 1888), p. 49. Joseph Knight, the *Athenaeum* critic, wrote (*Theatrical Notes*, London, 1893, p. 19): "Othello was the weakest of his Shaksperian performances. So weak was it, that men who, with the present writer, contemplated in it the most intellectual of Tragedians for the first time doubted whether his reputation was merited, and were scarcely disposed to see him in a second part."

⁴ Junius Browne, in *Galaxy*, XVI (Dec., 1873), 819.

⁵ *Nicholas Nickleby* (Imperial Edition, London, 1901), p. 489. Dickens, who dedicated the manuscript of the novel to Macready, may have had his acting friend in mind. Macready, it is said, would work himself into an anger offstage by "cursing *sotto voce* and shaking violently a ladder." Lewes, *On Actors and the Art of Acting* (New York, 1956), p. 44.

⁶ The *Spectator*, XXII (1849), 966–967, quoted in Alan Downer's "Players and Painted Stage—Nineteenth Century Acting," *PMLA*, LXI (June, 1946), 2, 522–576. (Like Downer's essay on eighteenth-century acting, previously quoted, this is a very useful study.) See also Joseph Knight, note 3 above.

⁷ *Bell's Weekly Messenger*, Nov. 17, 1822. See Barry Cornwall, *The Life of Edmund Kean* (London, 1899), p. 237.

⁸ *Works*, vol. V, pp. 339–340.

⁹ *Theatrical Inquisitor and Monthly Mirror*, IX, 312.

¹⁰ Lewes, *op. cit.*, p. 41; William Archer, *William Charles Macready* (London, 1870), pp. 202–203; Lester Wallack, *Memories of Fifty Years* (New York, 1889), p. 132, quoting an actor named Fredericks. Wallack wrote that Macready looked more like a very tall woman than a soldierly man (p. 131).

¹¹ W. C. Macready, *Reminiscences*, ed. Sir Frederick Pollock (New York, 1875), pp. 276, 356, 358 (Oct. 21, 1835); Toynbee, *op. cit.*, vol. 1, p. 28. Later in 1836 Macready felt better—though not satisfied—with his performances: see *ibid.* pp. 354, 356; *Reminiscences*, pp. 359, 566 (March, 1845).

¹² Trewin, *op. cit.*

¹³ George Vandenhoff, *Leaves from an Actor's Notebook* (London, 1860), p. 223. Vandenhoff was not exactly a friend of Macready's; but he was fair enough to say that Macready's splendid Macbeth and Iago were so far beyond the rest of contemporary acting as to be of another

century (See Coleman, *op. cit.*, p. 49). His comments on Macready's stage vanity are repeated by others over and over. See also how Macready treated his heroines in the chapter on the Victorian Desdemona.

[14] See *Othello, Charles Fechter's Acting Edition* (London, 1861), preface, where the actor proposed to destroy the "unwholesome prison" of tradition where "Dramatic Art languished in fetters."

[15] J. W. Cross, *Life of George Eliot*, vol. II, p. ii, quoted in Matthews and Hutton, vol. IV, p. 221.

[16] Lewes, *op. cit.*, p. 117.

[17] *Ibid.*, p. 131.

[18] *Ibid.*, p. 128.

[19] *Ibid.*, p. 130.

[20] *Once a Week*, V (Nov. 30, 1861), 630. Henry Morley, *Journal of a London Playgoer* (London, 1866), pp. 274, 275 was troubled by his "curious French politeness" here.

[21] Lewes, *op. cit.*, p. 132.

[22] See Morley, *op. cit.*, p. 275, and Lewes, *op. cit.*, p. 132.

[23] Morley, *op. cit.*, p. 275, J. R. Towse, *Sixty Years of the Theater* (New York, 1916), p. 79.

[24] Lewes, *op. cit.*, pp. 132–134.

[25] Fechter lost his effect of introducing the trance by suggesting an almost physical disease beforehand (Morley, *op. cit.*, p. 275), and then withdrawing the seizure offstage so that, in Ottley's words (Henry Ottley, *Fechter's Version of Othello Critically Analyzed*, London, 1861, pp. 10–11), "Fancy Othello, on the rise of the curtain of the fourth act, being discovered 'stretched unconscious on the Divan' [Fechter's stage direction] . . . Othello now lies on his back on a narrow settee, which is much too short for him, his head dangling at one end, his legs at the other . . ." He might as well have been dozing, Lewes thought, for "when he rises . . . he is indeed as calm and unaffected by the fit as if he had only been asleep." (Lewes, *op. cit.*, p. 135). When Fechter attempted to point up the racial insecurity in Othello by looking in the mirror, Lewes thought he muffed the point, and Morley was simply confused (Morley, *op. cit.*, p. 274). It was generally agreed that the essence of the actor's failure was distilled in his business in Othello's last speech, of first seizing Iago as the "circumcis'd dog" before finally stabbing himself: "it was in the worst taste of a small melodramatic theatre" (Macready, *Reminiscences, op. cit.*, p. 720).

[26] *Athenaeum* (Oct. 26, 1861), 549.

[27] Nov. 16, 1861, 654.

[28] Lewes, *op. cit.*, p. 130; the *Morning Advertiser*, Nov., 1861, quoted in W. May Phelps, *The Life and Life Work of Samuel Phelps* (London, 1886), p. 200.

[29] Charles Hiatt, *Henry Irving* (London, 1899), p. 138.

[30] *Athenaeum* (Feb. 19, 1876), 276.

[31] Dutton Cook, *Nights at the Play* (London, 1883), p. 308.

[32] Quoted in James Agate, *The Contemporary Theatre* (New York, 1945), pp. 36–37. But she liked his address to the Senate.

[33] See the *Athenaeum* (Feb. 19, 1876), 276: "No great conception animates and intensifies the impersonation."

[34] J. Ranken Towse, in Matthews and Hutton, *Actors and Actresses* . . . (New York, 1886), vol. V, p. 146.

[35] *Athenaeum* (Feb. 19, 1876), 276.

[36] *Ibid*. And the passionate scenes were "more frequently violent than intense."

[37] *Academy*, IX (Feb. 19, 1876), 182.

[38] *Saturday Review of Politics*, XLI (Feb. 19, 1876), 239 ff.

[39] William Archer and R. W. Lowe, *The Fashionable Tragedian* (London, 1877), pp. 14–18. It was a mark of special praise when a critic wrote that all Irving said was clear. See Laurence Irving, *Henry Irving* (London, 1951), p. 377.

[40] *Ibid*.

## Chapter 6
BOOTH
(Pages 80–88)

[1] This quality can still be perceived in the old Booth recordings.

[2] *Boston Evening Transcript*, May 10, 1867.

[3] *Ibid*., March 6, 1878. A few years earlier, Booth's Salvini-like Othello had been less impressive. The reviewer recalled preferring the actor's "sweeter and tenderer" Moor of the past. (*Ibid*., March 18, 1875). Booth himself liked Salvini, and admired his Othello conception. See Edwina Booth Grossman, *Edwin Booth* (New York, 1894), p. 71.

[4] T. B., "Edwin Booth in Germany," quoting the *Börsenzeitung*, the *Nation*, 36 (April 26, 1883), 359.

[5] See note 3, above.

[6] For a summary of Booth's style, see Garff Wilson's "Versatile Tragedians: Edwin Booth and James E. Murdoch," *Speech Monographs*, 19 (March, 1952).

[7] *New York Herald*, Oct. 4, 1862, quoted in G. C. Odell, *Annals of the New York Stage* (New York, 1931), vol. VII, p. 476. The *Herald* said they were depicted with "thrilling truth and earnestness."

[8] Though the *Athenaeum* (Jan. 22, 1881), p. 141, doubted if *any* English-speaking actor now could do any more than make a "character part" out of Othello.

[9] *Macmillan's* (July, 1881), 214.

[10] *Nation, op. cit.* The indignant American who relayed this German report said this German really wanted a savage "let loose to do murder."

[11] See William Winter, *Shakespeare on the Stage* (New York, 1911), p. 268.

[12] *Saturday Review of Politics,* LI (Feb. 5, 1881), 177; LI (May 7, 1881), 593.

[13] *Academy,* XIX (May 7, 1881), 344–345.

[14] Harping on its old theme, the journal added: "That passion is inadequately expressed . . . we own with resignation since things may not be otherwise . . . Failure, however, attends all Mr. Booth's attempts to go outside his limits, and within these limits there is so much that is excellent, we are content to keep him there." May 7, 1881, p. 633.

[15] Booth's directions, unless otherwise identified, are from the Furness *Variorum.* See note 20, below.

[16] M. E. Sherwood in the *New York Times,* January 20, 1875. In Matthews and Hutton, *Actors and Actresses* . . . (New York, 1886), vol. V, p. 72.

[17] *Saturday Review of Politics,* LI (Feb. 5, 1881), 177.

[18] *Ibid.*

[19] *Ibid.*

[20] See *Variorum,* pp. 32, 38, 54, 62, 113, 164–165, 186, 194, 198, 203, 204, for quotations from Booth to this point.

[21] Feb. 5, 1881, 177.

[22] *Nation, op. cit.*

[23] *Boston Transcript,* March 6, 1878.

[24] *Variorum,* p. 214.

[25] Ellen Terry, *The Story of My Life* (New York, 1909), p. 223.

[26] *Variorum,* pp. 217, 223, 208, 297.

[27] *Ibid.,* p. 300.

[28] Junius Browne, *Galaxy,* XVI (Dec., 1873), 824.

[29] Winter, *op. cit.*

[30] *Variorum,* pp. 326, 332.

[31] William Winter, *Shakespearean Plays of Edwin Booth* (Philadelphia, 1899), and Hinton's edition, which has a few variations.

[32] See appendix.

[33] *Athenaeum, op. cit.*

[34] Winter, *Shakespeare on the Stage,* p. 268.

[35] *Galaxy,* XVI (Dec., 1873), 822, 824.

## Chapter 7
### FORREST
(Pages 89–101)

[1] Gabriel Harrison, *Edwin Forrest* (New York, 1889), p. 64.

[2] W. R. Alger, *Life of Edwin Forest* (Philadelphia, 1877), vol. II, p. 497. The story of the divorce and the verbatim references are taken from Alger, pp. 486–503, and from Richard Moody, *Edwin Forrest* (New York, 1960), pp. 245 ff.

[3] John Foster Kirk, "Shakespeare's Tragedies on the Stage," *Lippincott's,* XXXIII (June, 1884), 604, 605.

[4] See Alger, *op. cit.,* vol. II, p. 480, and Herman Vezin, in the *Dramatic*

*Review*, quoted in Matthews and Hutton, *Actors and Actresses* . . . (New York, 1886), vol. IV, p. 57.

5 Kirk, *op. cit.*, p. 606. Barbara Alden, "Edwin Forrest's Othello," *Theatre Annual*, XIV, 1956, concludes that Forrest's ranting diminished as the actor developed. Forster (*Dramatic Essays*, 17) thought Forrest was generally poor in the role. But Forster was a friend of Macready, Forrest's rival. John Forster, *Dramatic Essays* (London, 1896).

6 See the *London Sun*, quoted in Alger, *op. cit.*, vol. I, p. 305. For a New York opinion of his superiority to Kean, see *New York Mirror*, Nov. 30, 1833.

7 Alger, *op. cit.*, vol. II, p. 770.

8 Kirk, *op. cit.*, 606–607.

9 *New York Mirror*, Nov. 26, 1836, p. 174.

10 Alger, *op. cit.*, vol. II, p. 770. Alger has a very full description of Forrest's Othello (vol. II, pp. 768–780). Further references not specifically identified will be from this section.

11 Dec. 14, 1833.

12 *New York Literary Gazette and American Athenaeum*, III (Nov. 11, 1826), 118.

13 This description of Forrest's early jealousy is from the detailed account by Harrison, *op. cit.*, pp. 84–87.

14 Quoted in Alger, *op. cit.*, vol. I, p. 308.

15 *John Bull*, quoted in Alger, *op. cit.*, vol. I, p. 306. There was an early time when he actually imitated the sounds he mentioned in the Farewell: he neighed "the neighing steed," and shrilled "the shrill trumpet." But he learned better (*ibid.*, vol. II, p. 649).

16 Alger, *op. cit.*, vol. II, p. 775. See also *New York Mirror*, *op. cit.*, Harrison, *op. cit.*, pp. 89–90.

17 Harrison, *op. cit.*, p. 64.

18 *Galaxy*, XVI (Dec. 1873), 820–821.

19 Alger, *op. cit.*, vol. II, pp. 773–774, 775. Alger describes Forrest's technique in these "sudden and violent transitions from extreme to extreme with exact truth to nature, by that constant interchanging of intense muscles and languid eyes with intense eyes and languid muscles."

20 Kirk, *op. cit.*, 606. This change does not appear in Forrest's promptbook, nor does his use, as noted further in the text, of "O the world hath not a sweeter creature."

21 Alger, *op. cit.*, vol. II, pp. 773–774, 775.

22 Though Kirk (*op. cit.*, 607) thought it ludicrously exaggerated: " 'Twas I that did it' with the exaggerated emphasis on the first word and the exaggerated prolongation of the second, accompanied by a vigorous thumping on the breast, like some barbarian chief boasting of his warlike exploits."

23 Alger, *op. cit.*, vol. II, p. 777.

24 *New York Mirror*, Dec. 14, 1833, Nov. 26, 1826.

25 This is the *Mirror*'s account; Harrison remembered him dying on the kiss.

26 *Galaxy*, *op. cit.*

27 Matthews and Hutton, *op. cit.*, vol. IV, p. 46.

28 See Garff Wilson's excellent summary of "The Acting of Edwin Forrest," *Quarterly Journal of Speech*, XXXVI (Dec., 1950), 483–491.

29 Alger, *op. cit.*, vol. II, pp. 768–769.

30 Harrison, *op. cit.*, p. 91.

31 See Wilson, *op. cit.*, for a thoughtful statement of Forrest's limited imagination.

## Chapter 8
### SALVINI
(Pages 102–119)

1 Fanny Kemble, "Salvini's Othello," *Temple Bar*, 71 (July, 1884), 376; J. R. Towse, *Sixty Years of the Theatre* (New York, 1916), p. 158.

2 Henry James, *The Scenic Art* (New York, 1957), p. 175.

3 *Ibid.*, p. 172.

4 April 10, 1875.

5 XVI, Dec., 1873, 824.

6 James, *op. cit.*, p. 189.

7 Edwina Booth Grossman, *Edwin Booth* (New York, 1894), p. 71. See also Salvini, *Leaves from the Autobiography* (New York, 1893), *passim.*

8 Towse, *op. cit.*, p. 161.

9 E. T. Mason, *The Othello of Tommaso Salvini* (New York, 1890), p. 61.

10 W. E. Henley, "Salvini," *Littell's Living Age*, CLXI (April, May, June, 1884), 470.

11 *Ibid.*, 469.

12 Mason, *op. cit.*, pp. 12, 13. Henley agreed that Salvini was rhetorical here; Miss Lazarus (see note 16, below) cites a somewhat more restrained performance—though it, too, included occasional "oratorical" moments here. The *Academy* (April 10, 1875), 385, saw "no artifice whatever of rhetoric." Clement Scott (*The Drama of Yesterday, and Today*, London, 1899) thought the speech "exquisitely graceful."

13 Mason, *op. cit.*, p. 13. Mason's description of Salvini's Othello is done in close detail, and anyone interested in its minutiae should consult his little book. Hereafter, quotations not otherwise identified will be drawn from it. The cuts in Salvini's text are reported from *Othello, The Italian Version as performed by Signior Salvini* [the English text on facing pages], (New York, 1873).

14 *Athenaeum*, April 10, 1875.

15 Henry Austin Clapp, *Reminiscences of a Dramatic Critic* (Boston, 1902), p. 146; *Galaxy* (Dec., 1873), 824.

16 Emma Lazarus, "Tommaso Salvini," *Century Magazine*, XXIII (Nov., 1881), 114.

[17] The *Academy, op. cit.* Towse thought he retorted to Brabantio's hint "with a superb gesture of smiling confidence." Winter (and Browne, in *Galaxy, op. cit.*), thought there was an early show of jealousy here. But Salvini says he was only reacting here to a "blasphemy . . . yet it leaves its impression."

[18] *Athenaeum,* April 10, 1875.

[19] Kemble, *op. cit.,* 375.

[20] *Ibid.*

[21] *Ibid.*

[22] *New York Herald,* Sept. 19, 1873; *Athenaeum,* April 10, 1875.

[23] Henley, *op. cit.,* 469; Frank Archer, *An Actor's Notebooks* (London, n.d.), pp. 166–167.

[24] *Athenaeum, op. cit.*

[25] Winter, *Shakespeare on the Stage* (New York, 1911), pp. 290, 298.

[26] Lewes, *On Actors and the Art of Acting* (New York, 1956), p. 226.

[27] Henley, *op. cit.,* 470. See also Lazarus, *op. cit.,* 115, on this same passage: ". . . not only defies criticism but makes even praise seem impertinent."

[28] Salvini felt the gap in motivation was taken care of by his comment, in V, that he had seen the handkerchief in Cassio's hand. See *Variorum,* p. 237.

[29] Towse, *op. cit.,* p. 160.

[30] *Variorum,* p. 251.

[31] Towse, *op. cit.,* p. 163.

[32] *Galaxy, op. cit.,* 823–824.

[33] Towse, *op. cit.,* p. 159.

[34] Archer, *op. cit.,* p. 168.

[35] James, *op. cit.,* pp. 174–175.

[36] See Appendix.

[37] "Impressions of Some Shakespearean Characters," in *Century Magazine,* XXXIII (Nov., 1881), 122–124.

[38] James, *op. cit.,* p. 175.

[39] Winter, *op. cit.,* pp. 295–297.

[40] For instance, Dillon (see the *Athenaeum,* Dec. 6, 1856), and Fairclough (*ibid.,* Sept. 12, 1868). See also Winter, *op. cit.,* and T. R. Gould, *The Tragedian* (Cambridge, 1868), on the elder Booth's Othello.

[41] *Dame Madge Kendal,* by herself (London, 1933), pp. 86–87.

[42] *Illustrated London News* (July 3, 1858).

[43] Theophile Gautier, *Voyage en Russie* (Paris, n.d.), pp. 154 ff. Herbert Marshall and Mildred Stock, in their exhaustive study of Aldridge (*Ira Aldridge, The Negro Tragedian,* London, 1958) note other reports of his characterization as "intellectual," and like Macready's. See pp. 84, 124, 144. While some enthusiastic reviews are reported, the book as a whole confirms the London consensus that Aldridge's Othello was not one of the great ones.

[44] W. J. Lawrence, *The Life of Gustavus Vaughan Brooke* (Belfast, 1892), p. 244.

Chapter 9
THE VICTORIAN IAGO
(Pages 120–134)

[1] *John Cumberland's British Theatre* (London, 1829), vol. II, p. vi.

[2] See the *News* (London), Oct., 1816 (on Young); *Theatrical Inquisitor*, Oct. 23, 1817 (on Maywood). The *Edinburgh Dramatic Review* (March 14, 1823) thought Young displayed "all the machinations of the petty devil." See *Letters from a Theatrical Scene Painter*, Twynihoe W. Erle (London, 1880), pp. 48–50, for a satirical sketch of the stock villains of the day.

[3] James R. Anderson, *An Actor's Life* (London, 1902), p. 128.

[4] *Academy*, LI (May 29, 1897).

[5] Barry Cornwall, *The Life of Edmund Kean* (London, 1835), p. 74.

[6] See F. H. Hawkins, *Life of Edmund Kean* (London, 1869), vol. I, p. 135, for a description of how he hovered over the dead Roderigo in the last act—one of his brilliant bits of business.

[7] Cornwall, *Life, op. cit.*, p. 74.

[8] Hazlitt, *Works*, vol. XVIII, pp. 200 ff. Hazlitt was partly answering Leigh Hunt, who replied (*Examiner*, Sept. 18, 1814) that his meaning had been mistaken.

[9] Hazlitt, *Examiner* (Aug. 7, 1814), in *Works*, vol. V, p. 221.

[10] Hazlitt, *Morning Chronicle* (May 9, 1814), in *Works*, vol. V, p. 190.

[11] *Ibid.*

[12] *Punch*, XLI (Nov. 16, 1861), 194.

[13] W. J. Lawrence, *The Life of Gustavus Vaughan Brooke* (Belfast, 1892), p. 51. Forrest himself was an Iago in the Kean fashion, but he, too, dropped the part—he did not like to play villains. The *New York Gazette* (Dec. 23, 1826) found him often "too colloquial . . . passionless."

[14] Lawrence, *op. cit.*, pp. 66, 132.

[15] Quoted in Harold Hillebrand, *Edmund Kean* (New York, 1933), p. 129.

[16] *Saturday Review of Politics*, XLI (Feb. 18, 1876), 239.

[17] *Athenaeum* (Feb. 19, 1876), 276.

[18] This had always been the mark of a good Iago. See the account of Macklin, above, and see *Essays of Elia* (New York, n.d.), "On Some of the Old Actors," pp. 163–164, for Lamb's account of Bensley's "honest" surface: "His confession in soliloquy alone put you in possession of the mystery."

[19] George Vandenhoff, *Leaves from an Actor's Notebook* (London, 1860). Though Vandenhoff told Coleman that the performances of other actors were not in the same century with Macready's Iago. John Coleman, *Players and Playwrights I Have Known* (London, 1888), p. 49.

[20] Macready, *Reminiscences*, ed. Sir Frederick Pollock (New York, 1875), p. 90.

21 *Ibid.*, 273.

22 *Ibid.*, 309.

23 Coleman, *op. cit.*, p. 40.

24 Lady Pollock, *Macready as I Knew Him*, pp. 110–113.

25 Macready, *Reminiscences*, p. 648. All other actors, he felt, had only achieved superficial characterization. But even this moment of completion was tinged with self-pity: "But what is the difference to an audience? To how many among them does the deep reflection, the toil of thought, carried out into the most animated and energetic personation, speak its own necessary course of labour? By how many among them is the 'poor' player appreciated?"

26 *Morning Chronicle*, quoted in *Public Opinion* (March 8, 1862), 642.

27 "On Mr. Fechter's Acting," *Atlantic Monthly*, XXIV (Aug., 1869), 243.

28 In *Public Opinion*, *op. cit.*

29 Quoted in *ibid*. The *Morning Post* (Nov. 16, 1861, 654), which was not partial to Fechter's Othello, thought his Iago was his masterpiece.

30 See Henry Morley, *Journal of a London Playgoer* (London, 1866), p. 283.

31 *Ibid.*

32 *Ibid.*

33 *Athenaeum* (May 7, 1881), 633.

34 *Academy*, XIX (May 7, 1881), 345.

35 *Macmillan's*, XLIV (July, 1881), 210.

36 *Ibid.*, 212.

37 *Athenaeum* (May 7, 1881), 633. The *Daily Telegraph* (May 5, 1881) said: "In such a magnitude of study what is an extra pull of the moustache or a scratch of the head, a too marked jingle of the silver chains . . ."

38 H. M. Walbrook, "Henry Irving: His Personality and His Art," *The Stage Year Book* (New York, 1928), in Sprague, *Shakespeare and the Actors* (Cambridge, 1948), 189. Sprague notes that Ryder, earlier, had a somewhat similar business.

39 Sprague, *op. cit.*, p. 209. Alternately, he is said to have kicked the corpse "as if it had been carrion."

40 Ellen Terry, *The Story of My Life*, p. 224.

41 *Macmillan's, op. cit.*

42 *Macmillan's, op. cit.*

43 Henry Irving, "My Four Favorite Parts," *Forum* (Sept., 1893), 36.

44 *Macmillan's, op. cit.*, 213.

45 See note 37 above.

46 Laurence Irving, *Henry Irving* (London, 1951), p. 376.

47 Ellen Terry, *op. cit.*

48 Henry Irving, *op. cit.*, p. 36. Irving blandly disavowed the possibility that a true-born Englishman could be such a man. It was not easy, he wrote, "to impersonate the veritable spirit of a creation so foreign to our native thought and atmosphere."

[49] *Variorum*, p. 214. Booth's other *Variorum* notes will not be indicated separately in this chapter, since the scenes involved are always given.

[50] *Macmillan's, op. cit.*, 212. Booth could get lost in the part in real life. He wrote to Furness: "In Act III I made some remark regarding *Desdemona's* boldness which, I'm sure, does not express my opinion of her. I was *Iago* when I wrote it, not my cold-blooded self; his opinion of the 'guinea-hen' influenced me when I said 'she was bolder than her father supposed.'" Edwina Booth Grossman, *Edwin Booth* (New York, 1894), p. 256.

[51] Winter, *Shakespeare on the Stage* (New York, 1911), p. 271.

[52] See *New York Times*, Dec. 17, 1860.

[53] *Galaxy*, VII (Jan., 1869), 83.

[54] Though Towse (*Sixty Years of the Theatre*, New York, 1916, p. 190) thought Booth grew more stiff and labored with age.

[55] *Boston Evening Transcript*, May 11, 1886.

[56] *New York Herald*, April 30, 1886.

[57] Richard Lockridge, *Darling of Misfortune* (New York, 1932), 292; Grossman, *op. cit.*, p. 71.

[58] See Lockridge, *op. cit.*: "*The Evening Post* said Salvini's 'greatness' was never exhibited to better advantage than in [that] trying scene in New York."

[59] Tommaso Salvini, *Leaves from the Autobiography* (New York, 1893), p. 210.

[60] *Boston Transcript*, May 11, 1886. Even in younger days, Booth was not always at his best. The *New York Herald* once (April 27, 1869) was disappointed in his Iago: "a muddy-mettled rascal."

[61] Towse, *op. cit.*, p. 191.

[62] Winter, *Shakespeare on the Stage* (New York, 1911), p. 271.

[63] Richard Dickins, *Forty Years of Shakespeare on the English Stage* (London, 1907), 40; quoted in Sprague, *Shakespearian Players and Performances* (Cambridge, 1953), 129.

[64] Winter, *op. cit.*, pp. 271–272.

[65] Salvini, *op. cit.*, p. 124.

## Chapter 10
THE VICTORIAN DESDEMONA
(Pages 135–140)

[1] Frances A. Kemble, *Records of Later Life* (London, 1882), pp. 111, 380.

[2] *Ibid.*, pp. 368, 386.

[3] See *ibid.*, p. 378.

[4] *An Account of the Life of that Celebrated Actress, Mrs. Susannah Maria Cibber* (London, 1887), p. 11.

[5] Kemble, *op. cit.*, p. 368.

6 Robert W. Lowe, "Helen Faucit," in Matthews and Hutton, *Actors and Actresses* . . . (New York, 1886), vol. IV, p. 181.

7 This was not, of course, the last gasp. See Sir Theo. Martin, *Helen Faucit* (London, 1900), pp. 99–101.

8 See Appendix.

9 *Dramatic Opinions and Essays* (New York, 1906), pp. 11, 279. Ellen Terry's "unconventional" Desdemona is a little reminiscent of the heroine of *Captain Brassbound's Conversion*, Lady Cicely, whom Shaw modeled for Miss Terry.

10 Ellen Terry, *Four Lectures on Shakespeare* (London, 1932), pp. 129 ff.


# PART IV
## The Twentieth Century
(Pages 141–144)

1 Walter Kerr tells the story. See the *San Francisco Chronicle*, "This World" (July 7, 1957), p. 14.

2 *Shakespeare Quarterly*, IX (Spring, 1958), 198.

3 Herbert Farjeon, *The Shakespearean Scene* (London, n.d.), p. 163.

4 *Ibid.*


## Chapter 11
### THE MODERN OTHELLO
(Pages 145–154)

1 Raymond Mortimer, *New Statesman and Nation*, 15 (Feb. 19, 1938), 287. For other examples of Iago dominating his Othello, see for instance Gordon Crosse, *Shakespearean Playgoing*, p. 44; John Russell Brown, *Shakespeare Quarterly*, VII (Autumn, 1956), 408; *New Statesman and Nation*, 2 (Nov. 14, 1931), 610; Margaret Marshall, *Nation*, 157 (Oct. 30, 1943), 507–508.

2 *Athenaeum* (Nov. 16, 1907), 627.

3 Herbert Farjeon, *The Shakespearean Scene* (London, n.d.), p. 163.

4 James Agate, *First Nights* (London, 1934), p. 90; Peter Fleming, in *Spectator* (April 9, 1932), p. 507.

5 *Times* (London) (May 30, 1956), 5.

6 *Theatre Arts Monthly*, 21 (March 1937), 181; John Mason Brown, *Two on the Aisle* (New York, 1938), pp. 45–48.

7 *Times* (London) (Jan. 22, 1935), 10. See also reviews of Sofaer in *New Statesman and Nation*, 9 (Feb. 2, 1935), 141–142; *Punch*, 188 (January 30, 1935), 132; and of Merivale, Grenville Vernon, *Commonweal*, XXII (Oct. 18, 1935), 612; *Time*, 40 (Aug. 24, 1942), 66–67.

8 Audrey Williamson, *Contemporary Theatre* (New York, 1956), p. 128.

[9] Walter Kerr, in *San Francisco Chronicle*, "This World" (July 7, 1957), p. 14. But in a later performance at Stratford, Connecticut, Kerr thought Hyman lacked weight against a fully armed Iago. See also Brooks Atkinson in the *New York Times* (June 30, 1957), and John Beaufort, in the *Christian Science Monitor*, June 29, 1957. However, the *Boston Daily Record* (June 25, 1957) praised this performance highly.

[10] Roger Wood and Mary Clarke, *Shakespeare at the Old Vic* (New York, 1957).

[11] T. C. Worsley, *New Statesman and Nation*, 42 (Oct. 27, 1951), 460.

[12] Peter Fleming, *Spectator*, 187 (Oct. 26, 1951), 536.

[13] Eric Keown, *Punch*, 221 (Oct. 31, 1951), 500.

[14] *Spectator, op. cit.*

[15] *Spectator, op. cit.*

[16] *Times* (London) (Oct. 19, 1951), 8.

[17] Eric Keown, *Punch*, 216 (June 29, 1949), 715.

[18] *Times* (London) (June 20, 1949), 7.

[19] *New Statesman and Nation*, 3 (March 19, 1932), 363.

[20] Farjeon, *op. cit.*, p. 167.

[21] *Shakespearean Playgoing*, pp. 77, 78.

[22] Peter Fleming, *Spectator*, 149 (March 12, 1932), 366.

[23] Richard David, "Stratford 1954," *Shakespeare Quarterly*, V (Autumn, 1954), 387. David feels that later Quayle turned to "whimpering," left Othello too helpless, but he suspects a weak Iago was the cause.

[24] *Times* (London) (March 17, 1954), 11.

[25] Rosamund Gilder, *Theatre Arts*, 27 (Dec., 1943), 701.

[26] *Othello*, Alice Walker and John Dover Wilson, eds. (Cambridge, 1957), Introduction.

[27] Howard Barnes, *New York Herald Tribune*, Oct. 24, 1943.

[28] *Newsweek*, 22 (Nov. 1, 1943), 93.

[29] Otis L. Guernsey, Jr., *New York Herald Tribune*, Oct. 17, 1943.

[30] *Ibid.*

[31] Farjeon, *op. cit.*, p. 165.

[32] April 13, 1959, 540.

[33] April 10, 1959, 501–503.

[34] See the *Times* (London), April 8, 1959, 14, and *Punch*, April 15, 1959, 529. Caryl Brahms, *Plays and Players*, 6 (May, 1959), 9, was most critical. Kenneth Tynan (*The New Yorker*, 35, Sept. 26, 1959, 117) wrote, "[Robeson] seems to be murdering a butterfly on the advice of a gossip columnist."

[35] Much criticism was directed at the cramped stage levels and the foggy lighting. Micheál Mac Liammóir, the *Observer* (April 12, 1959), thought that if Robeson and his director could agree to eliminate "the abrupt movements of his hands which reduce his leonine grandeur," and allow him to rely "on the profound reality of his voice, the black lightning of his eyes, the sorcery of his tortured and smiling face, he would be the finest Othello of his day."

[36] Stark Young, *New Republic*, V (Nov. 1, 1943), 621–622.
[37] 39 (Nov. 5, 1943).
[38] *Theatre Book of the Year, 1943–44* (New York, 1944), pp. 90–93.
[39] Gilder, *op. cit.*, 702.


## Chapter 12
### THE MODERN IAGO
(Pages 155–160)

[1] Richard David, *Shakespeare Quarterly*, V (Autumn, 1954), 388;
Roger Marvell, *New Statesman and Nation*, 24 (Aug. 1, 1942), 75–76.
[2] Nicholas Bentley, *Spectator*, 166 (Jan. 31, 1941), 115–116; *Punch*, 236
(April 15, 1959), 529; Kenneth Tynan, *The New Yorker*, 35 (Sept. 26,
1959), 117.
[3] T. C. Worsley, *New Statesman and Nation*, 42 (Oct. 27, 1951), 460.
[4] Eric Keown, *Punch*, 221 (Nov. 14, 1951), 556; Peter Fleming, *Spectator*, 187 (Nov. 9, 1951), 600.
[5] *Punch*, 142 (April 17, 1912), 296. Interesting stage note: this Iago had
to step into a real gondola in real water—and when it started off without
him "though he escaped actual immersion, he sustained a very nasty jar."
[6] *Nation and Athenaeum*, 29 (May 7, 1921), 227–228; *New Statesman
and Nation*, 9 (Feb. 2, 1935), 141–142.
[7] *More First Nights* (London, 1937), p. 103.
[8] Jan. 30, 1935, 132.
[9] *Times* (London), March 9, 1932.
[10] Peter Fleming, 148 (March 13, 1932), 366.
[11] *New Statesman and Nation*, 3 (March 19, 1932).
[12] *First Nights* (London, 1934), pp. 85–89.
[13] Herbert Farjeon, *The Shakespearean Scene* (London, n. d.), p. 166.
[14] Nathan, *Theatre Book of the Year, 1943–44* (New York, 1944), p.
93.
[15] *New Republic*, 109 (Nov. 1, 1943), 621–622.
[16] *Commonweal*, 39 (Nov. 5, 1943), 72.
[17] Margaret Marshall, *Nation*, 157 (Oct. 30, 1943), 507–508.
[18] *Time*, 42 (Nov. 1, 1943), 70.
[19] Felix Barker, *The Oliviers* (New York, 1953), p. 165.
[20] Farjeon, *op. cit.*, p. 122.
[21] A. V. Cookman, *London Mercury*, XXXVII (March, 1938), 533;
Alan Dent, *Preludes and Studies* (London, 1942), p. 118.
[22] Rupert Hart-Davis, *Spectator*, 160 (Feb. 11, 1938), 223.
[23] Raymond Mortimer, *New Statesman and Nation* (Feb. 19, 1938),
287. Years later, a somewhat similar Iago was played by Richard Burton,
and it reminded Audrey Williamson of Olivier's in that the "humour was
played too obviously to the audience and too pleasant altogether." And
here, too, beyond the guilelessness and charm, "his sadness had an interesting psychopathic ring, and his emphasis on 'She *must* change, she

*must . . .'* like the talk on sex, had an element of festering disgust that gained a rather frightening suggestiveness at a moment, as his poison worked, where he lightly caressed Othello's hair. Somewhere, here, was the seed of a characterization not yet come to flower." *Contemporary Theatre* (New York, 1956), p. 128.

24 *New Statesman and Nation* (March 12, 1938), 405.

25 John Gassner, in *Educational Theatre Journal,* IX (Oct., 1957), 215.


## PART V
Othello and the Critics
(Pages 161–165)

1 Thus G. Wilson Knight produced the play, and I did (and acted Iago).


## Chapter 13
IN DEFENSE OF IAGO
(Pages 166–184)

1 It is an old libel, first appearing in "An Apology for the Character and Conduct of Iago," in *Essays, by a Society of Gentlemen* (1796), pp. 395–409. See the *Variorum,* pp. 408–409, and *Monthly Review,* XXII (1796), 7.

2 Tucker Brooke, "The Romantic Iago," *Yale Review,* VII (Jan., 1918), 349–359.

3 Allardyce Nicoll, *Studies in Shakespeare* (London, 1927), pp. 94, 103.

4 J. W. Draper, "*Othello* and Elizabethan Army Life," *Revue Anglo-Americaine,* IX (April, 1932), 324.

5 John Jay Chapman, *A Glance toward Shakespeare* (Boston, 1922), p. 47.

6 Lytton Strachey, *Characters and Commentaries* (New York, 1935), pp. 295–296.

7 E. E. Stoll, *Shakespeare and Other Masters* (Cambridge, 1940), pp. 231, 246.

8 Robert Heilman, "Dr. Iago and His Potions," *Virginia Quarterly Review,* XXVIII (Autumn, 1952), 568–584. Heilman has a curiously different imagistic approach to the same problem in "The Economics of Iago and Others," *PMLA,* LXVIII (June, 1953), 555–571. S. L. Bethell, "Shakespeare's Imagery: The Diabolic Images in *Othello,*" in *Shakespeare Survey* (Cambridge, 1952), pp. 62–80, comes to pretty much the same conclusion on the basis of the "devil" images.

9 J. I. M. Stewart, *Character and Motive in Shakespeare* (London, 1949), p. 108. The split-ego concept of Shakespearean heroes was sug-

gested as applying to Macbeth by Freud (Sigmund Freud, *Collected Papers* [London, 1925], vol. IV, 332. For Jekel's expansion of the idea, see L. Jekels, "Shakespeare's Macbeth," *Imago*, V [1917–19], 170–195). It has been applied several times to Othello. See also Derek Traversi, *"Othello," The Wind and the Rain*, VI (Spring, 1950), 268–269, Bodkin (see note 11 below), Leavis (see note 15 below), T. F. Connolly, "Shakespeare and the Double Man," *Shakespeare Quarterly*, I (Jan., 1950), 30–35, and Feldman, below. Kenneth Burke, *"Othello:* An Essay to Illustrate a Method," *Hudson Review*, IV (Summer, 1951), 166–168, seems, in his curious and complex study of the play, to go one further and find that Othello, Iago, and Desdemona are all expressions of one "inseparable integer."

[10] A. B. Feldman, "Othello's Obsession," *American Imago*, IX (June, 1952), 151–152, 156. See also Martin Wangh, "Othello: The Tragedy of Iago," *Psychoanalytic Quarterly*, XIX, 2 (April, 1950), 202–212.

[11] G. W. Knight, *Wheel of Fire* (London, 1930), pp. 127, 131. Maud Bodkin, *Archetypal Patterns in Poetry* (London, 1934), pp. 220–221, follows Knight's imagery, although she also considers the possibility of the split ego conception, of ". . . Iago as a projected image of forces present in Othello . . ."

[12] John R. Moore, "The Character of Iago," *University of Missouri Studies*, XXI, 39–46.

[13] Robert Bridges, *The Influence of the Audience on Shakespeare's Drama* (London, 1927), p. 23. See also J. W. Abernethy, "Honest Iago," *Sewanee Review*, XXX (July, 1922), 336–344.

[14] Bernard Spivack, *Shakespeare and the Allegory of Evil* (New York, 1958), pp. 47–58. This old Vice was "so traditional and popular," Spivack argues, "that he had to be disguised, because he could not be abandoned"; Shakespeare's attempted addition of motivation is "superfluous, never really fits him, invariably fails to fuse with his archaic nature and function, so criticism writhes." To assert this, Spivack (p. 17) must insist that Iago is passionless; he finds the "gnaw my inwards" outburst an inexplicable exception, but "Everywhere else his [Iago's] emotions are simply variations on the monolithic passion of laughter." Clearly, Spivack does not perceive the look and sound and feeling of Iago. He is, in fact, trying to measure one work of art by generalizations he deduces from other works different in time, in design, and certainly in artistic reach. There are traces of the traditional in Iago—as in all Shakespeare's works; and beyond this Iago resembles conventional figures of evil, back beyond the morality, for indeed all dramatizations of villainy spring essentially from a common source; but where Shakespeare used tradition, it was to create something entirely new. A rather more interesting speculation on the playwright's model is Paul A. Jorgensen's " 'Honesty' in *Othello*," *Studies in Philology*, XLVII (Oct., 1950), 557–568, which sees Iago as a knave posing as the morality Honesty. Another pigeonhole is suggested by Theodore Spencer, who finds some qualities in Iago common with Marston's Malevole, and—for the convenience of classification—lists him

as a "malcontent" ("The Elizabethan Malcontent," in *Joseph Quincy Adams Memorial Studies* [Washington, 1948], p. 530). Against the efforts of those who assume Shakespeare's intentions from the supposed intentions of his colleagues and predecessors, Stauffer has a pertinent warning: "For the ordinary reader"—and I would dispense with the qualification—"the most barren and dangerous practice of teachers and scholars is the pointing out of analogues, influences, sources, and Elizabethan stage conventions and devices, and stock characters and situations. This tends to make the unwary reader believe"—as the scholar himself often believes—"that Shakespeare is a product of his environment and predecessors. It explains everything but Shakespeare." Donald Stauffer, *Shakespeare's World of Images* (New York, 1949), p. 359.

[15] F. R. Leavis, partly in reaction to his impression that Bradley thought Othello was Iago's foil, argues instead that Iago was a "dramatic mechanism," an auxiliary, and he also suggests the split-ego concept noted above. "Diabolic Intellect and the Noble Hero: A Note on Othello," *Scrutiny*, VI (Dec., 1937), 261 ff.

[16] *Essays, op. cit.* (note 1), p. 409.

[17] See, in the last century, S. J. Snider, *System of Shakespeare's Drama* (St. Louis, 1877), vol. II, p. 97. J. A. Heraud, *Shakespeare, His Inner Life* (London, 1865), p. 270, says the adultery was "not impossible." Interestingly enough, S. A. Tannenbaum, "The Wronged Iago," *Shakespeare Association Bulletin*, XII (Jan., 1937), 57, in expanding this argument, noted that most critics were too squeamish to discuss the adultery issue and added "From nineteenth century critics nothing else could have been expected."

The basic Snider-Heraud interpretation of Iago as a deeply jealous personality was, it seems to me, a step in the right direction. It has been elaborated effectively by modern critics: John W. Draper, "The Jealousy of Iago," *Neophilologus*, XXV (1939), 50–60; F. P. Rand, "The Over-Garrulous Iago," *Shakespeare Quarterly*, I (July, 1950), 155–161; and Kenneth Muir, "The Jealousy of Iago," in *English Miscellany*, II (Rome, 1951), pp. 65–83. Muir emphatically denies the possibility of a relationship between Emilia and Othello; Draper and Rand are not certain.

[18] Tannenbaum, *op. cit.*, 58–60, catalogues the arguments.

[19] See H. J. Webb, "The Military Background in *Othello*," *Philological Quarterly*, XXX (Jan., 1951), 40–51. For more on the title subject, see J. R. Moore's answer to Webb, "Othello, Iago, and Cassio as Soldiers," *Philological Quarterly*, XXXI (April, 1952), 189–195; J. W. Draper, "Honest Iago," *PMLA*, XLVI (Sept., 1931), 724–737; "Captain General Othello," *Anglia; Zeitschrift fur Englische Philogie*, LV (Halle, 1931), 296–310, and Paul Jorgensen, *Shakespeare's Military World* (Berkeley and Los Angeles, 1956).

[20] Rand (*op. cit.*, 158) sees Iago's treachery as perhaps the sudden outbreak of what may have been a predisposition: ". . . he could hardly have been the Iago we know when Emilia married him, or during the

years when he was becoming the 'honest Iago' to the Venetians." H. H. Jordan, "Dramatic Illusion in Othello," *Shakespeare Quarterly*, I (July, 1950), 146–152 also finds Iago a brooding egoist at loose ends between wars, moved by his intelligence to desert a life of honesty to plunge into treachery for the first time when he seems unfairly treated. Here Jordan follows Nicoll (*op. cit.*, pp. 94–97). Rand, Jordan, and Nicoll take for granted, as do—among others—Kittredge (*Othello*, ed. G. L. Kittredge [New York, 1941], p. x), W. H. Hallett, "Honest, Honest Iago," *Fortnightly Review*, LXXIX, 275–286, Mario Praz, in *Proceedings of the British Academy*, XIV (1928), 76, Wyndham Lewis, *The Lion and the Fox* (New York, n.d.), p. 197, Thomas D. Bowman, "A Further Study in the Characterization and Motivation of Iago," *College English*, IV (May, 1943), 460–469, John B. Shackford, "The Motivation of Iago," *Shakespeare Newsletter* (Sept., 1953), 30, and Tannenbaum, Draper, Webb and Brooke, that Iago was definitely motivated to revenge by his loss of the appointment and/or the suspicion of Emilia's infidelity with Othello. Donald C. Miller, "Iago and the Problem of Time," *English Studies*, XXII (June, 1940), 97–115, speculates that Othello had made a secret "contract marriage" with Desdemona well before the play opened, and that Iago suddenly realized, with the overt elopement, that he had been superseded by a man (Cassio) merely better able to act as an assistant in the courtship.

[21] Brooke, *op. cit.*, pp. 351–359.

[22] Draper, "*Othello* and Elizabethan Army Life," 324–326.

[23] Nicoll (p. 102) finds that Iago evinces, after setting Othello aflame, ". . . a hesitation which betrays a certain fear . . . that he has gone too far. . . ." But in performance, Iago seems to gain assurance as he goes alone. It is Iago after all who urges Othello on to "strangle her in her bed," and who brings the Moor back to the murderous purpose when he wavers momentarily (IV.i), remembering Desdemona's gentle qualities.

[24] Brooke, *op. cit.*, 358. H. C. Goddard, *The Meaning of Shakespeare* (Chicago, 1951), pp. 481–485, also suggests that after this scene and Desdemona's pathetic appeal to him, Iago, profoundly disturbed, his power sapped, goes haltingly to his end. Goddard cites as his chief support the scene following with Roderigo, where ". . . we see Iago for the first time at his wit's end, unable to devise anything by way of answer to Roderigo's importunities." As customarily staged, the scene points entirely in the other direction. Iago is more disdainful than ever of Roderigo, until the gull threatens to go to Desdemona, whereupon Iago promptly—and with some humor—flatters him again into temporary submission. (Recall Booth here.) Surely Iago is shown as never more resourceful and purposeful than in the opening scene of the fifth act, where, pressed at last to take a hand in the violence he has initiated, he almost kills Cassio, does kill Roderigo, and blames the whole thing on Bianca with hardly a stop for thought.

[25] See note 22, Chapter 1.

[26] The Satanists tend to talk around the point. See, for instance, John Palmer, *Studies in the Contemporary Theatre* (1927), p. 78.

[27] Knight, *op. cit.*, p. 129; *Principles of Shakespearean Production* (1936), p. 57. Italics mine.

[28] *Macmillan's*, LXIV (July, 1881), 210; Hazlitt, *Works*, vol. V, p. 213.

[29] See Virgil Whitaker, *Shakespeare's Use of Learning* (San Marino, 1953), pp. 275 ff. for a discussion of theories of will in relation to *Othello*. For other psychological theories, see Lily B. Campbell, *Shakespeare's Tragic Heroes—Slaves of Passion* (Cambridge, 1930), pp. 21–23, 29–45, *et passim*. But it seems clear that when Shakespeare picked his way among such theories it was not to find what to say, but to find what would be most suitable for his characters to say. Nor can any of his characters be circumscribed by contemporary psychological theories— which were of a wide variety. How conflicting, for instance, the popular humoral psychology was is evident in John Draper's *The Humors and Shakespeare's Characters* (Durham, 1945). Draper's careful research seems mainly to show that there are many types (e.g., choleric), within types, that types overlap or duplicate (e.g., choleric and sanguine), that humors may be counterfeit, may change, or may be mixed, with one or the other dominating. Clearly individual interpretations could be wildly contradictory. See in this connection L. C. Forest, "A Caveat for Critics against Invoking Elizabethan Psychology," *PMLA*, LI (Sept., 1946), 651.

[30] A. C. Bradley, *Shakespearean Tragedy* (New York, 1957), p. 182, is frankly bewildered to find that Iago ". . . has *less* passion than an ordinary man, and yet he does these frightful things." Bradley accepts in principle the suggestions of Hazlitt and Swinburne (p. 171), and he accepts Coleridge's "motive-hunting" figure too (p. 183); Bradley's point is that Coleridge's estimate does not equate with "evil for evil's sake." H. Granville-Barker, *Prefaces* (Princeton, 1947), pp. 98 ff., allows Iago the emotion of hate, but even this is seen as cold. For the view that Iago is all laughter, see Spivack, *op. cit.*, pp. 17, 18, 23. See also note 14, above.

For the Satanist view of Iago's lack of passion, see Chapman, Stoll (p. 247), and Palmer.

[31] Kittredge, *op. cit.*

[32] Karen Horney, *Self-Analysis* (New York, 1942), pp. 56 ff. See also, by the same author, "The Quest for Power, Prestige, and Possession," and "Neurotic Competitiveness," in *The Neurotic Personality of Our Time* (New York, 1937), pp. 162–206. This and the next quotation are syntheses of several pages.

[33] Karen Horney, *Neurosis and Human Growth* (New York, 1950), pp. 197–213. Bradley, I think, was reaching for some such explanation for Iago's humanity in his emphasis on the Ancient's urge to "plume up my will" (Bradley, *op. cit.*, pp. 229 ff.). Bradley saw, too, that Iago did not understand the power of love; but the critic stopped short of the

further insight that it was some repression of the passion all humans share, and not the utter lack of it, that accounted for the power of Iago's characterization. Perhaps a greater tolerance for seeing *Othello* in the theater would have helped Bradley here. Kittredge, though he tended to justify Iago's actions on the basis of external provocation, sensed more acutely the "torment" within the Ancient.

34 B. Mittelman, H. G. Wolff, and M. Scharf, "Emotions and Gastro-duodenal Functions," *Psychosomatic Medicine*, IV (1942), 5, 16.

35 Peter de la Primaudaye, *The French Academy*, trans. T. B(owes) (1586), quoted in Lily B. Campbell, *op. cit.*, p. 153.

36 The *Variorum* translation, "in great favor with the Moor," is usually followed, but it falls short of the personal relationship implied.

37 Henry Austin Clapp, *Reminiscences of a Dramatic Critic* (Boston, 1902), p. 136. Inside, Booth's Iago was the very "spirit of hate" (George Woodberry, *Studies in Letters and Life*, New York, 1891, p. 171).

38 Percy Fitzgerald, *Henry Irving* (London, 1893), pp. 165–166.

39 And if, after consultation, a psychiatrist found repressed homosexual impulses of this sort, he would treat them as part of a larger character problem. Similarly, if Shakespeare had meant to create a homosexual motivation for Iago, he could have done so by a sharp focus on this in the character design; but consciously at least he specifically avoided it. It may be that what Dr. Jones had in mind was that Shakespeare was subconsciously expressing through Iago latent impulses in his own psyche.

## Chapter 14
IN DEFENSE OF OTHELLO
(Pages 185–205)

1 J. L. F. Flathe, *Shakespeare in seiner Wirklichkeit* (Leipzig, 1863), pp. 321–348. See especially pp. 312–338, 380–428.

2 T. S. Eliot, "Shakespeare and the Stoicism of Seneca," *Selected Essays* (New York, 1932), p. 130. Eliot's interpretation pairs interestingly with Tolstoy's attack on Othello for his "false pathos and . . . unnatural speeches" (*Tolstoy on Shakespeare*, New York, 1907, pp. 64 ff.); where Tolstoy sees an author's shortcomings, Eliot sees a design. Here Peter Alexander's observation is most apt: ". . . had [Eliot] studied Tolstoy's earlier condemnation and seen the fantastic conclusions Tolstoy develops from it, Mr. Eliot would . . . have realized its extravagance." (*Review of English Studies*, IX, May, 1958, 188–193.)

3 I do not mean to suggest that any of these critics borrowed from Flathe or from each other. There is much independent parallel discovery in criticism.

4 F. R. Leavis, "Diabolic Intellect and the Noble Hero: A Note on Othello." *Scrutiny*, VI (Dec., 1937), 259, 283. Maud Bodkin, *Archetypal Patterns in Poetry* (London, 1934), also represents this view.

[5] Leo Kirschbaum, "The Modern Othello," *English Literary History*, II (Dec., 1944), 283–296.

[6] Robert Heilman, *Magic in the Web* (Lexington, 1956), pp. 144–145. Heilman's notes provide a very useful survey of many aspects of critical interpretation of Othello.

[7] Kirschbaum, *op. cit.*

[8] Heilman, *op. cit.*

[9] *Ibid.*, pp. 164–165.

[10] Kirschbaum, *op. cit.* Heilman, *op. cit.*, p. 275, cites this in support of his visualization of a "tendency to violence, even to spectacle, here."

[11] Heilman, *op. cit.*, pp. 148–150.

[12] *Stanislavsky Produces Othello* (London, 1948), pp. 109 ff.

[13] *Othello*, ed. by John M. Kingdom (New York, 1876), p. 10; see Chapter 4, note 12.

[14] 1. Wolfit. 2. Sofaer. 3. Quayle. 4. Walter. 5. Hyman. 6. Robeson.

[15] 1. Walter. 2. Robeson. 3. Wolfit. 4. Sofaer. 5. Quayle. 6. Hyman.

[16] Emma Lazarus, "Tommaso Salvini," *Century Magazine*, XXIII (Nov., 1881), 114.

[17] Hyman.

[18] A. W. Schlegel, *Lectures on Dramatic Art and Literature* (London, 1815), p. 189.

[19] 1. Quayle. 2. Wolfit. 3. Walter. 4. Robeson. 5. Hyman. 6. Sofaer.

[20] T. Reik, *Psychology of Sex Relations* (New York, 1945), p. 79.

[21] 1. Wolfit. 2. Walter. 3. Sofaer. 4. Hyman. 5. Robeson. 6. Quayle.

[22] 1. Sofaer. 2. Robeson. 3. Walter. 4. Quayle. 5. Wolfit. 6. Hyman.

[23] Walter.

[24] Quayle. This is a point of view I particularly welcomed, since it confirmed the opinion I expressed on Shakespeare's actors.

[25] Paul Jorgensen is particularly valuable on the conflict between soldier and society, in *Shakespeare's Military World* (Berkeley and Los Angeles, 1956), pp. 208–314.

[26] Shakespeare, in *Henry V* (*Chorus V*), had made a unique pause to hope that Essex would return in triumph from Ireland. But the Earl returned in failure, eventually to attempt his rebellion; and the night before it, at the urging of Essex' men, the Globe players performed the then subversive *Richard II*, with its story of the deposition of an unfit monarch. The players were officially questioned about this, but were let off.

[27] *Works* (Birmingham, 1884), The English School's Library, 871. See, in the same vein, a letter from Thomas Bernhere, June 24, 1600, in Samuel Purchas, *Purchas, His Pilgrimes*. By 1550 those Englishmen who read Italian may have known the encyclopedic study of Leo Africanus, himself a "More." The work was soon translated into French and Latin, and into English in 1600. By 1585, a few years after Alcazar, there was a translation of Nicholas Nicolay Dauphinois' *The Navigations, peregrinations and voyages, made into Turkie* . . . which somewhat reluctantly speaks of civilized treatment accorded to him by the Moors. Most in-

fluential on popular images of the Moor would be the book's illustrations of Moorish men and women of powerful figures and considerable dignity. See also E. W. Bovill, *The Golden Trade of the Moors* (London, 1958), pp. 111 ff.

[28] See Richard Hakluyt, *The Principal Navigations Voyages Traffiques and Discoveries of the English Nation* (London, 1907), vol. IV, p. 275.

[29] In a letter to me, February 6, 1958. Two Moors, "noble men," had been in England as early as 1551 (see Hakluyt, *op. cit.*, pp. 32–33). See also Henry de Castries, *Sources inédites de l'Histoire du Maroc* (Angleterre), 1. He suggests the two men were carrying letters from Charles V, and were passing through England on their way home.

[30] See Bernard Harris, "Portrait of a Moor," in *Shakespeare Survey*, 1958, pp. 89 ff.

[31] See *Arrivall and intertainments of the Embassador Alkaid Ben Jaurer Abdella with his Associate . . . from Mulley Mahamed Sheque . . .* (London, 1637).

[32] See *Chrysanaleia: The Golden Fishing: or Honour of Fishmongers. Applauding the advancement of Mr. John Leman, Alderman, to the dignitie of Lord Mayor of London . . .* (London, 1616). "Before, on either side, and behinde him, ride sixe other his tributarie kings on horsebacke, gorgeously attired in faire guilt Armours . . . shewing thereby, that the Fishmongers are not unmindful of their combined brethren, the worthy company of Golde-Smithes, in this solemne day of triumph."

[33] Albert Feuillerat, *Documents relating to the Revels at Court in the time of King Edward VI and Queen Mary*, in W. Bang, *Materialen*, vol. XIV, pp. 33, 190, 191 (see also the following volume, *. . . in the time of Elizabeth*, index, "Moors"); George Peele, *The Device of the Pageant borne before Woolstone Dixi, Lord Mayor of the Citie of London* (London, 1585), in George Peele, *Works* (London, 1888), vol. 1, p. 351.

[34] Ben Jonson, *Works* (London, 1871), vol. VII, pp. 6 ff.

[35] The old gossip had it that Elizabeth's partiality for Falstaff helped shape *The Merry Wives*, and more recently we have been told that Shakespeare wrote *Twelfth Night* for the queen and *Macbeth* for James. See Leslie Hotson, *The First Night of Twelfth Night* (New York, 1954), and Henry N. Paul, *The Royal Play of Macbeth* (New York, 1950).

[36] *Progresses, Processions, and Magnificent Festivities of King James I*, collected by John Nichols (London, 1828), p. 474.

[37] Jonson, *op. cit.*

[38] Thus one critic feels Othello should have turned on Desdemona when she begged before the Duke to go to Cyprus with him. "Her husband's duty was utterly to silence her and make her see how utterly unreasonable her prayer was. But Othello . . . carried away . . . by his love and admiration for his bride . . . forgets everything except his irrepressible desire 'to be free and bounteous to her mind' . . . All of this of course is very beautiful. But if the sentimental among the spec-

tators have felt nothing but admiration for such forgetfulness of all contingencies, what will the wiser sort have thought of it? Is not the great general blinded by his infatuation? . . . Has not his love unbalanced him, deprived him of common sense? Has he not let the passions get the better of his reason and rule it instead of being ruled by it?" G. Bonnard, "Are Othello and Desdemona Innocent or Guilty?" *English Studies*, XXX (Oct., 1949), 175–184. This argument is intended to prove Othello—and Desdemona—guilty, and therefore deserving of the catastrophe. The writer seems surprised that English criticism has not recognized the clear evidence of this guilt in their submitting to passion and going together to Cyprus. See also H. J. Webb, "The Military Background in *Othello*," *Philological Quarterly*, XXX (Jan., 1951), 40–51, on Othello's "lovesickness."

[39] Stanislavsky, *op. cit.*, pp. 17, 78.

[40] E. T. Mason, *The Othello of Tommaso Salvini* (New York, 1890), p. 17.

## Chapter 15

IN DEFENSE OF DESDEMONA
(Pages 206–217)

[1] Thomas Rymer, *A Short View of Tragedy* (London, 1693), in J. E. Spingarn, *Critical Essays of the Seventeenth Century* (Oxford, 1908), vol. II, pp. 221–248.

[2] John Quincy Adams, in *Notes, Criticism, and Correspondence upon Shakespeare's Plays and Actors* (New York, 1863), pp. 224 ff.

[3] Henry James Pye, *Comments on the Commentators on Shakespeare* (London, 1807), p. 335.

[4] Friedrich Bodenstedt, in *Jahrbuch der Deutschen Shakespeare-Gesellschaft* (1867), p. 259, in *Variorum*, pp. 440–441. See also, in Augustus Ralli, *A History of Shakespearean Criticism* (London, 1932), references to J. L. Geoffroy, *Cours de Littérature Dramatique* (1825), p. 210; Franz Horn, *Shakespeare Schauspiele erläutert* (1823), p. 234; G. G. Gervinus, *Shakespeare Commentaries* (1849–1850), p. 345; Alfred Mèziéres, *Shakespeare, Ses Oeuvres et Ses Critiques* (1860), p. 375; Hans Koester, *Marginalia Zum Othello und Macbeth* (Jahrbuch, 1, 1865), p. 445.

[5] J. A. Heraud, *Shakespeare, His Inner Life* (London, 1865), pp. 273 ff.

[6] C. Cowden-Clarke, *The Shakespeare Key*, quoted in *Variorum*, p. 69.

[7] Allardyce Nicoll, *Studies in Shakespeare* (London, 1927), p. 91.

[8] For instance by Stopford Brooke, *Ten More Plays of Shakespeare* (London, 1932), p. 172.

[9] Robert Speaight, "Reflexions sur 'Othello,'" *Mercure de France*, number 1079 (July, 1953), 478–493.

[10] Hazlitt, Mrs. Jameson, A. C. Bradley, for instance. See below.

[11] J. W. Draper, "Desdemona, A Compound of Two Cultures," *Revue de Littérature Comparée*, 13 (1933), 338 ff. G. B. Shaw, in a little whimsy, once suggested that Shakespeare originally intended a super-subtle Desdemona to ruin Othello, but she got away from him (*Short Stories, Scraps, and Shavings*, New York, 1933, 85 ff.).

[12] A. W. Schlegel, *Lectures* (London, 1815), pp. 11, 192. Schlegel calls her, "an offering without blemish . . . full of simplicity, softness, and humility . . . she seems calculated to form the most yielding and tender wife."

[13] William R. Turnbull, *Othello, A Critical Study* (London, 1892), p. 345.

[14] A. C. Bradley, *Shakespearean Tragedy* (London, 1951), p. 164.

[15] Robert B. Heilman, "Light and Dark in Othello," *Essays in Criticism*, 1 (Oct., 1951), 324 ff.

[16] G. W. Knight, *Wheel of Fire* (London, 1930), pp. 127 ff. As noted elsewhere, Knight later produced the play and wrote intelligently: ". . . the moment any of this [symbolism] is allowed to interfere with the expressly domestic and human qualities of the drama, you get disaster." *Principles of Shakespearean Production* (1936), p. 157. S. L. Bethell accepts Knight's hell-heaven imagery ("The Diabolic Images in Othello," *Shakespeare Survey*, 1952, pp. 66 ff.). Bethell even extends the imagery, in a rather curious way: "Deceitful appearance . . . thus characterizes all the main figures in *Othello*"—including Desdemona because she "deceives expectation: though a Venetian, she is not a 'cunning whore' as Othello was led frantically to believe." For other versions of this devil-versus-divine imagery, see Paul Siegel, "The Damnation of Othello," *PMLA*, LXVIII (Dec., 1953), 1068–1079, and Robert Heilman, "Dr. Iago and His Potions," *Virginia Quarterly Review*, XXVIII (Autumn, 1952), 582 ff.

[17] Thomas Campbell, *Life of Mrs. Siddons* (London, 1834), vol. II, pp. 60–61; James Boaden, *Memoirs of the Life of John Philip Kemble . . .* (London, 1825), pp. 258 ff.; C. E. L. Wingate, *Shakespeare's Heroines on the Stage* (New York, 1895), p. 327.

[18] *Monthly Mirror*, N.S. III (Jan., 1808), 51; Stark Young, *New Republic*, 109 (Nov. 1, 1943), p. 622.

[19] Dutton Cook, *Academy*, XIX (May 7, 1881), 345.

[20] *Athenaeum* (May 7, 1881), 633.

[21] *Macmillan's*, LXIV (July, 1881), 218.

[22] *Variorum*, p. 247.

[23] A. C. Bradley, *Shakespearean Tragedy* (New York, 1955), p. 147.

[24] *Nation and Athenaeum*, 29 (May 7, 1921), 228.

[25] Desmond MacCarthy, *Drama* (New York, 1940), p. 24.

[26] Thornton Wilder, in *Theatre Arts Monthly*, LX, 3 (March, 1925), 153.

[27] Peter Fleming, *Spectator*, 187 (Oct. 26, 1951), 536.

[28] Herbert Farjeon, *The Shakespearean Scene* (London, n.d.), p. 165.

[29] Douglas Woodruff, *Punch*, 188 (Jan. 30, 1935), 132.

[30] E. V. R. Wyatt, *Catholic World*, 158 (Dec., 1943), 297; Rosamund Gilder, *Theatre Arts*, XXVII, 12 (Dec., 1943).

[31] *Punch*, 206 (March 8, 1944), 208.

[32] This Desdemona, playing with a weak Othello and a dominating Iago, was "in a fair way to rule the production, and some critics hailed her for this feat." John Russell Brown, *Shakespeare Quarterly*, VII (Autumn, 1956), 4, 408.

[33] *Ibid.*, 164.

[34] *Othello, Charles Fechter's Acting Edition* (London, 1861), pp. 72 ff.

[35] See J. W. Draper, "*Othello* and Elizabethan Army Life," *Revue Anglo-Americaine*, 9 (April, 1932), 326; G. Bonnard, "Are Othello and Desdemona Innocent or Guilty?", *English Studies*, XXX (Oct., 1949), 175–184.

[36] Farjeon, *op. cit.*, pp. 169–170.

[37] Moody Prior, "Character in Relation to Action in *Othello*," *Modern Philology*, XLIV (May, 1947), 225–237.

[38] Peter Fleming, *Spectator*, 187 (Nov. 9, 1951), 600.

[39] In a letter dated November 14, 1949. Similarly, in the nineteenth century, she was too often represented by "any pretty puppet." *European Magazine* (Jan. 1816), 53.

[40] See the earlier chapter on Desdemona in the nineteenth century.

[41] *Ibid.*

[42] See Dutton Cook, "Othello in Paris," the *Theatre*, II (Oct. 1, 1880), 209–214. Unfortunately Bernhardt played in an excerpted version of the play which was not successful; but her singing, and particularly her "death," was said to have "sauvé la soirée."

[43] M. E. W. Sherwood in *New York Times* (Jan. 20, 1875), quoted in Matthews and Hutton, *Actors and Actresses* . . . (New York, 1886), vol. V, 72.

[44] See chapter on Desdemona in the nineteenth century.

## Chapter 16
IN DEFENSE OF THE PLAY: I
(Pages 218–229)

[1] E. E. Stoll, *Othello, an Historical and Comparative Study* (Minneapolis, 1915), p. 17 *n.*

[2] Rymer's objections are particularly unsavory when set against his own play. To spare others an onerous task, here is a brief synopsis of *Edgar, or the English Monarch, an Heroic Tragedy* (London, 1678). Edgar, the noble king of England, has sent his favorite, Duke Ethelwold, to seek out the beautiful Alfrid, of Cornwall. Ethelwold has found her to be as beautiful as rumor said, but he modifies her loveliness in his description to the king. Then he arranges to marry his own daughter, Ethelgede, to King Edgar, and to marry Alfrid himself. All this is told

in long labored expository dialogue that begins the play. Now Alfrid appears, and sees Edgar, and at once—much more quickly than Othello becomes jealous—they fall in love. Ethelwold plots against the king, and finally, fearing he will lose Alfrid, plans to kill her. Alfrid, meanwhile, feeling she is legally betrothed to Ethelwold, plans to renounce the king's love. She tells Ethelgede she will lead the king by her voice to a dark tower, where Ethelgede "Having aswag'd his Amorous Heat, He will applaud the innocent Deceit," and all will be well. But Ethelwold, creeping to the rendezvous, kills daughter Ethelgede by mistake and (the action occurs offstage of course, and is reported by a soldier):

> In their mixt Goar he swims
> And with stiff Arms still grasps her congeal'd Lims.

Thus, Rymer says in his Advertisement, "The Tragedy ends Prosperously." It is a collection of long speeches in stiff heroic couplets because "Rhyme is more proper for this sort of Tragedy, which ends happily."

[3] *Op. cit.*, 121. I wrote to Mr. Eliot to ask if he had changed his opinions about this, and about his comment on the dynamic theater form (see chapter 1). My letter was acknowledged by his secretary, but I have not heard from Mr. Eliot, so I am unable to say what his present attitude is. However, in September, 1958, he was quoted as saying: "I'm just beginning to grow up, to get maturity. In the last few years, everything I'd done up to 60 or so has seemed very childish." *Time*, 72 (Sept. 29, 1958), 98.

[4] E. E. Stoll, *Shakespeare and Other Masters* (Cambridge, 1940), p. 272.

[5] And his quotations from others about the operational stage are not rewarding. Thus Stoll quotes (*From Shakespeare to Joyce*, New York, 1941, p. 174) from Samuel Barron, who declared that the stage has no means of projecting character motives and "subjective causes" of action in purely theatrical terms. This conclusion led Barron to call his piece "The Dying Theater." It was another premature obituary for a fabulous invalid. One of the most interesting developments in the modern theater has been its successful experiments with the externalization of inner life, in dramatized fantasy and reminiscence.

[6] *Othello* . . . ; see also, for a restatement of Stoll's position on *Othello*, *Art and Artifice in Shakespeare* (Cambridge, 1933), and *Shakespeare and Other Masters*, p. 200.

[7] See, further, in the text, the discussion of Miss Bradbrook's views.

[8] Controversy has a value as well as a satisfaction for Stoll, as he notes in his preface to *Shakespeare and Other Masters* (*op. cit.*). For his side in some recent debates involving *Othello*, see "Mainly Controversy: Hamlet, Othello," *Philological Quarterly*, XXIV (Oct., 1945); "An Othello All Too Modern," *English Literary History*, XIII (March, 1946); "Another Othello Too Modern," in *J. Q. Adams Memorial Studies* (Washington, 1948); "A New 'Reading' of Othello," *Modern Philology*, XLV (Feb., 1948); and "A Freudian Detective's Shakespeare," *Modern Philology*, XLVIII (Nov., 1950).

⁹ This is apparent in both his specific and general references. In more recent writings he has spoken of "the bad tidings out of Vienna" (*From Shakespeare to Joyce*, p. 340), and of how "Recent psychology and literature" have " 'sexualized the universe.' " ("Iago Not A 'Malcontent,' " *Journal of English and Germanic Philology*, April, 1952, 162 n.). Though Stoll may use such concepts as the subconscious in his criticism, a scholar sympathetic to the findings of the Freudians and post-Freudians is likely to doubt that Stoll had absorbed them or the dynamics behind them. Note that Stoll finds it curious that critics influenced by modern psychology should be open-minded to new or diverse opinion: "In the Freudian and symbolist critics . . . there is now and then . . . something a little disarming: they are hospitable to interpretations other than their own, if also Freudian or symbolical" ("A Freudian Detective's Shakespeare," p. 131).

¹⁰ See *Othello* . . . , p. 21 *et passim.*

¹¹ *Ibid.,* p. 24.

¹² Stoll apologizes for agreeing in part with "captious and clumsy Rymer"; (*ibid.,* p. 17) but what is significant is not the similar opinion, but the similar kind of thought. Both Rymer and Stoll refuse to suspend disbelief in the given dramatic situation, both restructure the situation according to their preconceived "decorum" for the tragic hero they feel Othello ought to be. Where Stoll feels Othello did not act as a typical jealous or noble man should, Rymer felt Othello did not act as a typical soldier should. Rymer, too, had a proper idea of how the Moor might have behaved, that is, "He might have set a Guard on Cassio, or have lockt up Desdemona, or have observed their carriage a day or two longer."

¹³ T. Reik, *Psychology of Sex Relations* (New York, 1945), p. 79.

¹⁴ Stoll himself has made the point that art and life are different; but does he not go too far when he argues that for plays to be faithful to life implies that they are ". . . not the product of art at all . . . [but] the record of an oracle, the vision of a seer" (*Othello* . . . , p. 67)?

¹⁵ *Ibid.,* p. 29 n.

¹⁶ J. M. Robertson, *The State of Shakespeare Study* (London, 1931), p. 30.

¹⁷ *Othello* . . . , p. 2. Iago does *not,* by the way, *supplant* Cassio until the end of the temptation.

¹⁸ In "This World," *San Francisco Chronicle,* June 19, 1950.

¹⁹ *Othello* . . . , p. 17 n. Nor, apparently, did Stoll change his early impression; for more than a quarter of a century later he wrote of the speed of Othello's succumbing that he had not emphasized it enough: "This matter I have in later discussions too much neglected. But see my *Othello* (1915) . . ." He refers to such quotations as those in the text. "Another Othello Too Modern," *op. cit.,* p. 363 n.

²⁰ Stanislavski, *My Life in Art* (New York, 1956), p. 269.

²¹ E. T. Mason, *The Othello of Tommaso Salvini* (New York, 1890),

p. 35. The papers Othello originally worked on were probably the maps of the fortifications he went to inspect in III, ii (a scene usually cut, at least since the eighteenth century).

[22] *Othello, Charles Fechter's Acting Edition* (London, 1861), p. 126.

[23] *Shakespearean Plays of Edwin Booth*, ed. William Winter (Philadelphia, 1899), vol. 1, p. 62.

[24] Mason, p. 41. Stanislavski confirms this (*op. cit.*, p. 270).

[25] For examples of praise for slow jealousy—besides those in the text—see, for instance: *Athenaeum*, Dec. 6, 1856 (on Dillon), Oct. 26, 1861 (on Fechter), Sept. 12, 1868 (on Fairclough), April 10, 1875 (on Salvini), and Feb. 19, 1876 (on Irving). Kean was criticized for being jealous too soon, but even he waited until midway in the scene. I think any actor of Othello would find inconceivable Stoll's notion of changing in a moment from quiet dignity to groans or sobs in this scene.

[26] 1. Hyman and Wolfit. 2. Quayle and Robeson. 3. Sofaer. 4. Walter.

[27] *Othello* . . . , p. 56. In a footnote, he gives us an illuminating clue to what he demands from a playwright in the way of "psychology" (p. 62 *n*):

"Even Pinero, in the *Second Mrs. Tanqueray*, could make shift so to psychologize . . . only by dint of a bit of exposition at the end. 'What am I maundering about?' she (Paula) cries as she pulls herself together. How then could Shakespeare, even if he happened to carry all modern psychology *in petto*, dispense with a comment like that? If he knew anything, it was how to express himself, and make his point in the inelusive language of the stage."

Cannot a character express "that undertow of passion which sweeps us—considering or debating, choosing or refusing" unless he says he is doing so? Surely we would know Paula is under this tension, whether she says so or not. Similarly, in *Othello*, what are the Moor's "trance," and the incoherency preceding it, and the beautiful "wavering scene," but visibly charted manifestations of a man's ego tormented by conflicting passions and emotions? Do we need Othello to say "what am I maundering about" to know the strain he is under? What of the sound of torture in his voice, the sight of it in his face? Are not these integral to the "inelusive language of the stage"? If Stoll does not perceive this language, is he following his own precept to judge a work with the same spirit that the author writ? (*From Shakespeare to Joyce*, p. ix).

[28] *Elizabethan Stage Conditions* (Cambridge, 1932), p. 86. Miss Bradbrook credits Stoll with having "treated the question at great length."

[29] *Themes and Conventions of Elizabethan Tragedy* (Cambridge, 1935), p. 63.

[30] *Othello* . . . , p. 61.

[31] *Ibid.*, p. 67.

[32] Sir John Squire, *Shakespeare as Dramatist* (London, 1935), p. 74.

## Chapter 17
IN DEFENSE OF THE PLAY: II
(Pages 230–242)

[1] See Marvin Rosenberg, "Public Night Performances in Shakespeare's Time," *Theatre Notebook*, VIII (Jan.–Mar., 1954), 44–46.

[2] A. C. Bradley, *Shakespearean Tragedy* (New York, 1957), p. 151.

[3] Victor Hugo, *William Shakespeare* (Paris, 1899), pp. 193 ff.

[4] For a summary of this position, see Lawrence J. Ross, "The Shakespearean Othello" (unpublished dissertation, Princeton, 1956).

[5] See Thomas Wilson, *A Compleat Christian Dictionary* (1645), definitions of "black," "blackness."

[6] Paul Siegel, *Shakespearean Tragedy and the Elizabethan Compromise* (New York, 1957), pp. 89, 90.

[7] Caroline Spurgeon, *Shakespeare's Imagery* (New York, 1935), p. 335.

[8] Specific marvels from Africa are reported by the Englishman who told of the coming of a Moorish ambassador to Charles II (*Arrivall and intertainments . . .* London, 1637): ". . . it is said that there are a people called Aramaspians, with one eye in the Fore-head; some with their Feete naturally growing backward, some with heads like Dogges, some with long tailes, some with but one legge, that doe hop very swift . . . some without Heads, with Eyes in their shoulders . . . some with eares so great they cover the whole body . . . I am persuaded that many of these things are true, or else so many Grave and approved Authors would never have written of them, and divulged them to the world."

[9] For further explorations of Shakespeare's imagery, see Edward Armstrong, *Shakespeare's Imagination* (London, 1946); W. H. Clemen, *The Development of Shakespeare's Imagery* (Cambridge, 1951); Donald Stauffer, *Shakespeare's World of Images* (New York, 1949); and among useful articles, S. L. Bethell, "Shakespeare's Imagery: The Diabolic Images in *Othello*," and R. A. Foakes, "Suggestions for a New Approach to Shakespeare's Imagery," both in *Shakespeare Survey*, V, 1952. But also see Moody Prior's excellent warning to imagery hunters, "Imagery as a Test of Authorship," *Shakespeare Quarterly*, VI (Autumn, 1955), 381–386.

[10] See William Empson, *The Structure of Complex Words* (London, 1951), pp. 218–249.

[11] See J. A. S. McPeek, " 'The Arts Inhibited' and the Meaning of *Othello*," *Boston University Studies in English*, III (Autumn, 1955), pp. 129–147.

[12] Allegorists of *Othello* lose the figure of the play entirely in the ground of a larger, nondramatic scheme. Miss Winstanley firmly picks out Venice behind Desdemona, Spain—or Philip—behind Othello, and behind Iago a personal enemy of Philip's. The play becomes really an attempt to counter the pro-Spanish policies of James. Dr. Creighton goes as far afield in another direction: Desdemona is "the traditional

Sacrament of the Altar"; Othello, the Lollard heretic (blackness equating with heresy in this system), discovered ". . . under the tutelage of Iago that he had inadvertently married the Mass. The fanaticism of the Lollard breaks out when the truth comes to him, for he recalls that the Mass had become a thing for sale." Nobody can object to these as private visions of the play; but clearly they are valueless for anyone interested in the qualities of the tragedy. (Lillian Winstanley, *"Othello" as the Tragedy of Italy* [London, 1924]; Charles Creighton, *An Allegory of Othello* [London, 1912]).

13 Sigmund Freud, *Collected Papers* (London, 1925), vol. IV, p. 332. For other references, see note 9 in the chapter "In Defense of Iago."

14 Knight, *Wheel of Fire* (London, 1930), p. 130.

15 See Arthur Sewell, *Character and Society in Shakespeare* (Oxford, 1951), p. 97; and Geoffrey Bush, *Shakespeare and the Natural Condition* (Harvard, 1956), p. 61.

16 *The Counter-Renaissance* (New York, 1950), pp. 619, 666–667.


## Appendix
### A KIND WORD FOR BOWDLER
(Pages 244–256)

1 *Memoirs of the Life of John Bowdler* (London, 1824), p. 319. The British Museum Catalogue of 1910 lists the first Family Edition as edited by Thomas Bowdler. This is probably an error, based on the commonly held assumption that he initiated the project. However, it has been suggested (by Stanley Yonge, in *Notes and Queries*, V, Sept. 1958) that the catalogue note refers to another Thomas Bowdler, perhaps Bowdler's nephew of the same name, who was author of the memoir cited above. But the younger man specifically credits the first edition to one of "T. Bowdler's *nearest relatives*"—among whom a nephew is not usually counted. Nor does there seem to be any reason why he should not have admitted—or boasted—of beginning the project, if he had done so, or have identified any other man responsible. The sister seems to be the only one whose anonymity would need to be preserved.

2 Thomas Bowdler, *A Letter to the Editor of the British Critic* (London, 1823), pp. 12–13.

3 William Jaggard, *Shakespeare Bibliography* (Stratford, 1911), p. 504. I am indebted to Philip Highfill for the following note on the Bell volumes:

"The collection of Shakespearean plays which has gone under the name of the "Bell" edition (even though the curious footnotes and introductory material were contributed by actor-author Francis Gentleman) was issued both separately by the plays and bound in volumes from early 1772. Bell at first brought out the texts of plays popular in the theaters—from the prompt books of the patent houses, it was claimed, a claim which seems substantially true. Eventually, virtually the whole canon as then established was put out, including the non-dramatic poetry as well as all the plays, both those which were habitually acted and those which never were. For the latter, Gentleman suggested excisions to bring them into line with contemporary critical tastes. He also wrote a brief "Introduction to Shakespeare," which was included in the bound sets. There is copious evidence of the popularity of the "Bell" edition, which was available in both small demy and large royal papers, with sumptuous *ad vivam* plates of actors, illustrations which set the pace for such prints for years to come."

[4] Bowdler, *op. cit.*, pp. 6–7.

[5] *Ibid.*, p. 15.

[6] *Ibid.*, pp. 16–17.

[7] *Ibid.*

[8] *Ibid.*

[9] *Ibid.*, p. 22.

[10] *Edinburgh Review*, XXXVI (Oct., 1821), p. 53.

[11] *Monthly Mirror*, N.S. III (Jan., 1808), p. 51.

[12] His mutilation, never published, resides in an interleaved edition in the Boston Public Library.

# Index

303

humor

put money speech ?

169 +

158 - funny
179